CRIMINAL INTERROGATION and CONFESSIONS

The present (1974) reprinting of this book contains several up-datings with respect to the legal rules governing interrogations and confession admissibility. The page numbers, however, remain the same.

SECOND EDITION

CRIMINAL INTERROGATION and CONFESSIONS

Fred E. Inbau PROFESSOR OF LAW, NORTHWESTERN UNIVERSITY
Former Director, Chicago Police Scientific Crime Detection Laboratory

John E. Reid DIRECTOR, JOHN E. REID AND ASSOCIATES
Former Staff Member, Chicago Police Scientific Crime Detection Laboratory

THE WILLIAMS & WILKINS COMPANY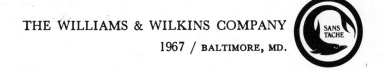
1967 / BALTIMORE, MD.

Copyright ©, 1967
THE WILLIAMS & WILKINS COMPANY
428 E. Preston Street
Baltimore, Md. 21202 U.S.A.

Made in the United States of America

Library of Congress Catalog Card No. 67-18901

This book is a second edition of an extensive revision and enlargement of
the second part of the previously published third edition (1953) of
Inbau & Reid: *Lie Detection and Criminal Interrogation*

Reprinted January, 1970
Reprinted July, 1970
Reprinted June, 1971
Reprinted 1972
Reprinted January 1973
Reprinted March 1974
Reprinted November 1974
Reprinted 1977
Composed and printed at the
WAVERLY PRESS, INC
Mt Royal and Guilford Aves.
Baltimore, Md. 21202 U.S.A

THE AUTHORS ARE ALSO CO-AUTHORS OF
THE COMPANION BOOK

Truth and Deception:
The Polygraph ("Lie Detector") Technique

PUBLISHED IN 1966 BY THE WILLIAMS & WILKINS CO.,
BALTIMORE, MD. 21202

PREFACE

This second (1967) edition of *Criminal Interrogation and Confessions* has been made necessary by the June, 1966, decision of the Supreme Court of the United States in *Miranda v. Arizona*. In that case the Supreme Court altered very substantially the law governing criminal interrogations and the admissibility of confessions.

In effecting the present revision we have made a conscientious effort to conform to the requirements recently established by the Court. We hasten to add, too, that our original edition was also in conformity with the then prescribed legal requirements. Moreover, throughout that book—as well as in this one—we repeatedly urge that no interrogator should ever employ a tactic or technique that is apt to make an innocent person confess. And we know of not one case in which any of the interrogation methods we describe has elicited a confession from an innocent suspect.

The time may arrive when most criminal offenses can be solved or effectively prevented by technological non-interrogational means—and we hope for this eventuality. Meanwhile, however, reliance must be placed upon the present, less sophisticated methods for achieving these two objectives. One is the currently indispensable police procedure of interrogating criminal suspects— by means that will induce confessions from the guilty, without the risk of provoking confessions from the innocent.

We trust that this second edition of our book will continue to be of value to criminal investigators as they go about their ever increasingly difficult task of protecting the lives and property of law abiding citizens.

ACKNOWLEDGMENTS

We again wish to express our gratitude to our colleagues and friends who assisted us in the preparation of our original publication. We are also indebted to Professor James R. Thompson of Northwestern University School of Law for his many valuable suggestions as we were preparing the revisions contained in the present discussion of the law governing criminal interrogations.

Fred E. Inbau/John E. Reid

CONTENTS

ix

GENERAL INTRODUCTION

As we interpret the June, 1966, five to four decision of the Supreme Court of the United States in *Miranda v. Arizona,*[1] all but a very few of the interrogation tactics and techniques presented in our earlier publication are still valid if used after the recently prescribed warnings have been given to the suspect under interrogation, and after he has waived his self-incrimination privilege and his right to counsel. The Court's critical comments about the procedures we advocated were, we believe, for the purpose of establishing the necessity for the warnings rather than as a condemnation of the procedures themselves. And this interpretation is shared by some of the applauders of all that the Court has been doing in the past few years in its efforts to "police the police."

If we are in error with regard to our interpretation of the *Miranda* case, then the Supreme Court has but one more move to make, and that is to outlaw all interrogations of criminal suspects. We say this because of our confidence that effective interrogations can only be conducted by such procedures as the ones we herein describe.

In our opinion, the *Miranda* rules that were established by a one man majority of the Court were unnecessary for the protection of the innocent and they are not soundly derived as constitutional requirements. Nevertheless, the rules are now the law of the land and they must be followed by police interrogators, no matter how deleterious the police may think the consequences will be with respect to public safety and security. They have no alternative, either legally or morally, other than to follow the new rules. Their only responsibility insofar as the consequences of the rules are concerned is to function as best they can within the confines laid down by the Court. The unfortunate consequences will not rest upon their shoulders but rather upon the shoulders of the makers of

[1] 384 U.S. 436 (1966).

1

the rules.[2] At most, the police may look forward hopefully to the future when perhaps a change in the composition of the Court may result in a return to its earlier interpretation of the pertinent constitutional provisions. Such changes of interpretation have occurred before, even in the interrogation-confession area itself. For instance, in the 1958 decision in *Crooker v. California*,[3] the Court held, five to four, that there was no constitutional right to a lawyer in the police station, whereas in the 1964 case of *Escobedo v. Illinois*[4] the Court held, again by a five to four margin, that the right did exist. Then, too, in a related constitutional area, that of search and seizure, the Court appears to have made almost a full circle in its vacillations.[5] The force of unfavorable circumstances resulting from the *Miranda* rules may impel the Court to overrule or greatly modify the scope of that decision.

[2] Concern over such consequences was forcefully expressed by some of the dissenting Justices. Justice Harlan, for instance, had this to say:

"What the Court largely ignores is that its rules impair, if they will not eventually serve wholly to frustrate, an instrument of law enforcement that has long and quite reasonably been thought worth the price paid for it. There can be little doubt that the Court's new code would markedly decrease the number of confessions. To warn the suspect that he may remain silent and remind him that his confession may be used in court are minor obstructions. To require also an express waiver by the suspect and an end to questioning whenever he demurs must heavily handicap questioning. And to suggest or provide counsel for the suspect simply invites the end of the interrogation.

". . . the Court is taking a real risk with society's welfare in imposing its new regime on the country. The social costs of crime are too great to call the new rules anything but a hazardous experimentation."

[3] 357 U.S. 433 (1958). Also see the companion case of Cicenia v. La Gay, 357 U.S. 504 (1958).

[4] 378 U.S. 478 (1964).

[5] In Trupiano v. United States, 334 U.S. 699 (1948), the Court held that if the police have the time in which to obtain a search warrant and they fail to do so, the evidence they seize, even if pursuant to an otherwise reasonable search, is inadmissible as evidence. Two years later, in United States. v. Rabinowitz, 339 U.S. 56 (1950), the Court overruled the earlier case, holding that even though time permitted, a failure to obtain a search warrant would not nullify the validity of evidence obtained from an otherwise reasonable search. Eleven years thereafter, in Chapman v. United States, 365 U.S. 610 (1961), the Court, in effect, overruled the second case and favored the first one.

In 1971 and 1974 the Supreme Court rendered two decisions which have greatly modified the effects of the *Miranda* rules. In one the Court held that a confession obtained without giving proper *Miranda* warnings could nevertheless be used to discredit ("impeach") the defendant confessor if he took the stand and denied his guilt. In the other case the Court held that "derivative use" could be made of a confession considered invalid by *Miranda* standards. This was a case where a defendant who had not been given full *Miranda* warnings supplied the police with the name of a false alibi witness, and that person was permitted to testify against the defendant at his trial.[6]

Congress, in the Omnibus Crime Act of 1968, enacted a provision which seeks to abolish the *Miranda* case warning requirements in federal cases. The provision is reproduced later in this text (p. 184). As of October, 1974, the Supreme Court had not considered a case involving its constitutionality, nor had the Court rendered any decision dealing with the issue of overruling *Miranda*. Until the rendition of any such decision to abandon *Miranda*, police interrogators, and particularly those on the state level, are well advised to continue to administer the *Miranda* warnings set forth on the next page, or as modified or enlarged by the directives of the department's legal advisor, or by the district attorney or attorney general of their particular jurisdiction. If a test case is to be attempted, by a deviation from *Miranda* or a failure to give any of the prescribed warnings, that effort can be made more appropriately by the federal government. This is based upon the fact that Congress has declared that a failure to issue the warnings would not in and of itself nullify the use of confessions in federal cases, whereas a similar declaration has not been made by the state legislatures.

A strong indication of the possibility that the Court may ultimately overrule *Miranda* is the fact (a) that two of the Justices who dissented in *Miranda* (Justices Stewart and White) have since then stated that *Miranda* should be abandoned, and (b) that there has been a replacement on the Court of three of the five Justices who were among the majority which decided *Miranda*.

[6] The two cases are, respectively, Harris v. New York, 401 U. S. 222 (1971), and Michigan v. Tucker, 94 S. Ct. 2357 (1974).

CRIMINAL INTERROGATION

THE WARNINGS AS TO CONSTITUTIONAL RIGHTS

Whenever a person who is about to be interrogated by a law enforcement officer "has been taken into custody or otherwise deprived of his freedom of action in any significant way," he must be given the following warnings, as prescribed by the Supreme Court of the United States in the *Miranda* case:

(1) That he has a right to remain silent, and that he need not answer any questions;

(2) That if he does answer questions his answers can be used as evidence against him;

(3) That he has a right to consult with a lawyer before or during the questioning of him by the police; and

(4) That if he cannot afford to hire a lawyer one will be provided for him without costs.

All of the warnings must be given in such a way that the suspect clearly understands what he is being told.

If the suspect indicates, at any time, or in any manner whatsoever, that he does not want to talk, the interrogation must cease. The interrogator is no longer privileged to "talk him out of" his refusal to talk.

If the suspect says, at any time, that he wants a lawyer, the interrogation must cease until he has the opportunity to confer with a lawyer, and no further questions may be asked of him outside the lawyer's presence or without the lawyer's permission. Nor can the interrogator "talk him out of" his desire for a lawyer.

In instances where the suspect requests a lawyer but he cannot obtain one, and no lawyer is provided for him by the police, the interrogation must be terminated.

As now prescribed, the only time a police interrogation can be

4

conducted of a suspect who is in custody or otherwise restrained of his freedom is *after* he has been given the required warnings and *after* he has expressly stated that he is willing to answer questions, without a lawyer being present. Once that waiver is given the interrogator may then proceed to employ the interrogation tactics and techniques which are subsequently described. They can also be used *without* prior warnings or waivers, on a suspected person who is not in police custody or "otherwise deprived of his freedom of action in any significant way." Moreover, they may be employed by non-police interrogators in personnel investigations without the prior issuance of warnings or waivers.

PRIVACY

The principal psychological factor contributing to a successfu. interrogation is *privacy*—being alone with the person under interrogation. This we all seem to instinctively realize in our own private or social affairs, but in criminal interrogations it is generally overlooked or ignored. For instance, in asking a personal friend or acquaintance to divulge a secret, we carefully avoid making the request in the presence of other persons; we seek a time and place when the matter can be discussed in private. Likewise, when anyone harbors a troublesome problem that he would like "to get off his chest," he finds it easier to confide in another person alone rather than in the presence of a third party. This is so even though the other person may also be one to whom the disturbed individual would like to reveal the same information. In other words, if *B* and *C* are equally good friends of *A*, and *A* wants to discuss his troubles with both *B* and *C*, it will be easier for *A* to first talk to one of them alone, for example, to *B*, and then, on another occasion, to make the same disclosure to the other one, *C*. A moment's reflection by anyone upon his own past experiences will readily satisfy him regarding the privacy requirements for confidential or embarrassing disclosures. Nevertheless, in criminal interrogations, where the same mental processes are in operation, and to an even greater degree by reason of the criminality of the disclosure, interrogators generally seem to lose sight of the fact that a suspect or witness is much more apt to reveal his secrets in the privacy of a room occupied only by himself and his interrogator than in the presence of an additional person or persons.

Three cases with which the writers are familiar serve well to illustrate the point.

In a small mid-western town a citizen of the community was being questioned concerning the killing of his wife, who had been shot on a lonely road not far from a main highway. According to the husband's story, while he and his wife were riding in their automobile, they were held up and robbed by a man who then fired upon the deceased when she called for help. For a number of reasons, the husband's account of the occurrence was viewed with considerable skepticism. The husband was suspected of being the actual killer.

For several hours, upon two or three different occasions during the twenty-four hours following the shooting, the husband was subjected to considerable questioning—*but always in the presence of several persons.* Later, at the request of the state's attorney, one of the writers interrogated the suspect. A private room was selected for this purpose, and everyone else was excluded.

From the very moment the suspect entered the room he displayed every indication of guilt, and from the very outset it appeared quite evident that here was a man who *wanted* to confess. He wanted to unburden himself of his troubles generally. As the interrogator already knew, the subject had experienced a very unhappy married life—meddling relatives, sexual incompatibility, etc. Now he wanted some sympathy, and he wanted to be told that the shooting of his wife was something which anyone else might have done during his weaker moments under similar circumstances. It was essential, however, that he be alone with the person who was to listen to his troubles and offer him the sympathy his mind so craved. Up to the time of his discussion with this interrogator he had not had the opportunity to do so. When the opportunity presented itself, however, he very soon told how and why he killed his wife.

This was the easiest sort of case. It should have been unnecessary for the local authorities to seek outside assistance. All that was really needed was a little privacy.

Another case in point involved an investigation into the rape and murder of a young girl who had been employed as a hostess in a cafeteria. Her nude body had been found in a ditch by the side of a cemetery road the morning after the night of her disappearance while on her way home from work. She was last seen in the company of a bus-boy employee of the same restaurant in which she served as hostess. The bus-boy stated he had merely walked to the streetcar with her and saw no more of her after that.

In an effort to obtain information concerning the character and habits of the deceased, and the relations between her and the bus-boy—in so far as such information might furnish some clue to her murderer—the local authorities began questioning other employees of the restaurant. This was undoubtedly a good starting point, but the procedure followed deserves no recommendation. In the presence of *eighteen* persons, gathered in a large office, five waitresses from the restaurant were asked to divulge any confidential information they might have as to the character and habits of the deceased and of the bus-boy, who upon several occasions had been the escort and companion of two of these girls. In answer to questions concerning the character and habits of the victim, the waitresses invariably replied, "She was a good girl." When questioned about the boy, and as to his behavior when alone with a girl, the answer was: "He is a good boy; on dates he behaves like a gentleman." What other sort of answers could be expected—even if the victim had been a girl of very loose morals or the boy a rake of the first order? It so happened, however, that other more thorough investigation resulted in a solution of the crime; the bus-boy was cleared and the good moral character of the victim was confirmed. But suppose one or more of these five girls had possessed valuable information on either the victim or the bus-boy. Was it not expecting too much of them to ask for confidential information in the presence of eighteen persons, whose number included several local politicians of the town and a few curious spectators having no official connections either with the city or the case itself?

In the foregoing case, each one of the girls should have been questioned alone, with no one else present but the interrogator.

For another kind of case, of course, where the girl or woman to be questioned is the suspect, or a person of an unsavory character with a possible motive for hampering the investigation, it may be advisable to have a policewoman or some other reliable female in a position to hear and see what transpires. In this way the interrogator may protect himself from a possible accusation that while in the interrogation room he made a sexual advance toward the subject. However, if the policewoman or other observer must be in the interrogation room, she should be seated in back of the subject and instructed to remain seated and to refrain from taking any part in the interrogation. In this way the element of privacy is essentially fulfilled.

In the famous Degnan murder case in Chicago (1945–1946), the importance of privacy was impressively revealed—*by the murderer himself!* William Heirens, a 17-year-old college student, was accused of the brutal killing of 6-year-old Suzanne Degnan. His fingerprints were found on a ransom note left in the Degnan home and the handwriting on the note was identified as his. There was also evidence that he had killed two other persons and committed twenty-nine burglaries. His attorneys, to whom he apparently admitted his guilt, advised him to confess to the prosecuting attorney and thereby afford them an opportunity to save him from the electric chair.

Arrangements were made, by Heirens' counsel, with the Cook County State's Attorney to take Heirens' confession, but at the appointed time and place Heirens refused to confess. The reason for his last minute refusal appears in the following headline from the Chicago Daily News of August 2, 1946: *"Youth asks Privacy at Conference. Blames Refusal to Talk on Large Crowd at Parley."* The newspaper account further stated: "It was learned that Heirens balked at a conference arranged for last Tuesday because [the prosecuting attorney] had invited almost 30 law enforcement officers and others to be present. . . . It was at the conference between the youth and his lawyers that he told them for the first time that there were 'too many' present on Tuesday. He said he would go through with the confession arrangements to escape the electric chair if it could be done under different conditions. The state's attorney told reporters that he had invited the police officials to the conference because they had all played a leading part in the investigation and he felt they should be 'in on the finish.' "

Another Chicago newspaper, the Chicago Times of August 2, 1946, reported: "It was hinted the original confession program was a flop because the youth was frightened by the movie-like setting in [the state's attorney's] office. Presumably he was frightened out of memory, too. To every question about the murders he answered, 'I don't remember.' His self-consciousness reportedly was deepened by the presence of several members of the police department, especially [the police officer] whose handiness with flower pots as weapons brought about Heirens' exposé in a burglary attempt."

At the second setting for the taking of Heirens' confession the number of spectators was reduced by about half, but a reading of the confession gives the impression that Heirens, though admitting his guilt, withheld—for understandable reasons—about fifty per cent of the gruesome details and true explanations of his various crimes.

It is indeed a sad commentary upon police interrogation practices when a seventeen-year-boy has to impart an elementary lesson to top-ranking law enforcement officials, i.e., that it is psychologically unsound to ask a person to confess a crime in the presence of thirty spectators.

Cooperation among Investigators

The authors are aware of the practical difficulties that may be encountered in arranging for a private interrogation, even after the interrogator is convinced of its desirability. In a case of any importance each investigator wants to be in on the interrogation, or at least be present when a suspect confesses, or when an informer or a witness divulges valuable information. He wants to improve his efficiency rating or otherwise demonstrate his value to the department or to his office, and the publicity in his community is considered valuable—to say nothing of the satisfaction to his own ego. All this is perfectly understandable and nothing more than normal human behavior, but it is something which must be controlled to some extent in the interest of efficient police procedure.

The person in charge of the investigation, or someone with command rank, should direct that the interrogation be conducted under conditions of privacy. In instances where all investigators are of equal rank, and each one seems to want to participate in the interrogation, they should work out some arrangement among themselves to insure the element of privacy. It will help if one of them suggests that one of the others should begin the interrogation, or that he himself will do so if they wish. In this way it may be possible to avoid the presence of more than one investigator during the interrogation.

Privacy in interrogations can be maintained without denying to any investigator assigned to the case the credit due him for his efforts. An understanding may be reached among the various investigators to the effect that if a "break" comes when any of them have absented themselves from the interrogation room for the purpose of insuring privacy between the interrogator and the suspect or witness, they will all share the credit for whatever results the interrogator himself obtains. Perhaps this suggestion may seem naive and impractical, but the authors have seen it operate successfully in a number of instances, and under the most trying conditions. For example, in one community where the prosecuting attorney and the sheriff were members of opposing political parties, they followed such a procedure, and their teamwork and cooperation simplified their respective duties to an immeasurable extent. Neither one hesitated to cooperate with the other because each one knew that the other would not seek any publicity to the exclusion of his co-worker.

The investigator who gains the reputation of publicity seeker in his casework soon will find it difficult to obtain the proper cooperation from his fellow officers. His own work then becomes considerably more of a burden when he has to operate alone, and, as most of us fully realize, criminal investigation is not a one-man job. Of course, there are investigators who are more capable than their colleagues, but, just as a star halfback on a football team needs the blocking of his teammates, the best of investigators must have the cooperation and assistance of other workers if he is to operate successfully. Consequently, in the interest of his community, as well as for his own selfish desires, the interrogator should make every effort to secure and maintain the respect and cooperation of his fellow workers by sharing with them credit as well as responsibility. Eventually his true merit and value to his department, office, and community will become known and recognized by his superiors and also by those members of the public who can be of most help to him in shaping his future career.

No set rules can be outlined for overcoming this practical difficulty of having investigators seemingly sacrifice their own interests in being present during an interrogation. Each community presents its distinctive problems. It may be a sheriff-prosecuting attorney relationship, or one between sergeant and patrolman, or between two separate units within a police department; but it is a problem which should and must be worked out in the interest of efficient investigation.

THE INTERROGATION ROOM

In providing for privacy during interrogations it is advisable to select a quiet room with none of the usual police surroundings, and with no distractions within the subject's view. If existing facilities permit, a special room, or rooms, should be set aside for this purpose. In any event, the room should be as free as possible from outside noises, and it should also be a room into which no one will have occasion to enter or pass through while the interrogation is in progress.

The less there is in the surroundings of an interrogation room to remind a criminal offender, suspect, witness, or other prospective informant that he is in police custody or in jail, or that the penitentiary awaits him or someone else about whom he may have incriminating information, the easier it is for him to make a frank statement or to supply the interrogator with the desired information. To this end, therefore, it is well to select a room without barred windows, or, better yet, one without any windows at all. If windows cannot be avoided, the bars should be replaced with some sort of ornamental grill work which would be just as effective for preventing possible escapes during the temporary occupancy of such a room. (As to the ventilation of a windowless room, a mechanical blower and exhaust system can be used without much difficulty or inconvenience.)

The interrogation room should contain no ornaments, pictures, or other objects which would in any way distract the attention of a person being interviewed; and this suggestion also refers to the presence, within the subject's reach, of small, loose objects, such as paper clips or pencils, that he may be inclined to pick up and fumble with during the course of the interrogation. Tension-relieving activities of this sort detract from the effectiveness of the interrogation, especially during the critical phase when a guilty subject may be trying desperately to suppress an urge to confess.

If pictures or ornaments are used, they should not be placed in that part of the room faced by the subject during the interview.

The lighting fixtures of the room should be arranged in such a way as to provide good but not excessive or glaring illumination of the subject's face, and certainly any lighting which interferes with the interrogator's full view of the subject's facial features and expressions should be avoided; nor should there be any glaring light shining on the interrogator's face, for this interferes with his observations of the subject and at the same time perhaps distorts the interrogator's facial indications of his feeling and attitude of understanding, sympathy, etc.

No telephone should be present in the interrogation room. Among other disadvantages, its ringing or use constitutes a serious distraction.

If available facilities permit, there should be an observation room adjoining the interrogation room. What we have in mind is a smaller adjoining room, in the wall of which there is inserted a two-way mirror—a panel of glass chemically treated so as to permit someone from within a relatively dark observation room to see into the lighted interrogation room without being seen. Then, in addition to the "mirror" arrangement, the interrogation room should be equipped with a concealed microphone so that a person or persons in the observation room may hear, as well as see, what occurs in the interrogation room. (State and local laws should be checked first, however, to ascertain whether or not there is any legal prohibition against "electronic eavesdropping.")

An interrogation-observation room arrangement of the type suggested above can be of considerable value in several respects. First of all, by affording an opportunity to investigating officers to observe and hear, it will be much easier for an interrogator to acquire the necessary privacy for his interrogation. Secondly, a fellow interrogator will be able to observe and listen and be that much better prepared for whatever role he may have to play in the interrogation. Thirdly, in cases where a female is the subject, a policewoman or other female may be stationed in the observation room to witness the proceedings as a safeguard against possible false accusations of misconduct on the part of the interrogator; and such a witness, whether male or female, is also helpful in other types of situations as a safeguard against false accusations of physical abuse, threats, or promises on the part of the interrogator. Fourthly, when a subject is left alone in the interrogation room, he can be kept under observation as a precaution against any effort to escape or perhaps even the remote possibility of an attempt at suicide.

PRELIMINARY PREPARATIONS

Prior to an interrogation, and preferably before there has been any meeting or contact with the subject, the interrogator should become thoroughly familiar with all the facts and circumstances of the offense which are known to the investigators up to that time. This information should be obtained from the most reliable source, for any inaccuracies will seriously interfere with the effectiveness of the interrogation.

It is also advisable for the interrogator to secure as much information as possible concerning the victim of the crime, and a similar effort should be made as regards the subject—particularly so if he is to be interrogated as a suspect rather than as a witness or other prospective informant.

Any oral, written, or recorded statements that the subject may have made to the investigating officers should be sought by the interrogator and carefully considered by him.

If an interrogation is conducted on the basis of inadequate or faulty information, the subject will be unfavorably impressed. If guilty, he will be more confident with regard to his lying; on the other hand, if he is innocent, he will feel insecure because of his lack of confidence in an unprepared interrogator. Moreover, even if the subject is to be interviewed only as a witness or other prospective informant, the interrogator certainly will not be able to ask the kind of pertinent, probing questions that he could employ if he had greater familiarity with the facts of the offense, the victim, and the subject himself. For these and other related reasons, therefore, the interrogation should begin only after the interrogator is in possession of such detailed information as the following:

1. As to the Offense Itself

The legal nature of the offensive conduct—e.g., forcible or statutory rape; robbery, burglary, embezzlement, or larceny, and the exact amount and nature of the loss.

Date, time, place of occurrence (in *accurate* detail).

Description of the crime area and of the crime scene itself.

The way in which the crime appears to have been committed and the known details of its commission, i.e., implement used, place of entry or exit, etc.

Possible motives for its commission.

Incriminating factors respecting a particular suspect.

2. As to the Suspect or Suspects

Personal background information, such as age, education, marital status, financial and social circumstances, and criminal record if any.

Present physical and mental condition, as well as medical history, including such facts as addiction to dope or alcohol.

Attitude toward the investigation (e.g., hostile, cooperative).

Relationship to victim or crime scene.

Incriminating facts or possible motives.

Alibi, or other statements (oral, written, or recorded) that the suspect has related to the investigators.

Religious or fraternal affiliations or prejudices.

Home environment.

Social attitudes in general.

Hobbies.

Sexual interests or deviations.

Abilities or opportunities to commit the offense.

3. *As to the Victim or Victims*

(a) If a company or other institution—
   Attitude and practices toward employees and the public.
   Financial status (insured against losses, etc.).
(b) If a person—
   The nature of injury or harm and the details thereof.
   Age, sex, marital status, family responsibilities (number of
      dependents).
   Social attitudes regarding race, nationality, religion, etc.
   Financial and social circumstances.
   Physical and mental characteristics.
   Sexual interests or deviations.
   Blackmail potentialities.

If none or very little of this kind of information is available, it is perhaps advisable, where time and circumstances permit, to defer the interrogation until the investigators have renewed their investigation in pursuit of such further details.

In cases where a suspect has given an alibi, it should be checked, if at all possible, before the interrogation begins. Any known defects in it will assist the interrogator very materially. Moreover, an alibi check may actually establish the innocence of the suspect, however much other circumstances may point to his guilt. In such instances the interrogator can direct his attention toward obtaining helpful leads from the suspect regarding other possibilities, or the interrogation may be abandoned altogether. All too often, time and effort are unnecessarily expended in the interrogation of a suspected innocent person when an alibi check could have readily established the fact of his innocence.

By way of illustrating the significance of the kind of information outlined above, we will refer to several of the listed items and point out their possible application to a specific case situation.

Assume a case in which the office building of a corporation is partly destroyed by a nighttime fire. An investigation of the scene clearly established that the fire was deliberately set and that it started in the bookkeeping section of the company office, to which entrance seems to have been effected by means of a door key rather than by force.

Not only had the fire started in the bookkeeping area, but also the company's financial records had been burned outside the cabinet in which they were customarily kept. Moreover, the fire occurred the day before a scheduled audit was to have been made by an independent auditing firm.

Although these facts clearly suggest that the fire was set for the purpose of concealing an embezzlement, in the absence of certain information regarding the company personnel to be questioned, an interrogator would be faced with a very difficult, if not impossible, task. He should, therefore, defer any intensive interrogation efforts until some sort of investigation is first made of the personnel who had an opportunity to commit the embezzlement.

Assume, then, that an investigation of the personnel revealed that a recently employed cashier was considerably in debt, and that his wife was a woman of expensive habits and tastes. Also, interviews with the cashier's previous employer disclosed that his accounts had been short on several occasions and that whenever the shortage was called to his attention he readily offered to make up the deficit out of his own funds. Furthermore, the former employer had experienced a sizable loss which had never been traced or otherwise explained.

Equipped with this additional information the interrogator is in a far better position to conduct an effective interrogation than if such facts were unknown or unavailable to him, for, in the latter situation, even if he did detect the fact of deception or otherwise suspected the cashier, there would still be lacking, to the interrogator's definite disadvantage, the interrogation leads implicit in the information about the possible motive and the losses at the cashier's previous place of employment. Moreover, and perhaps of equal importance, the interrogator who is equipped with such interrogation leads will be better able to avoid certain interrogation pitfalls that can have a very damaging effect, particularly with regard to the rapport between the subject and the interrogator. For instance, in the foregoing case of the cashier suspect, if the interrogator had been unaware of the wife's extravagance as a possible reason for the embezzlement, he may well have questioned the cashier on the basis of gambling activities or "another woman," both of which unfounded references may have justifiably angered the subject, since the real reason was his wife's extravagance. On the other hand, an awareness of the information about the wife's conduct as a contributing factor permitted the interrogator to invoke the very effective technique (to be subsequently described) of placing the moral blame for the offense upon someone else, in this case the wife.

ATTITUDE AND CONDUCT OF THE INTERROGATOR

It is difficult to attempt to formulate and propose any set rules with regard to the attitude and conduct of an interrogator during his interview with the subject. Much of this will depend, of course, upon the circumstances of each particular case, but, in general, the following recommendations should be helpful, particularly with respect to the interrogation of the criminal suspect himself:

1. Avoid creating the impression that you are an investigator seeking a confession or conviction. It is far better to appear in the role of one who is merely seeking *the truth*.

2. Keep pencil and paper out of sight during an interrogation. By recording or making notes of the subject's statements or comments during the course of an interrogation, the interrogator places before the subject a more or less grim reminder of the legal significance or implication of an incriminating remark. It is better, therefore, to avoid note-taking, or at least to postpone it until the latter stages of the interrogation. However, if the subject mentions a name or an address that the interrogator wants to be sure to remember, he can take a pencil and paper out of his coat pocket to note that information, but then the pencil and paper should be removed from the subject's view.

For much the same reason as the avoidance of note-taking, the interrogator should be in civilian dress rather than in uniform during an interrogation. Otherwise the subject will have before him a constant reminder of police custody and the possible consequences of an incriminating disclosure. If the uniform cannot be avoided altogether, the coat, star, gun, and holster should be removed for the duration of the interrogation.

The interrogator should wear a conservative suit or jacket and should avoid any loud ties or other conspicuous clothing accessories. Unless weather conditions demand otherwise, a coat or jacket should be worn throughout the interrogation. A short-sleeved interrogator does not command the respect his position requires.

3. Such realistic words or expressions as "kill," "steal," and "confess your crime" should not be used by the interrogator. It is much more desirable, from a psychological standpoint, to employ milder terminology like "shoot," "take," and "tell the truth."

A subject should never be told, "You've been lying to me." A better expression is, "You haven't told the whole truth."

4. The interrogator should sit fairly close to the subject, and between the two there should be no table, desk, or other piece of furniture. Distance or the presence of an obstruction of any sort constitutes a serious psychological barrier and also affords the subject a certain degree of relief and confidence not otherwise attainable.

Straight back chairs should be used for both the subject and the interrogator. Other types of chairs induce slouching or leaning back, and such positions are psychologically undesirable.

Whenever possible, the seating arrangement should be such that both the interrogator and the subject are on the same eye level.

As to the psychological validity of the above suggested seating arrangement, reference may be made to the commonplace but yet meaningful expressions such as "getting next" to a person, or the "buttonholing" of a customer by a salesman. These expressions signify that when a person is close to another one physically, he is closer to him psychologically. Anything such as a desk or a table between the interrogator and the subject defeats this purpose and should be avoided.

To preserve and maintain the advantage of this close seating arrangement it is very important that the interrogator be free of any offensive breath odor, whether due to food, such as garlic, or to some other factor. As a precaution, it is advisable, whenever possible, to pursue the practice of talking at close range to a fellow interrogator or other colleague just before entering the interrogation room, with the understanding that he will advise the interrogator of any possible offensive breath odors. In the event that any such odor is present a mouthwash or a chlorophyl mint should serve the purpose of being able to talk to a subject without having him offended or distracted by unpleasant breath odors.

A similar arrangement should prevail with respect to a check of the interrogator for any facial uncleanliness or disarrayed clothing, etc., all of which can interfere with the interrogator's effectiveness.

5. The interrogator should remain seated and refrain from pacing about the room. To give undiverted attention to the person being interrogated makes it that much more difficult for the subject to evade the detection of his deception. Moreover, actions of jumping up and down and walking around give evidence of the interrogator's impatience, with its consequent encouragement to the subject that if he can conceal his guilt and continue lying a little while longer the interrogator will give up. An entirely different impression is created by the interrogator who remains seated during the entire interrogation.

6. The interrogator should avoid or at least minimize smoking, and he should also refrain from fumbling with a pencil, pen, or other room accessories, for all this tends to create an impression of lack of interest or confidence. As to the smoking, there is an additional reason for its avoidance. If the interrogator is not smoking, the subject is less likely to attempt to smoke in an effort to relieve his emotional tension or to bolster up his resistance to an effective interrogation; and if such a request to smoke is made, the interrogator may with much justification and fairness suggest that the subject postpone his smoking until he leaves the interrogation room. However, if the interrogator must smoke, he should start off by offering a cigarette to the subject and then minimize his and the subject's smoking as much as possible. To smoke without permitting the subject to do so prevents the establishment of the re-

lationship of trust and confidence that is so essential to a successful interrogation.

To facilitate matters with respect to an avoidance of smoking by a subject, it will be helpful if there are no ash trays present, for when present they represent a tacit invitation to smoke. Their absence may carry the opposite impression, as well as afford a basis, if necessary, for a suggestion by the interrogator that any smoking be postponed until the subject leaves the interrogation room.

7. The interrogator should adapt his language to that used and understood by the subject. In dealing with an uneducated or unintelligent subject the interrogator should use simple words and sentences. And where, for instance in a sex case, the subject uses slang or commonplace expressions and gives evidence of his lack of knowledge of more acceptable terminology, the interrogator should resort to similar expressions. This can be done in a reserved manner without the loss of the subject's respect for the position occupied by his interrogator.

8. A subject should be treated with decency and respect, regardless of the nature of his or her offense; this is especially true with regard to homosexuals and female subjects generally.

If a woman subject is of loose morals, or even a prostitute, this is no invitation to treat her as such, and the interrogator defeats his own purpose when he does. The following actual case experiences of the authors serve well to illustrate this point.

A woman of about sixty years of age was suspected of murdering a male boarder in her rooming house. She had called the police to report that the man had died, apparently of natural causes. An autopsy revealed that he had been killed with a small caliber bullet in his back. Suspicion was directed toward the woman for several reasons, one of which was the fact that she had been the deceased boarder's sleeping companion. Arrangements were made for one of the authors to interrogate her. At the time of the scheduled interrogation she was accompanied by a police captain of about twenty years' experience as a police officer. He related the case history to the interrogator while the subject remained seated in another room. Then, when the interrogator was ready to proceed with the interrogation, the captain called out for the subject to come to the interrogation room. As she approached, he pointed to the room and said, "Get on in there you old whore; this man wants to talk to you!" She looked at him with considerable scorn as she entered the room and the captain departed. The interrogator proceeded to address the subject as "Mrs. ———" and asked her to sit down. He then inquired if she had been given any food during the time she had been in police custody and while being questioned earlier by the police. She said, "No," and readily accepted the interrogator's invitation to have coffee and a sandwich delivered to her in the interrogation room. Thereafter the interrogator continued to treat her as a "lady" rather than as a "whore." Shortly thereafter she confessed to the killing of the boarder and supplied information that definitely established her guilt. Moreover, before she was through talking she confessed to the killing, several years ago, of her husband, who was known to have died under suspicious circumstances.

In another case a prostitute was suspected of a robbery performed by the use of a drug administered to the victim. As she removed her coat in the interrogation room, the interrogator observed that a broken shoulder strap on her dress had caused one of her breasts to be exposed. Before proceeding with the interrogation the interrogator procured a towel and placed it over the prostitute's shoulder. After a relatively brief interrogation, during which she was addressed as "Miss" rather than by her first name, she confessed the crime and disclosed the identity of her accomplice. Without doubt, the interrogator's treatment of her as a lady facilitated his task, for here was a woman who basically preferred that status to her own calling.

In the interrogation of homosexuals the police are prone to refer to them as "queers" or "fruits." As a result, a resentment develops and the interrogation is rendered far more difficult. It is much more effective for the interrogator to treat such subjects as though their homosexual conduct was morally acceptable; in any event they or their companions should never be referred to as "queers," "fruits," or by any other similar designation.

No matter how revolting or horrible a sex crime may be (e.g., a sex-motivated, brutal killing of a small child), the suspected of-

fender should not be treated or referred to as a despicable, inhuman individual. A sympathetic, understanding attitude and interrogation approach, such as will be subsequently described, is far more effective. In one of many cases which we could use to illustrate this point, a sex offender, after his confession, said, "I would have told the officers about this earlier if they had only treated me with some decency and respect."

9. After catching a subject in a lie, the interrogator should never scold or reprimand him by the use of such expressions as, "Why in the hell do you lie to me?" or, "You lied to me once and you'll lie to me again." It is much better to conceal any reaction of resentment, or even of surprise. In fact, the more effective handling of the situation is to convey the impression that the interrogator knew all along that the subject was not telling the truth.

10. Since the interrogator should always occupy a fearless position with regard to his subject and to the conditions and circumstances attending the interrogation, the subject should not be handcuffed or shackled during his presence in the interrogation room. Moreover, a confession obtained under such circumstances may be rejected on the ground of coercion. For similar reasons the interrogator should not be armed. In other words, the interrogator should face the subject as man to man and not as policeman to prisoner.[7]

When these various precautionary measures are dispensed with, others may be substituted with comparable assurance that no escape will occur or that no physical harm will come to the interrogator as a result of such omissions. For instance, where circumstances so warrant, a guard may be placed outside the door of the interrogation room, on the alert for an attempt to escape or for possible acts of violence toward an unarmed interrogator.

[7] Another, though unrelated, reason for not being armed is the fact that in such close quarters, the subject, if so inclined, might be able to unexpectedly seize the interrogator's weapon for use on him or on others who may seek to prevent his escape. An additional factor to consider is the advantage to be gained at the trial by having a disclosure made that the interrogator was unarmed, especially in instances where the cross examiner may be trying to get the idea across that the subject was in a state of constant fear of physical harm from the interrogator.

11. In the interrogation of any subject, whether he be a suspect or merely a witness or other prospective informant, the interrogator should try to think in terms of what he himself would be thinking, doing, or saying if he were the subject under interrogation. In other words, he should place himself in the other fellow's shoes. By doing this the interrogator may meet with success comparable to that attained by the farmer in the story of the lost mule. It seemed that several persons had searched long and laboriously for a lost mule, but with no success. Finally another searcher, who made the least physical effort of anyone, returned with the missing animal. When questioned about the secret of his success he replied, "Well, sir, I just thought to myself, 'If I were a mule where would I go?'; that's where I went, and there was the mule."

Even before the interrogator has had any contact with the subject, but after having been fully informed about the crime and the subject's background, the interrogator should try to picture himself in the subject's position and then attempt to justify or excuse the crime in his own mind. In this way the interrogator can develop the proper attitude of sympathy and understanding.

12. The interrogator should always be mindful of the fact that regardless of the kind of crime a person has committed, he is nevertheless a human being and will probably be reacting to the interrogation in much the same way as would the interrogator himself if their situations were reversed. It is a mistake, therefore, to look upon the subject as an animal, even though his offense may be a very brutal sexual assault or killing.

Another necessary attitude is a recognition by the interrogator that there is some good in everyone, and he should seek to determine at the outset what are the desirable traits and qualities of the particular subject. Thereafter the interrogator can capitalize on those characteristics in the establishment of the kind of rapport required for a successful interrogation.

THE "SIZING-UP" AND CLASSIFICATION OF SUBJECTS FOR INTERROGATION PURPOSES

An interrogator's success will depend to a considerable extent upon his ability (1) to "size-up" his subject, and (2) to select and effectively apply the interrogation tactics and techniques most appropriate for the occasion. As to the first phase of the task—the sizing-up—there is not much an experienced interrogator can offer in the form of written instructions to less experienced persons. Even with the opportunity of utilizing actual case demonstrations for instructional purposes, the development of this ability to size-up a person must remain largely a matter of practical experience, although even then the degree of efficiency attainable by the interrogator will be dependent to some extent upon his own native ability and capacity for such psychological insight. However, with regard to the selection and application of available tactics and techniques, an experienced interrogator's recommendations may be reduced to writing and thereby rendered of value to other interrogators not possessed of comparable experience or training.

Rather than offer to the reader a random and generalized discussion of various interrogation tactics and techniques, an effort has been made to organize and classify the following material so as to render it of greater practical utility. First of all, there is a major classification on the basis of the subject's presumed relationship to the offense in question—that is, whether he is considered as (1) a suspect, or (2) merely as a witness or other prospective informant. Consequently, in conformity with this primary classification, one part of the following discussion of interrogation methods will deal with *Suspects* and the other part will be devoted to *Witnesses and Other Prospective Informants*.

THE INTERROGATION OF SUSPECTS

There are two general groups of suspects:

1. Suspects whose guilt is definite or reasonably certain.
2. Suspects whose guilt is doubtful or uncertain.

In dealing with suspects whose guilt is definite or reasonably certain, the interrogator will usually make known his belief in the suspect's guilt and attempt from the very outset to secure a confession or incriminating statement. On the other hand, with suspects whose guilt is doubtful or uncertain, the interrogator must "feel his way around" until he arrives at a decision of guilt or innocence. This difference in objective and interrogation approach obviously necessitates a separate discussion of the interrogation techniques to be used on each group of suspects.

TACTICS AND TECHNIQUES FOR THE INTERROGATION OF SUSPECTS WHOSE GUILT IS DEFINITE OR REASONABLY CERTAIN

The interrogation approach to be used in an effort to obtain a confession or other incriminating information will depend to a considerable extent upon the nature of the offense, the offender's motivation, and the offender's reaction to the commission of the offense. On the basis of these considerations, criminal offenders are subject to a rather loose and flexible classification as either *emotional offenders* or *non-emotional offenders.*

By *emotional offenders* we mean primarily offenders who commit crimes *against persons*—that is, the infliction of physical harm or the taking of a life, in the heat of passion, anger, or revenge (for example, a sex offense, or the killing of one's wife in order to marry another woman), or as the result of an accidental occurrence such as negligent homicides or "hit-and-run" automobile cases. This group also includes some first offenders in certain other types of cases.

We classify a person who commits an offense of this type as "emotional," because he usually experiences a greater feeling of remorse, mental anguish, or compunction as a result of his act than is true with most other types of offenders; he has a greater sense of moral guilt—in other words, a troubled conscience. Because of this feeling of guilt, the most effective interrogation tactics and techniques to use on him are those based primarily upon sympathetic considerations regarding his offense and his present difficulty. We refer to this as the *sympathetic approach.*

By *non-emotional offenders* we mean primarily offenders who commit crimes *for financial gain,* such as larceny, burglary, robbery, or killings and physical harms inflicted for money reasons. The individual who commits a crime of this type is considered as "non-emotional" because he ordinarily does not experience the troubled conscience that is so characteristic of the emotional offender, and when he does react in that manner, it usually is of a lesser degree than that experienced by members of the "emotional" group. As a rule, the only or primary concern of the money-motivated offender is whether he will be caught or convicted. On him, therefore, a sympathetic approach is usually not nearly so effective as it is on the emotional criminal. The most effective tactics and techniques to use on the non-emotional criminal are those which are based primarily upon a *factual analysis approach*. By this we mean the employment of tactics and techniques that appeal to the subject's common sense and reasoning rather than to his emotions; they are designed and intended to convince him that his guilt is already established, or that it will be established soon, and that consequently there is nothing else for him to do but to admit it.

In our previously published materials on criminal interrogation we prescribed separate sets of tactics and techniques for each of the main interrogation approaches: the sympathetic approach for emotional offenders, and the factual analysis approach for the non-emotional group. We intended it only as a matter of emphasis. In the present publication, however, we are departing from that mode of presentation in order to avoid creating the impression that there are no exceptions to be made, either as to the groups themselves or with respect to the individual subjects within each group. Accordingly, we will set forth all the various tactics and techniques that we consider effective in the interrogation of criminal offenders without placing them under one classification or the other. Then, as the individual tactics and techniques are discussed, we will point out wherein each one is more, or less, applicable or effective on one group than on the other, and we will also indicate the modifications that may be warranted by particular case situations.

The sequence in which these various interrogation tactics and techniques are discussed and the lettering used to identify them are merely for reference purposes. They in no way signify a letter-by-letter application.

A. Display an Air of Confidence in the Subject's Guilt

By an air of confidence we do not mean a supercilious or bullying attitude, but rather one which will convey to the subject the impression that the interrogator is sure of himself. As part of this impression, of course, the interrogator must give no indication that he is being influenced by what the subject may state by way of a disclaimer of guilt; and he should do this even when the interrogator actually realizes the reasonable implication of some fact or evidence referred to by the subject.

(Lest we be misunderstood we wish to make it make it clear that we are now talking, of course, about subjects whose guilt is definite or reasonably certain, and not about subjects whose guilt is doubtful or uncertain.)

The manner and form of the initial meeting or contact with the person to be interrogated are of considerable importance. What happens at this stage of the interrogation may determine the success or failure of the entire effort.

Following is an illustration of the way in which the interrogator might proceed; it describes a procedure which the authors have found to be effective:

Where circumstances permit, the subject should be escorted into the interrogation room by one of the investigators who instructs him to have a seat and that Mr. (giving the name of the interrogator) will be in shortly to talk to him. When the interrogator enters he should greet the subject in somewhat the same manner as a doctor greets a patient—cordially, but not in an overly friendly manner, and there should be no offer of a handshake. Only when the subject himself extends his hand should the interrogator indulge in any handshaking, and even then it is well to do it rather casually.

As previously suggested, the interrogator should occupy a chair relatively near to, and in front of, the subject, or else the interrogator should move a chair into that position. At the beginning of the interrogation the interrogator's chair may be two or three feet from the subject's chair, but after the interrogation is under way the interrogator should move his chair in closer, so that, ultimately, one of the subject's knees is just about in between the interrogator's two knees.

Following the *Miranda* warnings, the interrogator should proceed as follows, and while doing so the interrogator should look directly at the subject with an obvious air of confidence in what he says: "There's been a considerable amount of investigation in this case and it indicates that you haven't told the whole truth." The interrogator should then pause momentarily for the subject's reaction, since it can be very revealing. It will, for one thing, serve as a gauge as to whether the interrogator is correct in his assumption of the subject's guilt. If he registers an immediate and strong resentment following the accusation of his not having told the truth, that fact may be viewed as a possible indication of innocence. In such instances the interrogator's further interrogation should be conducted along the lines subsequently described for the interrogation of suspects whose guilt is doubtful or uncertain. On the other hand, if the subject displays no resentment to the accusation, that fact is consistent with the original assumption of guilt.

At various times during the interrogation the subject should be reminded that the investigation has established the fact that he committed the offense; that there is no doubt about it; and that, moreover, his general behavior plainly shows that he is not now telling the truth.

In the early stages of the interrogation, if the subject interrupts the interrogator and asks, "May I say something?" it is well to respond by telling him, "Wait until I've finished with what I have to say." Incidentally, a guilty person will usually drop his request "to say something"; he eventually just listens.

Care must be exercised to avoid having the subject indulge in repeated denials of guilt. If the interrogator hears him out on his denials of guilt he will become more and more fortified, and the chances of obtaining a confession from him become less and less. The psychological considerations involved are these: The more often a subject repeats his lie the harder it becomes for him to tell the truth, and the task of the interrogator is rendered that much more difficult. In such a case there will be two major factors standing in the way of a confession: not only the subject's basic reluctance to admit his guilt, but also, now, his reluctance to admit that he had previously lied to the interrogator. Consequently, every discreet effort should be made to prevent the subject from uttering denials of guilt. The innocent, truthful subject will not be adversely affected by this tactic, while at the same time it will materially assist the interrogator in his efforts to secure a confession from the guilty.

As part of this procedure for discouraging denials of guilt, the interrogator should direct his comments toward *the reasons why* the subject committed the act; in this way the interrogator avoids the issue of *whether* the subject did it.

To avoid any misunderstanding of what the authors have in mind with respect to the foregoing suggestions we wish to emphasize that we are talking here about a suspect whose guilt is definite or at least reasonably certain. Moreover, this recommended procedure for an avoidance of denials of guilt possesses the already stated attribute of disclosing responses evidencing truth-telling by an innocent person whom the interrogator may have mistakenly assumed to be guilty at the start of the interrogation. Then, too, this technique is not apt to induce a confession of guilt from an innocent subject; it involves no threats or other factors that tend to provoke false confessions.

In developing and maintaining an air of confidence in a subject's guilt, the interrogator must always remain in psychological control of the interview. A "big shot" subject such as the prominent business or professional man should never be allowed to capitalize on his status. One little procedure toward that end is to address such a person by his first name (e.g., Joe) rather than by the appellation Mr. ——.

The fact that a suspect has a criminal record or has served time in a penitentiary should not be assumed to present an insurmountable barrier to securing a confession. Subjects of that type—who have waived their self-incrimination privilege and their right to counsel—may still be vulnerable to the tactics and techniques which will be subsequently described. In any event, if an interrogator becomes concerned over the fact that his subject has a criminal record and is probably too "wised up" to confess, he will be defeating himself before he even starts.

Along this same line it should be pointed out that a person with a background as a law enforcement officer is not any more difficult to interrogate than anyone else; in fact he is frequently more vulnerable to sound interrogation techniques than the person without such a background. Perhaps the reason for this is the subject's acute awareness of the significance that will be attached to even minor contradictions and slip-ups in a false story; he also knows from his own professional experiences that a guilty person may exhibit symptoms of deception by his behavior and general conduct. He may also know something of the particular interrogator's skill in obtaining confessions. In short, the subject with a background in the field of law enforcement may have less confidence in himself as a liar than the ordinary criminal suspect.

An interrogator should never adopt or drift into an indifferent, passive, or lethargic attitude. If those are his usual personality characteristics, he probably should not be in the interrogation field at all. However, if that attitude is the result of only a temporary "let-down" mood, it is advisable to have someone else serve as interrogator until that attitude changes.

The most effective attitude is generally one which reveals a calm confidence, wherein there is a constrained display of a vital, intense interest in the interrogation mission, but which at the same time implies an understanding, considerate, and sympathetic feeling toward the subject himself. There will be some subjects, of course, for whom the interrogator will find it necessary to assume an abrupt, accusative attitude. The ones who may require this approach are those who are seemingly indifferent or lethargic, or those who indulge in a "know it all" kind of conduct and behavior. In general, however, the previously described attitude is the more appropriate one for the average criminal suspect.

With subjects who fall within the category of non-emotional criminals (i.e., those whose offenses were money-motivated, such as the thief, burglar, robber, etc.), the interrogator's display of an air of confidence in the subject's guilt is of even greater importance than when the subject is of the emotional type. As regards the non-emotional group, the interrogator should emphasize the futility of the subject's resistance. The suspect must be made to realize that his guilt is not only already known but also that it will soon be provable. The interrogator should imply that this is, or will be so, even without any incriminating statement from the subject himself.

B. Point out Some, but by No Means All, of the Circumstantial Evidence Indicative of a Subject's Guilt

A mistake which criminal interrogators frequently make is to reveal to the subject all that is known about the case and about the suspect himself. Seldom is anything gained by this approach, and frequently much is lost. On the other hand, it is helpful to point out to the subject some one piece of evidence bearing on his guilt. For instance, in a hit-and-run automobile case, let the subject know (if it be a fact) that a dent has been observed on the left front fender of his car and that human hair and blood have been found around the dented area. In a theft case, the subject can and should be told (if it be a fact) that the interrogator knows that a substantial loan was paid off by the subject soon after the theft. In other words, some one thing should be told the subject in order to satisfy him that there is good reason for questioning him, and that the investigators are not just on a "fishing expedition."

Another approach which should be avoided is that which may be described as "high pressure salesmanship," whereby the interrogator goes into a rapid fire monologue, indulging in accusations and perhaps telling the subject all the interrogator knows about the case and about the circumstances pointing toward the subject's guilt. In such instances very little of what the interrogator says will soak in or have any effect whatsoever.

Once the subject's attention is called to a particular piece of incriminating evidence the interrogator must be on guard to cut off immediately any explanation the subject may start to offer at that time. This can be done by saying, "Wait a minute. Wait until I'm through and then I'll hear what you have to say." In this way, the interrogator may retain control or mastery of the situation. On the other hand, to permit the subject to offer an explanation of the incriminating evidence will serve to bolster his confidence, for then he is putting the interrogator on the defensive and this should never be permitted to occur. The psychological considerations here involved are very important, for the impression created at this early stage of the interrogation may set the pattern for all that follows. (Again we wish to remind the reader that we are here speaking only of a person whose guilt is definite or reasonably certain.)

In addition to calling some particular circumstantial evidence to the subject's attention, the interrogator may resort to the following stageplay, in an appropriate case situation, for the purpose of having the subject believe there is considerably more evidence against him. It consists of having, on a table in the interrogation room, a large file folder or batch of papers, into which the interrogator may look at the beginning of the interrogation, and at other times too, for the purpose of leading the subject to believe that it contains information and material of incriminating significance. Where the interrogator does have something specific by way of incriminating evidence, he may mention it while going through the file, as though the information were actually contained therein. All this is done in a manner which conveys the impression that the particular bit of information or material is only a small part of the incriminating data embodied in the complete file.

The foregoing tactic is particularly effective when the subject is a professional or business man who is himself accustomed to working with files and records. To him the consultation of the file by the interrogator may have a special impact. However, it can be effective on certain other types of subjects as well.

Apart from the psychological considerations underlying the suggestion that a subject should not be told all the details known about the crime, there is another, and very practical, reason for withholding many of the details. On those rare occasions when a subject may be a pathological liar, or when the interrogator may have some concern over that possibility, it is extremely helpful to be able to check what the subject says against the known facts which had not been disclosed to him and which he could know about only by reason of his having actually committed the crime. Following is a case which illustrates the point.

An elderly woman was brutally assaulted sexually and killed while in the kitchen of her home. The suspect, who confessed to the offense, did so rather quickly and in such a manner that the interrogator wondered whether the confession was genuine. Fortunately, no one had told the suspect the details of the offense, such as the exact nature of the victim's injuries, and the place where certain objects had been thrown; nor had anyone described the kitchen itself to the subject. An accurate revelation by the subject of these various details, including an accurate description of the kitchen, quickly allayed the interrogator's concern as to the validity of the confession. Had the subject been told all this before his confession, the case would have given the interrogator considerable concern.

While on the subject of circumstantial evidence, perhaps a suggestion is in order regarding the rather common mistake criminal investigators make by failing to face up to the stark reality that *when circumstantial evidence points toward a particular person, that person is usually the one who committed the offense.* Some investigators and interrogators seem overwhelmed by the fact that the circumstantial evidence does point so strongly to a particular person—to someone closely connected to the victim or to the scene of the crime, or to someone with a good opportunity or motive for its commission. It all appears too good to be true, and thus the obvious is overlooked. This attitude develops quite often in cases in which the circumstantially incriminated person is one of social or professional prominence. A good example is that of a clergyman who is circumstantially implicated in a sex-motivated murder. By reason of his exalted position the clergyman may be interrogated only casually or perhaps not at all, and yet it is an established fact that occasionally clergymen do commit such offenses.

C. Call Attention to the Subject's Physiological and Psychological Symptoms of Guilt

An offender who is led to believe that his appearance and demeanor are betraying him is thereby placed in a much more vulnerable position. His belief that he is exhibiting symptoms of guilt has the effect of destroying or diminishing his confidence in his ability to deceive and tends to convince him of the futility of further resistance. This attitude, of course, places him much nearer the confession stage.

This technique of calling attention to various physiological and psychological phenomena as symptoms of guilt may be utilized somewhat as follows, but the reader should bear in mind that, with one possible exception, none of these phenomena is a reliable indication of guilt.

1. Pulsation of Carotid Artery

Although an accelerated pulsation of the carotid artery in the neck is experienced by some innocent persons as well as a certain number of guilty ones, such a phenomenon exhibited by a guilty subject can be commented upon to good advantage. In doing so, the interrogator, pointing to the pulsations of his own neck artery, may remark, "You are so concerned over the fact you have not told the whole truth that this artery in your neck is pumping away so fast it can be seen clear across the room; that sort of thing doesn't happen when a man is telling the truth, regardless of how nervous he may be."

2. Excessive Activity of the Adam's Apple

For much the same reason, and in much the same way as with No. 1 above, it is well to comment upon the over-activity of a subject's epiglottis or Adam's apple. The fact that an acceleration of its up and down movement is experienced by many offenders when questioned—and particularly when first accused—is well-recognized among experienced interrogators.

3. Looking at Floor or Ceiling Rather Than Looking the Interrogator "Straight in the Eye"; Swinging One Leg over the Other; Foot-Wiggling; Wringing of the Hands, or Tapping with the Fingers; Picking Fingernails; etc.

When a subject fails to look the interrogator straight in the eye (and looks at the floor, wall, or ceiling instead), or when he exhibits a restlessness by leg-swinging, foot-wiggling, hand-wringing, finger-tapping, the picking of his fingernails, or the fumbling with objects such as a tie clasp or pencil, it is well for the interrogator to get the idea across that he is aware of such reactions and that he views them as manifestations of lying. A glance at the subject's foot or hand movements, even without any accompanying comment, will probably cause the subject some concern that he is thereby "giving himself away." As to his not looking the interrogator straight in the eye (which many people associate with truth-telling) there are several procedures available. If the look at the floor, wall, or ceiling happens at the beginning or during the early stages of the interrogation, an emphatic mention of the subject's name, followed by a slight pause before anything further is said, will serve to convey the idea that the subject should look at the interrogator and not away from him.

No challenge should ever be issued to subjects who do not look the interrogator straight in the eye, such as, "Joe, you can't look me straight in the eye and tell me that," because the subject may respond by saying, "Oh yes I can," and proceed to look the interrogator straight in the eye. Thereafter the subject will have greater confidence in himself and succeed in keeping the interrogator on the defensive.

Many subjects who are on the verge of confessing will start picking their fingernails, or scratching themselves, or dusting their clothing with hand movements, or they will begin fumbling with a tie clasp or other small object. As politely as the interrogator can, he should seek to terminate such conduct. He may do so by gently lifting the subject's hand or by removing the object from his hand, always avoiding any rudeness as he seeks to end such tension-relieving activities.

4. The "Peculiar Feeling Inside"

When a subject of the emotional offender type is being interrogated, it is advisable to remind the subject that he "doesn't feel very good inside," and that this peculiar feeling (as if "all his insides were tied in a knot") is the result of a troubled conscience.

5. Dryness of the Mouth

A fairly reliable symptom of deception is a condition describable as "dryness of the mouth," provided the interrogator can be reasonably sure that the subject is not under some kind of medication that may have produced such a side-effect.

Dryness of the mouth may be observed in a subject by his

swallowing motions accompanied by repeated attempts to wet the lips, which are sometimes so dry and sticky that upon parting they emit a smacking sound. (This condition is apparently due to an inhibition in the functioning of the salivary glands, which thereby produces a deficiency of saliva in the mouth.)

Whenever this condition is observed, the interrogator should call it to the subject's attention by first asking the question, "Your mouth's very dry, isn't it?" After receiving the usual affirmative reply, it is well to supplement this question with another, "Feels like you have a mouthful of cotton, doesn't it?" Then the interrogator should comment as follows: "That's the result of your not telling the truth. The glands in your mouth that produce the saliva are not functioning properly—they've just about quit for the time being; you can drink all the water your stomach can hold without getting any relief. There's only one remedy, and that is to tell the truth."

6. Swearing to the Truthfulness of Assertions

Quite often a guilty subject will invoke such expressions as, "I swear to God I'm telling the truth," "I hope my mother drops dead if I'm lying," "I'll swear on a stack of Bibles," etc. Although expressions of this type cannot be considered as symptoms of deception, they frequently are used by guilty subjects in an effort to lend forcefulness or conviction to their assertions of innocence. Consequently, whenever the subject swears to the truthfulness of his statements, or, better yet, whenever he starts to raise his hand with that apparent purpose in mind, the interrogator should comment upon the psychological significance of his conduct somewhat as follows: "Put your hand down! When you're telling the truth I'll know it; you won't have to swear to it. The reason for your swearing is that you know you're not telling the truth and you know I know it. So you're trying to make your story sound convincing by swearing to it. From now on let's have no more of that."

7. "Spotless Past Record"—"Religious Man"

The same psychological motivation for swearing is involved in the use of such expressions as, "I have a spotless record," or, "I'm a very religious man; I couldn't do anything like that." In instances where expressions of this type are used, the interrogator should counter with comments to the effect that even assuming that to be true, he knows that the subject is still responsible for the act under investigation. Moreover, the interrogator should point out to him the reason for his assertions of a spotless past record or religious nature—that they are made in an effort to lend support to statements which he knows, and realizes the interrogator knows, to be false. The following comments will serve the purpose: "I don't care how religious you are; I don't care how many days a week you go to church; and I don't care how spotless your past record may be. The fact of the matter is you are not telling the truth now. You're dragging your religion into this and giving me this business about your spotless record in an effort to make your story sound convincing. The only thing that's going to be convincing to me is when you start telling the truth." At this point the interrogator should go right into his interrogation, without pausing for any comments or explanations from the subject.

8. *"Not That I Remember" Expression*

Very often a lying subject will resort to the use of a "Not that I remember" response when answering a question pertaining to facts or events which, in view of their nature, or the time and place of occurrence, might reasonably be expected to have been so definitely impressed upon the subject's mind that an unequivocal "Yes" or "No" answer should be forthcoming.

This response, or any other similar one such as, "Not that I recall," or, "As far as I know," should be treated as a veiled admission or "half-truth." The interrogator should immediately thereafter ask a detailed question regarding some aspect of the offense, and one that is based upon an assumption of the subject's guilt. For instance, in the investigation of the stabbing of John Jones at the corner of Fifth and Main Street, a suspect may be asked if it isn't a fact that he was at the corner about the time of the stabbing. If he says, "Not that I remember," the interrogator should immediately ask a question such as, "What did you do with the knife, Joe?" In other words, the "Not that I remember" should be treated as though he admitted the stabbing.

D. Sympathize with the Subject by Telling Him That Anyone Else under Similar Conditions or Circumstances Might Have Done the Same Thing

A criminal offender, and particularly one of the emotional type, derives considerable mental relief and comfort from an interrogator's assurance that anyone else under similar conditions or circumstances might have done the same thing. He is thereby enabled to at least partially justify or excuse in his own mind his offensive act or behavior. Yet there still remains the realization that a wrong has been committed or a mistake made that has been injurious or damaging to another person. The self-condonation, therefore, does not completely satisfy the offender's desire for relief from a troubled conscience. As a matter of fact, the comfort derived from the interrogator's assurances that another person might have committed a similar offense merely offers an added incentive to him for obtaining the greater degree of relief and comfort that would be provided by a confession of guilt. While the subject is in such a frame of mind, the solicitations of a sympathetic interrogator seem to cast a shadow over the subject's previously clear vision of the legal consequences of an exposure of his guilt.

An illustration of the type of case in which this technique may be used very effectively is one involving the interrogation of a hit-and-run driver in a fatal automobile accident. For instance, when a hit-and-run driver is made to believe—and often rightly so—that anyone else under similar conditions of panic might also have fled from the scene, he is afforded an opportunity to "square himself" with his own conscience. Meanwhile, his realization that he was less savage-like in his behavior than he first assumed himself to be renders his task of confessing a much easier one than would otherwise be the case. In the sense in which Orientals use the term, he is thus permitted to "save face."

Following is a presentation of the line of conversation that has been found to be effective in the interrogation of an offender such as a hit-and-run driver: "I'm sure in my own mind that a man like you wouldn't deliberately run over anyone. I think I know what happened; your car hit something, and only then did you realize it was a person. You then got so excited and nervous that you didn't think there was anything else you could do but to keep on driving. But the farther you went the worse you felt, and you feel pretty awful now. My advice to you is to tell what happened and get this load off your chest. You'll feel better deep down inside. I know you will. I have talked to a lot of people like you—good people—who got involved in things like this."

In hit-and-run cases, and in fact in all other types of crimes as well, it is helpful for the interrogator to bear in mind the various factors that may account for a person's behavior in such circumstances. For instance, in the published literature regarding hit-and-run automobile cases, the following factors are known to account for flight from the scene of the accident: the motorist responds to panic or is psychologically numbed by the shock of the occurrence; he is under the influence of alcohol; he is driving without a license; he fears financial loss or public shame; he has a passenger in the car whose presence would cause him or the passenger considerable embarrassment; or he has stolen goods or other evidence of a crime in the car, or else he is fearful of exposure for some other criminal offense.

Suggesting to the subject any appropriate one of the foregoing reasons why he fled the scene of the accident will contribute greatly to the success of the interrogation.

As regards non-emotional offenders, when financial gain is the objective, the subject may be told: "I know how financially pressed you are. You were so hemmed in you could see no way out but to do what you did. Anyone else confronted with a similar situation might have done the same thing."

In addition to utilizing this technique for the purpose of justifying or excusing the offense itself, the interrogator should pursue a similar course with regard to the subject's conduct in previously denying his guilt to the investigating officers or perhaps even to the present interrogator himself during the initial stages of the interrogation. Therefore, in an effort to pave the way for an incriminating statement, the subject should be told that neither the interrogator nor any of the investigators resent his previous or persistent lying up to the present time—since anyone else, including the investigators themselves, probably would have done likewise under similar circumstances. The interrogator should then state that now, however, he should proceed to tell the truth. By this assurance the interrogator removes another barrier from the subject's mind— namely, the deterrent effect of his previous lies told to a person, or persons, to whom he now desires to be truthful.

In applying the present technique the interrogator must be careful not to violate the legal prohibition against making promises of immunity or diminution of punishment as an inducement for confessing, but there is no legal objection to extending sympathy to an accused person in an effort to get him to tell the truth.

E. Reduce the Subject's Guilt Feeling by Minimizing the Moral Seriousness of his Offense

Although this technique is of value in many types of cases, it is particularly effective in sex cases. In such cases it is desirable for the interrogator to pursue a practice of having the subject believe that his particular sexual irregularity is not an unusual one, but rather one that occurs quite frequently, even among so-called normal and respectable persons. In this connection it has been found effective to comment as follows: "We humans are accustomed to thinking of ourselves as far removed from animals, but we're only kidding ourselves. In matters of sex we're very close to most animals, so don't think you're the only human being—or that you're one of the very few—who ever did anything like this. There are plenty of others, and these things happen every day and to many persons, and they will continue to happen for many, many years to come." In appropriate instances, with the so-called "intellectual" type of subject, it may be helpful to support these statements by a reference to the Kinsey reports, which reveal a high incidence of "irregular" sexual practices among both males and females.[8]

In sex cases it is also very helpful to tell the subject that the in-

---

[8] See KINSEY, POMEROY, AND MARTIN, SEXUAL BEHAVIOR IN THE HUMAN MALE (1948), and KINSEY, POMEROY, MARTIN, AND GEBHARD, SEXUAL BEHAVIOR IN THE HUMAN FEMALE (1953).

terrogator has heard many persons tell about sex activities far worse than any the subject can relate about himself.

Whenever referring to the particular sex act about which the subject is being questioned, the interrogator should never describe it in vulgar terms, unless, of course, the subject is incapable of understanding more acceptable terminology. If the act is of a homosexual nature, the harshly descriptive expression of the act itself should never be mentioned. It is far better to refer to the act as "kissing off," or some other similar expression. Then, too, the conduct itself should be discussed as though it were actually normal, either by reason of its prevalence among certain groups, or by reason of the particular physiological or psychological personality of the subject, in which event the interrogator should speak as though the subject had no control over the development of his homosexual tendencies.

With non-emotional offenders—a thief, for example—the interrogator can point out that most people will steal if given the opportunity. The subject's attention may be called to published reports which disclose the high incidence of larceny and embezzlement among employees, etc. A published article by one of the authors might be used for this purpose; the article contains the statement that "about 85 out of every 100 persons will 'steal' if the opportunity to do so is presented to them." [9]

Following is an illustration of the application of this technique in a wife-killing case, in which the investigation revealed that the deceased wife had treated the subject, her husband, very miserably over the years: "Joe, as recently as just last week my wife made me so angry with her nagging that I felt I couldn't stand it anymore, but just as she was at her worst the doorbell rang and we had some out-of-town company. Was I glad they came! Otherwise I don't know what I would have done. You were not as lucky as I was on this occasion. Wasn't it something like that? Or was it over her spending all your money? Or did you find out she was running around with some other man? It must have been something of this sort that touched you off, or maybe it was a combination of several

[9] Inbau, *The Social and Ethical Requirements of Criminal Prosecution*, 52 J. CRIM. L., C. & P. S. 209, 211(1961).

things like that. You've never been in trouble before, so it must have been something like what I've just mentioned—something that got you on the spur of the moment and you couldn't stop yourself."

Not only is it effective to compare the subject's conduct with that of "lots of other people," including the interrogator himself, but also, where circumstances permit, to compare the subject's present offense with his prior similar (or lesser) offenses. This too, serves to minimize the moral seriousness of the offense about which the subject is being questioned. The application of this technique in the interrogation of a rapist-murderer was instrumental in eliciting his confession of the killing of his latest rape victim. During the subject's interrogation, the interrogator told him that his rape-murder was no worse than the many other non-fatal rapes he had committed (and to which he had confessed during an earlier period of his interrogation). He was told that in the one case where death had resulted he merely "got a tough break"—as was true to a considerable extent, because from all indications he apparently only wanted to subdue his victim's resistance rather than kill her. (He had choked and slugged the victim in a fit of passion, which was his usual practice with others, but in this particular instance the girl failed to recover consciousness soon enough, with the result that he assumed she was dead and disposed of her body by throwing it from his car. Her life might have been spared if he had only given her sufficient time to recover from the effects of his prior acts of violence.) During an interview which one of the authors had with the subject a few days before his execution, the latter stated that at the time of his interrogation just prior to his confession he had been comforted by the interrogator's remarks regarding the "no worse" aspect of his present offense in comparison with his previous ones.

As previously stated with respect to Technique D, the interrogator must avoid any expressed or intentionally implied statement to the effect that because of the minimized seriousness of the offense, the subject is to receive a lighter punishment. Nevertheless, there is no legal objection to minimizing in the subject's mind the moral seriousness of the offense in his particular case.

F. Suggest a Less Revolting and More Morally Acceptable Motivation or Reason for the Offense Than That Which Is Known or Presumed

A criminal offender should always be afforded an opportunity to save face by letting him base his initial admission of guilt upon a motivation or reason that is less offensive, morally speaking, than the real motivation or reason for his act.

A good example of the application of the present technique is the sex-motivated arsonist. The true motivation for the offense is now very revolting to him, and it is difficult for him to acknowledge it right away. Consequently, the interrogator should suggest that perhaps the subject *accidentally* started the fire. The objective at this point is to have the subject place himself at the scene of the occurrence. Once that is done, an acknowledgment of the true facts is rather easily obtainable.

Another illustration is the sex-motivated murderer. The sex feature of the killing is now not only extremely revolting to the subject, but he also realizes that it is very revolting to others. Therefore, when he reaches the confession state—when he feels the compulsion to admit the offense—it is much easier for him to start by attributing the victim's death to an accident, or to the result of an attempted robbery, or to some other such factor. Intoxication at the time of the occurrence is another face saver. Therefore, in order to secure the initial admission of guilt, the interrogator should suggest such possible reasons, motives, or excuses. The important thing is to have the subject place himself at the scene or to connect himself with the event in some way or another. Thereafter it is relatively easy to obtain a full, truthful disclosure of the true reason or motivation.

As to the specific way in which this technique can be used in a case such as a sex-motivated murder, here is the language the interrogator may use: "Joe, what happened? Did this girl go along with you at first, and then all of a sudden she let out a scream? You then had no alternative but to stop her yelling, and that's all you were trying to do, but she caused you to use more force than you ever intended. That's about it, isn't it, Joe?"

In a robbery-killing case, the interrogator should suggest that the subject did not intend or plan to kill, and that his only motive was to get money, but that he had to shoot to save his own life after the person he tried to rob pulled a gun or knife on him.

The self-defense excuse can also be used in other types of killings or near-killings for the purpose of obtaining the initial admission of guilt. For instance, where the known or presumed motive for a shooting was revenge, the interrogator may say to the subject: "Joe, you probably didn't go out looking for this fellow with the purpose of shooting him. My guess is, however, that you expected something from him and that's why you carried a gun—for your own protection. You knew him for what he was, no good. Then when you met him he probably started using foul, abusive language and he gave some indication that he was about to pull a gun on you, and that's when you had to act to save your own life. That's about it, isn't it, Joe?"

Following an admission of the shooting in a case such as the one described above, the interrogator can then proceed to point out that the circumstantial evidence (location of the wound, position of the body, etc.) negates the self-defense explanation. Thereafter, with relative ease, the interrogator will be able to secure the true explanation. Even if he fails to do so, the inconsistency between the subject's original denial of the shooting and his present admission of at least doing the shooting will serve to deprive him of a self-defense "out" at the time of trial.

In the interrogation of an embezzler the suggestion may be offered that the subject only intended to "borrow" the money rather than steal it, and that had it not been for the untimely discovery of the shortage he would have replaced the money somehow.

Another approach with an embezzler is to suggest that he probably took the money for the benefit of a wife, daughter, or other person. This is particularly effective when the interrogator knows that such a person was in need of financial aid and did actually receive aid from some source. For instance, a suspected bank teller was known to be financing his son's attendance at a theological seminary, which the teller could not afford on his bank salary. The interrogator suggested that the teller's desire to assist his son was the motive for the embezzlement, although the interrogator knew that the embezzled funds far exceeded the money needed by the son. The suggested motive, however, served the purpose of securing the initial admission, after which the subject eventually disclosed the real reason for the theft.

Occasionally the real reason for an embezzlement is, in fact, the suggested one—a sick child or a pregnant wife and the need to pay doctor and hospital bills. In many such instances the authors have recommended to the employers that they continue such confessed embezzlers in their employment. Apart from the humanitarian considerations involved, a persuasive practical argument in support of this practice is the fact that there is no assurance that a replacement of the confessed embezzler would be any better security risk. On the other hand, if the motive for embezzlement was to cover up or recoup gambling losses, the embezzler should be dismissed. He is a poor security risk. Moreover, for his own future welfare it is probably better that he not continue in a situation where he has access to cash belonging to a bank or other employer.

A female thief or embezzler is particularly vulnerable to the suggestion that her stealing was for the benefit of someone else—a child, her husband, her boy friend, etc. In fact, that is very often the reason why a female steals. Her thievery ordinarily is less selfishly motivated than a man's.

In a theft case, the suggestion may be offered that the subject took the missing item (purse, money, etc.) by mistake and then later was afraid to return it because he thought the owner might not believe that it really was taken by mistake. Also, in a theft case where the interrogator knows or has good reason to believe that gambling losses or the subject's propensity to gamble constitutes the probable reason for his thievery, it is well to talk to the subject somewhat as follows: "Joe, we are all human beings and we all have our faults and weaknesses. There's the good and the bad in all of us. Some people go nuts over women; others over whiskey. In your case it's gambling, and, except for the fact that it got too good a grip on you, you're no different from a lot of other people. Ninety-nine out of a hundred people gamble at one time or another, and a good percentage of us are chronic gamblers—we can't keep away from it. But one thing about gambling; it's a cleaner weakness than some of the others—like an irresistible urge to rape, or to drink excessively, or to use dope. Joe, what bit of gambling got you in the hole so that you had to make up for it by taking this money the other day?"

In all cases where an interrogator uses this technique of suggesting a less revolting and more morally acceptable motivation or reason than the one that is known or presumed, it is very important that he follow up by seeking an admission of the actual one. He should do this even though the criminal responsibility is in no way altered by the kind of motivation or reason for the criminal act. For instance, although it is immaterial, in the legal sense, whether a person embezzles to aid a sick child or to gamble, the interrogator should nevertheless seek the true explanation for the offender's conduct. Preceding this, however, the interrogator should obtain from the subject a full disclosure of the various details of the offense.

The importance of securing a true explanation for the offense lies in the fact that, in many cases, the real reason or motivation for an offense may be subject to corroboration by subsequent investigation, whereas an untruthful one is obviously not subject to supporting proof.

There will be occasions, of course, when a subject adheres to the face-saving explanation suggested by the interrogator. This risk, however, is not a serious one, particularly in view of the fact that many subjects will resort to this face-saving device without the benefit of any suggestion from the interrogator himself. Moreover, it is also a fact that most confessors to crimes of a serious nature will lie about some aspect of the occurrence, even though they disclose the full truth regarding the main event. They will lie about some detail of the crime for which they have a greater feeling of shame than that which they experience with respect to the main event. For instance, a sex-motivated murderer may make a complete and truthful disclosure of the killing, but at the same time he may lie about his sexual conduct. A burglar-murderer may freely reveal all the details of killing but still lie about taking a gold crucifix from the victim's home. These are psychological realities and it is well for judges, prosecutors, defense counsel, and criminal interrogators to recognize them in evaluating the trustworthiness of confessions which are obviously lacking in completely accurate disclosures of the details of the admitted criminal offense.[10]

G. Sympathize with the Subject by (1) Condemning His Victim, (2) Condemning His Accomplice, or (3) Condemning Anyone Else upon Whom Some Degree of Moral Responsibility Might Conceivably Be Placed for the Commission of the Crime in Question

The psychological basis for this suggested technique can be appreciated quite readily by anyone who will reflect upon his own non-criminal wrongdoings and upon the occasions (particularly during childhood) when he had to "own up" to them. In such instances there is a natural inclination to preface the admissions with a condemnation of the victimized person or thing, or with a statement purporting to place part or even all of the blame on someone else. The same mental forces are in operation in matters involving criminal offenses—and to an even greater degree by reason of their more serious nature.

In view of the fact that self-condonation of this type so frequently accompanies a confession of guilt—with the offender seeking by this means to more or less justify or excuse the offense in his own mind—it seems only reasonable to presume that an interrogator's condemnation of the offender's victim, accomplice, or others would prove to be effective in provoking or expediting a confession. Moreover, actual experience has demonstrated this to be so.

The following description of several case situations illustrates the manner in which this technique can be applied.

1. Condemn the Victim

The propensity of a wrongdoer to put all or part of the blame for his conduct upon his victim will be readily apparent by a re-

[10] An excellent illustration of this point is the case of State v. Rogers, 233 N.C. 390, 64 S.E. 572 (1951), where the defendant had confessed to the killing of a woman who had been raped and robbed, but denied the rape and robbery, even though the evidence was conclusive of the defendant's responsibility for all three offenses.

flection upon our own childhood experiences. Let us recall an event such as this one, which must lurk in the memory of many of us. One Sunday morning you saw little Johnny, your next door neighbor, standing on the sidewalk all ready for Sunday school or church. Just because of your own disagreeable mood, and for no other recognizable reason, you pushed Johnny down. The fall tore a hole in the knee of his trousers. He ran crying to his mother, and then your mother had you before her for an explanation of the event and a possible reprimand or punishment. What was your initial reaction? To deny it all; to deny you pushed Johnny down! But that cannot be done under present circumstances since your own mother saw you push Johnny, and she only inquires of you, "Why did you do it?"

If you conducted yourself according to the usual pattern, you probably responded somewhat as follows: "Mother, he pushed me first," or, "He called me a bad name," (or better yet, "Mother, he called you a bad name!"). "That's why I pushed him." All this was untrue, of course, but you defended your actions in this manner. You condemned the victim, and in doing so you reacted in a perfectly normal way. Even today, as adults, we still resort to the same kind of blame-escaping tactics and techniques.

In view of the normality and prevalence of this victim-blaming characteristic in wrongdoers, what does this suggest, then, by way of an interrogation device? It suggests that the interrogator use it as "bait" in the interrogation of criminal suspects—in other words, during the course of an interrogation the interrogator should develop the thesis that the primary blame, or at least some of the blame, for what the subject did rests upon the victim himself.

For purposes of illustration, take the case of a man suspected of killing his wife, in which the investigation reveals that the wife had treated the suspect very miserably over the years. Under such circumstances it is well for the interrogator to let the subject know that he is aware of what the suspect was up against. The interrogator should condemn the wife for her conduct, and the point should be made that by her own conduct she herself brought on the incident of the killing.

In cases of this type, much can be gained by the interrogator's adoption of an emotional ("choked-up") feeling about it all as he relates what he knows about the victim's conduct toward her husband. This demonstrable attitude of sympathy and understanding may be rather easily assumed by placing one's self in the other fellow's shoes and asking himself, "What might I have done under similar circumstances?"

Some outstanding examples of the effectiveness of this technique are to be found in sex cases involving offenses in which the victims are children. In such cases, when an adult offender confesses, he almost always places the blame upon his victim, even though the victim may be an eight-year-old child. The presence of this trait should in itself suggest the technique to be used in the interrogation of offenders of this type—namely, the condemnation of the victim: the placing of the blame on the child for doing something that triggered the subject's emotional outburst.

In a case of one of the authors, which involved the interrogation of a fifty-year-old man who was accused of having taken indecent liberties with a ten-year-old girl, the subject was told: "This girl is well-developed for her age. She probably learned a lot about sex from the boys in the neighborhood and from the movies and TV; and knowing what she did about it, she may have deliberately tried to excite you to see what you would do." The offender then confessed, but, true to the characteristics of his group, he proceeded to place the blame on the child. Even if this were so, of course he would still be just as guilty in the eyes of the law.

Whenever a sex offense involving a child has resulted in some actual physical harm to her, it is well for the interrogator to supplement the placing of blame on the child with a statement that the subject must have been only trying to please the child—just trying to make her happy—and that any hurt to her was purely accidental.

The interrogation technique of condemning the victim can also be used advantageously in other types of sex cases—for example, a forcible rape—by suggesting to the subject that the victim was to blame for dressing or behaving in such a way as to unduly excite a man's passion. The discussion might go somewhat as follows: "Joe, no woman should be on the street alone at night looking as sexy as she did. Even here today she's got on a low-cut dress that makes visible damn near all of her breasts. That's wrong! It's too much of a temptation for any normal man. If she hadn't gone around dressed like that you wouldn't be in this room now."

If the forcible rape occurred in the suspect's car or in his or the victim's residence, she can be blamed for behaving in such a way as to arouse the subject sexually to a point where he just had to have an outlet for his feelings. For instance: "Joe, this girl was having a lot of fun for herself by letting you kiss her and feel her breasts. For her that would have been sufficient. But men aren't built the same way. There's a limit to the teasing and excitement they can take; then something's got to give. A female ought to realize this, and if she's not willing to go all the way, she ought to stop way short of what this gal did to you."

Where circumstances permit, the suggestion might be offered that the rape victim acted like she might be a prostitute and that the suspect assumed she was a willing partner. In fact, the interrogator may even say that the police knew she had engaged in acts of prostitution on other occasions; the question may then be asked, "Did she try to get some money out of you—perhaps more than you actually had, but once you were that close to her you couldn't help but complete what she started?" Any such condemnation will make it easier for the subject to admit the act of intercourse, or at least his presence in the company of the victim.

The degrading of the character of the victim can also be used in cases such as one in which the subject is being interrogated regarding the killing of a fellow criminal or of a police officer. The victim can be pictured as "no good"—as one who was always up to crooked deals, shakedowns, etc.

In assault cases, the victim may be referred to as someone who was always "pushing other people around," and that perhaps he finally got what was coming to him.

The main objective of the interrogator in many instances is to have the subject place himself at the scene, or in contact with the victim. Once that is accomplished the interrogator will later on be able to have the subject relate the true facts of what occurred. For instance, in an assault case, once the subject admits he was involved in the incident, the exercise of a little patience will ultimately result in a disclosure of a guilty subject's full responsibility for the occurrence.

In embezzlement cases—and here we refer particularly to first offenders and to those whose motive arises more or less from a need or desire for more money than is represented by their salary. rather than from a scheme to "get rich quick"—it is well to condemn the employer for paying inadequate and insufficient salaries, or for some unethical or careless practice which may have created a temptation to steal. For example, in interrogating a bank teller, the subject might be asked, "How much money do you make, Joe?" after which the interrogator mentions a purposely overstated amount. Then when the subject states the actual salary amount, the interrogator may say, "Ye gods, man, how in the world can anybody with a family the size of yours get along on that kind of money in this day and time? Moreover, the temptations you face every day! You handle thousands upon thousands of dollars, and for a salary like that. And you're not only supposed to live on it but be a first-rate dresser as well. That's something common laborers don't have to do. They can go around in old, dirty clothes, and they make twice as much money a day as you do. Joe, when did you start taking the money?" (Or "What did you do with the money, Joe?" or "Where is it now?" etc.)

Following is an example of how the technique of condemning the employer for his or her carelessness may be used with employees such as household maids. Assume that the missing item about which the maid is being questioned is a fur coat. "Helen, your employer had several fur coats and I'll bet she threw them down all around the house or else treated them like they were cheap pieces of cloth. Many times you probably had to pick them up and put them away yourself. You probably got the idea she didn't much care for the coats and wouldn't even miss one if it did disappear. That's probably what gave you the idea. Then after you took the coat maybe you got to thinking about what you had done and would like to have brought it back but couldn't. That's the story, Helen. Right?"

2. Condemn the Accomplice

For much the same reason that a youngster with a baseball bat in hand alleges to an irate home-owner near the playing field that "we" (he and his teammates) broke the window—rather than stating that "I" did it (meaning the batsman who struck the ball its damaging blow), the criminal offender is naturally inclined to have someone else share the blame or even be blamed altogether for the commission of the crime in question. Any line of interrogation, therefore, which tends to lift from him some of the burden of guilt he bears for his criminal act will make him that much less reluctant to confess.

It was always a temptation, or even an instinctive reaction, for us as children to blame our playmates, in full or in part, for the mischief we ourselves did, either alone or with their help. For instance, recall such an occurrence as this one.

You and one or more youngsters were at a loss as to what to do some summer afternoon. You gazed at a neighbor's tomato patch and got the idea that it would be fun to engage in a "tomato war" —plucking the ripe tomatoes and throwing them at each other. This you did, all as a result of your own bright idea, but when your father began to question you about the event after he received the neighbor's complaint, what did you say? Did you own up to the deed and accept responsibility for leading your playmates into the tomato patch? You did not! First of all you tried to lie about it all, to deny any participation whatsoever in the act of destruction. But someone saw you throwing the tomatoes, and this your father knew. So what next? You instinctively tried to put the blame on "the other fellows": "Dad, I didn't pull any tomatoes off the vines. The only ones I threw were the ones that had been thrown at me." Today, as adults, we would seek the same way out if we were confronted with an accusation of wrongdoing which involved the participation of other persons. All this suggests, then, that in the interrogation of a suspect in a case involving another participant or participants, it is well to suggest that the primary blame, or at least some of the blame, belongs to the other fellow.

The manner in which the technique of condemning the accomplice may be utilized is aptly illustrated in the following description of an interrogation of a property owner who was accused of arson.

The subject had invested heavily in a real estate project which, as it neared completion, seemed doomed as a financial failure. In charge of the property in question was a handy man whose mental capacity was somewhat deficient. After a fire of suspicious origin, in which a large and heavily insured building was destroyed, the handy man, upon being questioned by investigators, confessed that he had set fire to the place at the request of the owner. On the basis of this confession, together with the evidence that the fire was of incendiary origin, the owner was arrested and charged with the offense. At first he denied his guilt, and he continued to do so even when confronted with the testimony of his employee. However, during a subsequent interrogation period, another interrogator proceeded to apply the above suggested technique of condemning the accomplice. The interrogator's expressions in this respect were somewhat as follows: "We all know—and you know—that there's considerable truth to what your employee says about the fire. We also know that a man of your type may not have done such a thing had it not been suggested or hinted at by someone else. It looks to me as if this fellow you have working for you may be the one who conceived this idea. He knew you were having a tough time financially, and he probably wanted to be sure his pay would go on, or perhaps he was looking for even more than that. For all I know he might have done this just for the purpose of getting you in trouble. Maybe he wanted to get even with you for something he thought you had done to him. That I don't know, and we won't know the true explanation unless you tell us. We know this much: the place was set afire; your employee did it; he says you told him to do it. We also know you haven't told the whole truth." (Along with all this, of course, the interrogator also freely applied the previously described Technique D.)

After an hour or so of such conversation, the subject admitted that he knew the property was to be set afire and had approved of the burning. At first he insisted, as the interrogator had indicated ıs a possibility, that it was the employee's idea, etc. This version, of course, was false; nevertheless, for a few minutes the interrogator permitted the subject to bask in the sunshine of this partial and reflected guilt and to derive therefrom the attending mental comfort and relief. However, soon thereafter the interrogator began to point out the lack of logic and reasonableness in the subject's fixation of primary blame upon his employee. The subject was told that he still did not look as relieved as a man should look after telling the truth. Then the interrogator proceeded to explain sympathetically that by coming out first with only part of the truth he was doing what all human beings do under similar circumstances. Finally, as a climax to such comments, the interrogator urged the subject to tell the whole truth. He then admitted that the idea of burning the building was his own. For the purpose of inducing the subject to begin his confession, however, it was necessary and effective for the interrogator to start off by first blaming the accomplice.

Another example of the "condemning the accomplice" technique is the following case of a robbery-murder, in which the police were convinced of the guilt of a seventy-two-year-old man and a thirty-year-old accomplice. The younger man, during his interrogation, was told: "That guy's always getting younger men and boys into trouble. He's been in trouble all his life, but he's never been in jail himself, although he's certainly been responsible for some younger fellows going there. It's time he got what was coming to him; he's long overdue."

In applying this technique of condemning the accomplice, the interrogator must proceed cautiously and refrain from making any comments to the effect that the blame cast on an accomplice thereby relieves the subject of legal responsibility for his part in the commission of the offense. By suggesting the application of this technique we merely recommend a moral condonation in the form of expressions of sympathy for the subject's "unfortunate" experience in having been influenced by his "criminally minded associate."

3. Condemn Others

In addition to victims and accomplices, there are others who may be condemned to good advantage. Toward this end the interrogator in some instances may find it effective to cast blame on government and society for permitting the existence of social and economic conditions which are conducive to the commission of crimes such as that for which the offender is accused. On other occasions the offender's parents, wife, etc., may be alleged blameworthy for the offender's conduct. Numerous other possible recipients of the interrogator's condemnation might be mentioned, but the following case descriptions will suffice to illustrate the application and effectiveness of this technique.

In the interrogation of an accused wife-killer (the one referred to in the previous discussion of privacy), the interrogator proceeded to condemn the wife's relatives, who were known to have meddled in the offender's marital affairs. They were blamed for having deliberately set about to render the subject's married life an unhappy one. At one point the interrogator remarked that probably the relatives themselves deserved to be shot. During the discussion the interrogator did not spare the wife either—nor wives in general. The subject's wife was alleged to be a provocative, unreasonable, and unbearable creature, a woman who would either drive a man insane or else to the commission of an act such as that perpetrated by the subject. In this respect, however, the interrogator stated that the subject's wife was just like most other women. The subject was also told that many married men avoid similar difficulties by becoming drunkards, cheats, and deserters, but unfortunately the subject tried to do what was right by sticking it out, and it got the better of him in the end. All of this, of course, rendered the subject's offense less reprehensible in his own mind, and his self-condonation finally overcame his desire to avoid an exposure of his guilt.

During the interrogation of a married rape suspect, blame may be cast upon the subject's wife for not providing him with the necessary sexual gratification. The discussion may proceed upon the following lines: "If your wife had taken care of you sexually, as she should have done, you wouldn't be here now. You're a healthy male; you needed, and were entitled to, sexual intercourse. And when a fellow like you doesn't get it at home he seeks it elsewhere. Moreover, since you're not able to search for and court a female as a single man is free to do, a fellow like you has to take what he finds; and sometimes, because of his terrific, pent-up urge he has to go about it in a rather hurried-up fashion. That's what you did here; that's the reason you did it. That's the story, isn't it, Joe?"

When the offense is theft or embezzlement, a spendthrift wife or child may be blamed for the subject's thievery. He may be told: "Your wife (or daughter, or son, if such is the case) has been pressuring you for more money than you were earning. You cared enough for her so that you wanted her to have all she asked for— even though you didn't have it to give, Joe. What you did here was for her; not for your own selfish interests. She shouldn't have asked for all she got from you. Now she will probably understand, and she should stick by you in your present difficulty. It's time now, Joe, for you to tell the truth."

A person who has taken indecent sexual liberties with a child, or hurt her in some other way, may be told that her parents are to blame for letting the child roam around by herself as they did. In instances where the subject had lured the child into his car or elsewhere by offering her candy, or something else in the way of a gift, the parents may be blamed for not providing such things themselves. Along with the blame-fixing upon the parents, the child herself may be blamed, as was suggested in the discussion of the earlier technique of condemning the victim. A moral coward of this type finds it very comforting to have his conduct understood on the basis of one or more of these considerations.

A thief such as a burglar or robber may be told that if there were no "fences" who bought and sold such stolen goods, the thief probably would not have done what he did. The interrogator may talk to him somewhat as follows, and particularly where the prinicipal objective is to build up a case against the "fence" himself. "Men like you wouldn't do the things you do if there were no 'fences.' Fellows like that are making monkeys out of people like you. You go out and risk your neck doing the job and taking all the chances of getting shot and killed. Then you bring what you took to one of these jerks and he gives you about 10 per cent of its value, after which he unloads it at a 90 per cent profit, minus, of course, what he has to give to the police as a 'payoff.' He makes a big haul. You take the chances; he makes the money. If there were no such people like that, men like you probably wouldn't get into this kind of trouble, because if you couldn't get rid of the stuff there would be no use taking it. Did any of these fences ever help you or any other men like you when you got in trouble? Hell, No! When a fellow like you gets put away the 'fence' gets himself someone else to do business with, and when that one gets sent away he finds another replacement. Everyone knows this, but when a 'fence' is questioned he grins and says, 'You don't have anything on me; I didn't do anything.' " We want to get at these fellows. If we can shut them off, you and a lot of others wouldn't be getting in trouble. They've been making suckers out of you guys long enough. It's time they be put out of business. They've been riding in Cadillacs long enough. What's this guy's name, Joe?"

Blame may be cast on high interest moneylenders (the so-called "loan sharks") for pressuring the subject for the payment of his loan at a time when he was unable to pay; in other words, his creditors "forced" him to steal. In such instances the subject may be told: "Joe, I know that it's hard today to get by without going into debt. I'm in debt myself, but fortunately I'm not over my head and my creditors are not loan sharks. You, however, have those fellows breathing down your neck, and they don't give a damn about men like you. All they're interested in is the big interest rates they get. And they suck people like you into believing that they are giving you a pretty good, easy-to-handle deal when they make a loan to you. I can't understand why the state allows them to get by with that kind of operation. They know damn well at the time a loan is made that you can't possibly keep up with it. It's hard enough to keep up the interest payments, to say nothing of the loan itself. You end up working for the loan sharks, and finally when they have you backed to the wall, you find that the only way out is to take someone else's money, just as you did the other day. That's about what got you into this difficulty, isn't it, Joe?"

In an arson case, blame may be placed upon the insurance company for permitting the accused and others to take out excessive insurance and to insure property far in excess of its actual value. The point to be made is that by this excessive insurance practice the insurance company presented too much of a temptation to set property afire for the insurance money, and particularly in those cases where the owner is hard pressed financially.

When the subject has committed a theft or embezzlement because of the apparent or surmised necessity of replenishing losses he sustained as a result of his own gambling activities, it is well for the interrogator to blame the police, or the prosecuting attorney, or the community as a whole for permitting gambling opportunities to exist. For instance, the subject may be told: "Joe, I know you've been doing a bit of gambling, and you got into the habit through little or no fault of your own. Too much temptation was put in front of you. The police and politicians are the ones to blame for letting the gambling joints operate. If they had shut up these places you probably wouldn't be here now, Joe, because you wouldn't have gambled and there would have been no occasion for you to take this money (or property)."

A suspected embezzler can be told, to good advantage, that we are living in times when money is treated rather casually by everyone, and particularly by the national government. We have, therefore, lost the old time regard for the money or possessions belonging to others. As an illustration the subject may be told that since the government squeezes us with burdensome taxes to obtain money to waste on foreign countries, it is no wonder that individuals like himself lose their own sense of values with respect to the money and property of other individuals.

Where the subject's home or neighborhood environment appears to be a factor accounting for his criminal conduct (as is so often the case), the interrogator should point out that fact to the subject. The application of this technique may be illustrated by the following statements made to a young robbery-murder suspect, who had actually encountered many of the experiences to which the interrogator referred: "Joe, you started out about the same way I did—the same way as a lot of kids. You had a mother and father, and then your luck changed and your father died when you were ten. Your mother had other children too, with very little to live on. You had to scratch for a living, and whatever you got you had to share or give to your mother and brothers. A child is a child and soon you probably had to take things from other people; otherwise you got nothing. That became a habit when you were a kid and it looked easy and then this thing happened. This would not have happened to you if your father had lived and been able to care for you and give you, your mother, and your brothers the necessities of life. If he had lived, you probably wouldn't be in this room today. Society should be blamed for not having found some way to help your poor mother when your father died so that it would have been unnecessary for you to develop the habits you did."

In a case where one or both parents were drunkards or otherwise neglected the subject as a child, the interrogator may say: "I can pretty well understand what would have happened to me if that condition existed in my home. No one to cook your meals or care whether you were living or dead. No wonder you finally got into something like this. You were worse off than an orphan. There are good homes for orphan kids but you couldn't have gotten into one because you were supposed to have a home and a father and a mother. Actually you didn't, and that's why you're in this trouble now."

H. Utilize Displays of Understanding and Sympathy in Urging the Subject to Tell the Truth

Although expressions of understanding and sympathy are essential factors in the successful application of the preceding techniques, under the present title we wish to suggest specific overtures which may be made toward that objective.

1. Extend Sympathy by Such Gestures as a Pat on the Shoulder or a Grip of the Hand

It is surprising how effective a well-timed pat on the shoulder or a grip of the hand can be in obtaining a confession. Coming as a climax to a series of sympathetic expressions constituting the basis for the previously employed techniques, a gesture of this sort may expedite a confession of guilt.

Considerable discretion must be exercised in the usage of the above suggested gestures. The pat on the shoulder should be reserved for males who are either (a) younger or of approximately the same age as the interrogator, or (b) of the first offender type. It should not be employed on a career criminal, or on the "cocky" type of person. Only rarely should it be used on older people, since to them the pretentiousness of the gesture may be too obvious.

With female offenders, it is most effective for the interrogator to place his hand on top of the subject's hand or hold her hand in the palm of his. If she begins to cry during the interrogation the interrogator may offer her the support of his shoulder, but within a very short time he should have her straighten up and the interrogation should be resumed.

Gestures of this type produce a very desirable pyschological effect. They impart to the subject an attitude of understanding and sympathy far better than any combination of words the interrogator can put together.

2. Tell the Subject That Even if He Were Your Own Brother (or Father, Sister, etc.) You Would Still Advise Him to Speak the Truth

A statement to this effect helps to establish the subject's confidence in the interrogator and thereby renders it easier for the subject to tell the truth.

3. Urge the Subject to Tell the Truth for the Sake of His Own Conscience, Mental Relief, or Moral Well-being, as Well as "for the Sake of Everybody Concerned," and Also Because It Is "the Only Decent and Honorable Thing to Do"

In urging or advising an offender to tell the truth the interrogator must avoid expressions which are objectionable on the grounds that they constitute illegal promises or threats. However, by speaking in generalities such as "for the sake of your conscience," or "for the sake of everybody concerned," etc., the interrogator can remain within permissible bounds.

A line of discussion which has been used to good advantage on many occasions (particularly in sex or embezzlement cases) is one in which the subject is advised that by telling the truth he performs somewhat of a mental operation on himself—an operation equally as important and necessary as the removal or destruction of injurious tissue in a cancer patient. In this respect it may be helpful to draw a circle on a piece of paper, mark off a small area on the rim of it, and tell the subject that in effect the marked-off portion represents a piece of infected tissue on his mind or soul which, if unarrested and unremoved, will continue to spread and produce other and more serious offenses than the one for which he is now accused. He should then be told that there is only one way that the necessary mental operation may be performed, and that is by telling the truth.

"For the sake of everybody concerned" is an expression which lends itself to many interpretations conducive to truth-telling. One consideration which it seems to bring to mind is the suffering of the victim or of his dependents, etc., or the wrong committed against other persons adversely affected as a result of the offender's conduct. It is advisable, therefore, to briefly mention these consequences for the purpose of placing the subject in a more regretful mood.

The expression, "It's the only decent and honorable thing to do," appears to constitute somewhat of a challenge for the offender to display some evidence of decency and honor. This is particularly so in sex cases where, in the absence of a plea of guilty, it would become necessary for the victim to undergo the ordeal of publicly relating the details of the offense committed against her; and in such instances it is occasionally helpful to ask the subject how he would like to have his own sister or mother appear in court as his victim may have to do. In playing upon this potential weakness, if the subject happens to be a religious person, discuss with him the tenets of his particular creed. Mention to him the fact that his religion becomes meaningless unless he tells the truth with regard to the offense in question. Likewise, if he belongs to a fraternal order, appeal to him in its name. It is also quite helpful if the interrogator can state that he or his parents or close friends belong to the same church or fraternity and that therefore he, the interrogator, knows and appreciates what the subject's moral obligations are in the present situation.

In a sex-murder case, in which the interrogator knew that the subject had an invalid mother, the appeal to the subject's "decency" was somewhat as follows: "Joe, a mother—and particularly one like yours—is the most understanding person in the world. Her real concern is about the reason for your doing this. That's what we all want to know—the reason. And your mother, in particular, is most entitled to know." The subject eventually responded by saying. "I'll tell you the whole story if I can first talk to my mother." The interrogator agreed and said he would send a car for the mother, but within a few minutes after making the request to see his mother, the subject made a full confession.

4. The "Friendly-Unfriendly" Act

When the various techniques of sympathy and understanding have proved ineffective, the interrogator may resort to a so-called "friendly-unfriendly" act. It may be carried on either by two interrogators cooperating together, or by one interrogator working alone.

When two interrogators are used, the technique may be applied somewhat as follows: Interrogator *A*, after having employed a sympathetic, understanding approach throughout his interrogation, expresses his regret over the subject's continued lying. *A* then leaves the room. Interrogator *B* enters and he proceeds to berate the subject, by referring to him as a rather despicable character, or perhaps as one who probably has been in a penitentiary or at least in prior police difficulties. (Or, *B* may enter while *A* is still in the room, and *B* can start his efforts by admonishing *A* for wasting his time on such an undesirable person; whereupon *A* will leave the room with pretended hurt feelings over the subject's refusal to tell him the truth.)

After Interrogator *B* (the unfriendly one) has been in the interrogation room for a short while, Interrogator *A* (the friendly one) re-enters and scolds *B* for his unfriendly conduct. *A* asks *B* to leave, and *B* goes out of the door with a pretended feeling of disgust toward both the subject and *A*. *A* then resumes his friendly, sympathetic approach.

This technique has been effectively applied by using a detective as the friendly interrogator and a police captain as the unfriendly one. As the captain leaves the room after playing his unfriendly role, the detective may say, "Joe, I'm glad you didn't tell him a damn thing. He treats everybody that way—persons like you, as well as men like me within his own department. I'd like to show him up by having you tell me the truth. It's time he learns a lesson or two about decent human behavior."

The psychological reason for the effectiveness of the friendly-unfriendly act is the fact that the contrast between the methods used by each interrogator serves to accentuate the friendly, sympathetic attitude of the first one and thereby renders his approach more effective.

In the employment of the friendly-unfriendly act, the second (unfriendly) interrogator should resort only to verbal condemnation of the subject; under no circumstances should he ever employ physical abuse or threats of abuse or other mistreatment.

Although the friendly-unfriendly act is usually performed by two persons, one interrogator can play both roles. In fact, the authors are of the opinion that this is the more effective way to apply the technique.

When a single interrogator acts out both parts he feigns impatience and unfriendliness by getting up from his chair and addressing the subject somewhat as follows: "Joe, I thought that there was something basically decent and honorable in you but apparently there isn't. The hell with it, if that's the way you want to leave it; I don't give a damn." The interrogator then sits down in the chair again, and after a brief pause, with no conversation at all, may say, "Joe, you'd tax the patience of a saint the way you've been acting. But I guess there is something worthwhile in you anyway." Or the interrogator may even apologize for his loss of patience by saying, "I'm sorry. That's the first time I've lost my head like that." The interrogator then starts all over with the reapplication of the sympathetic approach that formed the basis for his efforts prior to the above described outburst of impatience.

Now, by reason of the contrast with which he has been presented, the subject finds the interrogator's sympathetic, understanding attitude to be much more appealing. This places him in a much more vulnerable position for a disclosure of the truth.

The friendly-unfriendly act is particularly appropriate in the interrogation of a subject who is politely apathetic—the person who just nods his head as though in agreement with the interrogator, but says nothing in response except possibly a denial of guilt. With a subject of this type, a change in the interrogator's attitude from friendly to unfriendly and back to friendly again will at times produce a change in the subject's attitude. He may then become more responsive to the interrogator's efforts at truth disclosure.

I. Point out the Possibility of Exaggeration on the Part of the Accuser or Victim or Exaggerate the Nature and Seriousness of the Offense Itself

In many instances when an offender is accused by his victim, or by a witness to the crime, the interrogator should tell the subject that even though there must be a basis for the accusation there is the ever present possibility of exaggeration—which, if true, can be determined only by first obtaining the subject's own version of the occurrence in question. For example, in a case where the subject is accused of rape—and he denies not only the rape but even the act of intercourse itself—it is effective to interrogate the subject as follows: "We know that there's some truth to what the girl says. We also know that you're not telling the whole truth—even though she may be lying about certain things. For instance, perhaps she had intercourse with you voluntarily, and then after it was all over she became fearful of a possible pregnancy or of a venereal disease, or of her indiscretion being otherwise discovered by her parents. So in order to have an explanation for the occurrence, she concocted the rape story. If this is what happened, we have no way of finding out—unless we hear your own explanation. Now I'm not saying that this is what happened. I'm merely looking at this matter from all possible angles, but in any event we're interested in the truth. If the truth is what she states, we want to know it; on the other hand, if it's anything less than that, we're just as anxious to find that out. My advice to you, therefore, is to tell the truth." (All this may be preceded or supplemented, of course, by a condemnation of the victim, or of women in general, etc., as previously suggested in Technique G).

After an offender has succumbed to this technique, he may try to cling to his partial admission as representing the whole truth, but once he has acknowledged the fact that previously he had lied to the interrogator, it becomes very difficult for him to continue his resistance. He then can be told that if his present admission represented the complete truth he would not have delayed so long in stating it, and that he still does not have the relieved look of a man who has told the truth.

Pointing out the possibility of exaggeration on the part of an accuser is not only helpful in obtaining confessions from the guilty, but it may also serve the purpose of exonerating the innocent. A good illustration of the point is a case in which the thirty-five-year-old daughter of a police lieutenant accused a taxicab driver of rape. The interrogator was satisfied that the accused was telling the truth when he denied raping the accuser, but it also appeared that the subject lied when he denied having the accuser as a passenger in his cab. The interrogator then talked to the subject as follows: "Joe, you're not telling the whole truth. We also know that this woman is at least telling part of the truth. It may well be that she's grossly exaggerating what happened. But she was in your cab, and she probably had intercourse with you voluntarily. Then when she left she may have feared a pregnancy, or a venereal disease, or she may have had some other reason for coming up with this rape story. But unless you tell us the truth as you know it, we'll just have to take what she says at its face value. My advice to you, Joe, is to tell the truth." To this the subject responded by saying, "All right. Now that you put it up to me that way, I'll tell you what actually happened." He then related that the accuser had hailed his cab from in front of a tavern; that she was intoxicated; that as he approached the address she gave him, she directed him to go into an alley back of her family home, and told him to stop at a particular place and to turn the lights out;

that she invited him to have sexual intercourse with her, which he did. The interrogator then confronted the accuser with the cab driver's statement, and she admitted that he was telling the truth. She explained her false accusation by saying that after the affair she feared pregnancy and also was concerned over the possibility that a member of her family had seen her get out of the cab in the alley, and that her ruffled clothing would provoke suspicion. Furthermore, she did not think the cab driver would be located since she had only hailed a passing cab and was not in one sent to the pickup location by the cab company, which would have a record of the driver sent out on the call. But once she started with her lie it was difficult for her to retract her accusation.

In this case, therefore, had it not been for the utilization of the exaggeration technique the accused probably would have been sent to the penitentiary for a crime he did not commit.

Following are a number of case illustrations of the utility of the other phases of the present technique, whereby the interrogator himself actually exaggerates the accusation or the nature and seriousness of the offense.

In the interrogation of a person who is guilty of statutory rape, the interrogator may report to the subject that the girl has accused him of forcible rape. The subject will usually react immediately by making a denial of any force, while at the same time admitting the act of intercourse itself.

Where the case is one of a theft of money or property by means of larceny, embezzlement, or burglary, the interrogator should refer to the reported loss in terms of just about double or triple the actual amount involved. For instance, where the amount is reported to be $500, the interrogator may talk in terms of $1000 or $1500. He may also say that at the time the money was taken, other items of value were also carried away (e.g., a diamond ring, a negotiable bond, etc.), according to the victim of the loss. The interrogator should then suggest that the actual amount of the loss may be much less than reported, that perhaps nothing but money was taken, or that the person or company reporting the loss may be trying to cheat the insurance company covering the risk by adding to the loss actually sustained. As an alternative, the interrogator may suggest that perhaps the person who reported the loss—for example, a company manager—may have taken some money or property himself and is now trying to cover his own thievery by adding that amount to the actual loss in question.

The suggestion that the manager or other boss may be dishonest will frequently strike a responsive chord because of the employee's dislike of him for one reason or another. In some instances, of course, the suggestion that a manager or other boss may be covering up his own thievery by exaggerating the loss is well founded in fact!

To add to the effectiveness of the exaggeration of the accusation or the nature and seriousness of the offense, the verbal statements of the interrogator may be augmented by resorting to some documentary "evidence" in support of the interrogator's exaggerated statement of the amount of money or property stolen. For instance, in the interrogation of an embezzler of $500, the interrogator may arrange to have a letter or a memorandum typed (perhaps even on the employer's stationery) and addressed to the insurance company, or to the police department, in which a statement is made that since the loss was originally reported it now appears that the amount taken was not just $500 but rather $1500, and that some negotiable bonds worth $3000 were also taken. The letter may even name the subject as the one the company manager believes to be responsible for everything. After some repeated foldings and handling of the letter or memorandum, to make it look more authentic, it should be shown to the subject. At that point the interrogator should proceed to suggest that the reported loss may be exaggerated and he should then give the possible reasons for the exaggeration (e.g., trying to cheat the insurance company, or a company manager covering up his own thefts).

For an idea of the specific conversation that may develop between the interrogator and an embezzler during the application of this exaggeration technique, consider the following case situation. A company sustained a considerable loss of merchandise over a period of several months. An audit and inventory disclosed the amount to be about $20,000. The manager of the company warehouse was strongly suspected. He had been observed in the warehouse on a Sunday night, in company with two other men, when the warehouse was closed for business, and when there was no reason in the interest of the company for the presence of anyone there at that time. Furthermore, auditors ascertained that carbon copies of a number of invoices were missing; the safekeeping of such carbon copies was the manager's responsibility.

When the manager was interrogated, on the well-founded assumption that he was responsible for all or part of the loss, the interrogator began by saying:

> "Joe, there's a big shortage of merchandise here at the company, and it looks like you're in the middle of it. You were seen at the warehouse with two other men on Sunday night, February 16, and the auditors found that a lot of carbon copies of your invoices are missing. Joe, you got $40,000 since you started taking this stuff, didn't you?"

Joe's reply was, "Ye Gods no!" Then followed this line of conversation:

> Interrogator: "Was it about $30,000?"
> Joe: "Hell, no!"
> Interrogator: "Was it about $20,000?"
> Joe (speaking less firmly now): "No."
> Interrogator: "Was it as little as $15,000?"
> Joe: "Not even that much."
> Interrogator: "Well, how much was it, Joe? Be fair and honest about it. Was it $14,000?"
> Joe: "It's not even $10,000 worth."
> Interrogator: "Joe, it's more than $10,000 worth, and you know it."

(At this stage of the interrogation the interrogator asked the subject to relate the details of the thefts—the ways and means employed, the specific items taken and the disposition made of them, or their present location. Then the interrogator confronted the subject with the audit figure of the actual value of the missing merchandise—$20,000. The point was also made that since all the merchandise disappeared in the same manner, the subject must be responsible for the entire loss. The manager soon thereafter admitted a total theft of merchandise valued at $20,000. He also revealed exactly how and where he had disposed of everything he had taken.)

In a case such as the one just described, which involves a series of thefts from a single source, it is essential that the interrogator start with a figure considerably higher than the specific amount of money or merchandise actually involved. The subject's reaction to that figure will be very revealing, for a statement such as, "Hell, no. They don't have that much around the whole place," is obviously not the response of an innocent person. An innocent person will almost always respond by saying, with a feeling of resentment, something like, "I didn't take anything!"

As the interrogator lowers the loss figure by various stages he should carefully observe the subject's physical activities, such as squirming about in the chair, dusting his trousers, crossing his legs, picking his fingernails, fumbling with a tie clasp or other object, etc. Such activities, along with the subject's verbal responses, will furnish some indication of his approach to the confession stage, and, where the exact amount of the actual loss is not presently known, may even furnish a clue as to the correct figure which is in the subject's mind.

The person who becomes involved in a series of losses such as the kind to which we have been referring is usually one who is well-liked by fellow employees and who has been in a position to give them, or let them take, company merchandise, etc., in small amounts, acts for which he has a strong ulterior motive. He has thereby sought immunity from other employees reporting his own irregular activities, such as violating various company rules, or even his own thievery. He is the one who may say to a new employee, as he hands him some item of merchandise, or a tool, etc., "Here, take this home with you." If the new employee says, "But that would be stealing," or words to that effect, the response is apt to be, "This company's rich. And you're a damn fool if you don't take something; all the rest of the employees do." On rare occasions, of course, such efforts may backfire; the induced employee may become conscience-stricken and confess his own wrongdoing and at the same time reveal what he knows about the other employees too.

When an investigation of a series of losses involving a substantial sum of money or merchandise is being conducted, it is well to first interrogate the newly employed personnel, and in doing so they should be told that "someone is a *big* thief around here and it's got to be stopped." New employees will confess their own wrongdoing more readily than the confirmed employee-thief, and they are less reluctant to reveal what they know about those who are responsible for the much larger thefts.

J. Have the Subject Place Himself at the Scene of the Crime or in Some Sort of Contact with the Victim or the Occurrence

The value of the present technique—having the subject place himself at the scene of the crime or in contact with the victim, even though he denies doing the act itself—has been referred to earlier in our discussion of certain other techniques (e.g., F and I). However, since the present technique is, in itself, a major one, we will treat it as such under the present heading.

The technique's basic validity is illustrated in the questioning of a child regarding his mischievous conduct, or even the taking of something which did not belong to him. If he will admit that he was present when the act occurred, or that he saw the missing object earlier, his acceptance of full responsibility is not far off. For instance, if he took some money or some object from his parent's bedroom, he may first be asked, "Johnny, did you see that dollar bill on my dresser when you were in my room a while ago?" An admission that he saw the money, or that he was merely in the room from which it was taken, will constitute a substantial step toward a disclosure of the taking itself.

In an actual criminal case situation the technique can be utilized in the following fashion. Assume that money has been taken from a company safe, to which only a few employees had access during the day when it was kept open. As regards any other employee who may be under suspicion, it is important to establish by his own admission that he had an opportunity to take the money. Therefore, the interrogator may say to him, "Joe, I understand that the company safe is left open all day. That's right, isn't it?" (Assume "Yes" is the answer.) "You saw it open last Friday. Right?" (Assume that again the answer is "Yes.") "Joe, how many times did you go into the office that day?" These questions will then be followed by others of a more specific nature; finally the interrogator makes it clear that he believes that the subject took the money, and then proceeds to utilize the other techniques that are appropriate for such cases.

The placing of the subject at the scene should be done early during the interrogation and before the subject fully realizes the implication of his presence there.

K. Seek an Admission of Lying about Some Incidental Aspect of the Occurrence

Once a subject has been caught in a lie about some incidental aspect of the occurrence under investigation, he loses a great deal of ground, for thereafter, as he tries to convince the interrogator he is telling the truth, he can always be politely reminded that he was not telling the truth just a short while ago. This will bring him much nearer the confession stage.

An illustration of the present technique is a case involving indecent liberties with a child, where the subject had denied to the investigators that he even saw the child. In such instances the interrogator should try to get the subject to admit he saw the child and that he talked to her. The interrogator may say, "Joe, there's no question but that you were in this kid's presence and that you talked to her, and there's nothing wrong with that! There's also nothing wrong with giving her candy, or even patting her on the head. Joe, what did she say to you?" At this point the subject may think he can avoid any further suspicion by acknowledging the conversation with the child. Thereafter the interrogator can proceed to utilize the other appropriate techniques such as blaming the child, etc.

In the application of the present technique the interrogator must bear in mind that there are times and circumstances when a person may have lied about some incidental aspect of the offense without being guilty of its commission. Here is an actual case illustration: An investigation of the murder of a married woman disclosed that the subject, who was also married, had been having an affair with the deceased. When the subject was questioned about his whereabouts at the time of the murder he gave an alibi which was quickly established to be a falsehood. This convinced the investigators that he was the murderer. Subsequently, however, the subject admitted to a more skillful and cautious interrogator that at the time of the murder he was in bed with *another* married woman, and that was the reason for his having lied when he gave his previous alibi; in other words he lied in order to avoid an exposure of his latest indiscretion. The second alibi proved to be a truthful one!

Whenever a subject appears to be telling the truth regarding an event under investigation but is reluctant to tell where he was at the time of its occurrence, the interrogator may say, "Joe, if what you were doing at the time has nothing to do with this case, I give you my word I'll treat whatever you tell me as confidential. I'm not interested in your personal affairs. So tell me where you were at the time;" and whatever an innocent person says in response should be kept confidential!

Following is a case illustration of the fact that a person may be telling the truth about a principal offense but lying about some particular aspect of it: A delivery truck driver reported to the police that he had been robbed of his employer's money collections. Because of the driver's general behavior and certain other factors the police suspected him of making a false report and taking the money himself. He finally admitted that although a robbery had actually occurred, only a small amount of money had been taken because he had previously hidden most of the collection money in the truck as a precaution against just such an eventuality. Nevertheless, after the robbery the driver decided to, and did, take the remaining funds, which, but for his foresight of concealment, would have been taken by the robber.

Another practical consideration that must be kept in mind regarding the present technique is that in the investigation of a particularly large embezzlement an employee suspect who will admit taking a much smaller sum or sums of money is rarely the one who is guilty of the principal sum under investigation. The guilty party, however, will seldom admit any smaller thefts or even any kind of wrongdoing, because, since he knows he is guilty of taking the large sum, he assumes that any minor admission will have the effect of creating a presumption of guilt regarding the principal sum. An exception to this general rule occurs, of course, in cases involving a series of losses, such as stock shrinkage of merchandise over a period of time, or a series of relatively small money shortages; in this type of case the minor admissions of any employee are of considerable significance as regards his possible responsibility for all, or a large part of, the accumulated losses.

L. Appeal to the Subject's Pride by Well-Selected Flattery or by a Challenge to His Honor

It is a basic human trait to seek and enjoy the approval of other persons. In our professional activities or in our ordinary, everyday living most of us receive a satisfying amount of approving remarks or compliments. At times, of course, it comes from members of our immediate family and actually may not be deserved. However, persons who engage in criminal activities, and particularly those who operate alone, may seldom receive approving remarks and compliments; moreover, the need for such attention and status is just as great or even greater than it is with the rest of us. In the course of the interrogation of a criminal suspect, therefore, the establishment of effective rapport between interrogator and suspect may be aided very considerably by praise and flattery.

Consider the case of a juvenile or even an adult who is being interrogated as the suspected driver of a "getaway car" used in the robbery-murder of a gas station attendant. Assume that a police patrol car had given chase but was outdistanced by the fleeing vehicle because the officers could not run the risk of injuring innocent pedestrians or motorists. The driver of the fleeing vehicle, of course, had no such consideration, and his reckless driving made the escape possible. In such cases there is much to be gained by speaking to the subsequently apprehended suspect somewhat as follows: "Joe, the officers who were chasing that car tell me that in all their years on the force they have never seen a car maneuvered like that one was. It really took the corners on two wheels."

Why is flattery of this type helpful? Perhaps the explanation rests upon the following considerations, and again, for purposes of illustration, we use the case of the driver of the "getaway car." The driver may have developed into a criminal offender by reason of parental neglect and other such circumstances. At home he was accorded no love, affection, attention, or status. In school the only way he could attract attention or acquire any status was by being unruly and mischievous. To further distinguish himself he may have resorted to destructive acts such as breaking windows, stealing store merchandise; then automobile tires, automobiles, etc. A natural development beyond that was robbery, and murder. Here, then, may be a person starved for attention, recognition, and status. He is, in many instances, particularly vulnerable to an interrogator's compliments and flattery. This does not mean, of course, that ordinarily a confession is immediately forthcoming because of the flattering remarks, but along with all else the interrogator says and does, it can be very helpful in obtaining the confession of guilt.

In a case of one of the authors involving a robbery-murder suspect, the subject was told, with good effect, "I've been in investigative work a long time and I've talked to a lot of people who have done things like what you did, but I've never seen or talked to anyone who had as much guts as you do. I don't know how you could be as calm as you were under those circumstances. Moreover, this was the best planning job I've ever come across for a guy working alone. It's amazing how you found out where those materials [the stolen articles] were kept. And then when you got into action you made John Dillinger look like a piker. (The reference is to a well-known gunman in the early 1930's.) He had all kinds of help from others, but you worked alone. Joe, how did you feel before you pulled off a job? I guess your nerves of steel didn't have any room for nervousness."

In a case involving a rapist who was in military service and aspired to an advanced military career, the interrogator flattered the subject regarding his desire for public service and suggested that his interest in a military career was good evidence of the subject's basically honorable character. The interrogator then urged that the subject should be honorable as regards the case under investigation and tell the truth. A confession followed shortly thereafter.

A clergyman accused of taking indecent liberties with a child was complimented on his "dedication to God" and all the sacrifices he made as "a man of God." It was then suggested that basically he had the same human frailties as all the rest of us and that on this unusual occasion he just could not sufficiently suppress his feelings. He was then advised to go into the chapel of the jail where the interrogation was being conducted and there, while alone "with God," write out an account of what happened. Within an hour he presented the interrogator with a fully detailed confession.

Flattery is especially effective on women subjects. Reference may be made to their beauty, youthful appearance, attire, family background, good reputation, and unselfishness, etc.

The uneducated and underprivileged are more vulnerable to flattery than the educated person or the person in favorable financial or social circumstances. With the latter type, flattery should be used sparingly and very discreetly.

When interrogating persons of low social status, it is advisable to address them as "Mr.," "Mrs.," or "Miss," rather than by their first name. On the other hand, it is usually better to address persons of high social or professional status by their first name, or by their last name without attaching the "Mr.," "Mrs.," or "Miss." The advantages of this practice are as follows: The person of low social status is flattered and acquires a feeling of satisfaction and dignity from such unaccustomed courtesy. By according the subject this consideration the interrogator enhances the effectiveness of whatever he says or does thereafter. As regards the second type, the use of the first name, or the last name only (without the accustomed "Mr.," Mrs.," or "Miss"), has the effect of dispelling the subject's usual feeling of superiority and independence. He is made to realize that the examiner is in command of the present situation.

An exception to the foregoing suggestion should be made in a case involving the interrogation of a married woman criminal suspect who is known to have been having sexual relations with other men. It is better to address her by her first name rather than as "Mrs." In this way the interrogator minimizes to some extent the guilt feeling that may prevail because of the wife connotation in the "Mrs."

Occasionally a subject may attempt to utilize flattery on the interrogator in order to make a favorable impression. He may address the interrogator by a title obviously beyond that which the interrogator actually possesses—"Captain" instead of "Sergeant"; "Doctor" instead of "Mr." In such instances the subject should be corrected, and where the motive is obvious it is well to add, "Never mind trying to butter me up, Joe." In other words the subject should never be given the opportunity to think he has fooled his own interrogator.

It is occasionally helpful to appeal to the subject's loyalty to a group of persons or to an organization whose reputation and honor has been jeopardized by the subject's unlawful behavior. For instance, an appeal may be made in the name of the subject's church, or any other organization or group toward which the subject appears to have some loyalty or allegiance.

Another form of appeal to the subject's pride is challenging his honor, by calling into question his possible lack of manliness in not telling the truth about his offense. For instance, the interrogator may inquire, "Is the reason you're not telling me the truth the fact that you're afraid of the other fellows?"

In the interrogation of co-offenders it is well to anticipate and counteract the feeling of honor and loyalty a subject may possess with regard to his fellow participants. Toward this end the interrogator should speak somewhat as follows: "In asking you to tell me the truth I'm not trying to use you as a stool pigeon or to get you to squeal on anybody. I merely want you to tell the truth and to take your share of blame along with the others. And that's the difference between a stool pigeon or a squealer and a person in your position. You are not holding your hand out for any dirty money to sell someone down the river, and I'm not jingling any before your eyes. To the contrary, by assuming your share of the blame you put yourself above any blame from anyone. So don't let any false notion of honor stand between you and the truth."

M. Point out the Futility of Resistance to Telling the Truth

With all offenders, and in particular the non-emotional type, the interrogator must not only convince the subject that his guilt has been detected, but also that it can be established by the evidence that currently is available or which will be developed before the investigation is completed. In other words, an effort should be made to have the subject realize that it is futile for him to continue his resistance to telling the truth.

When the subject had accomplices in the planning or commission of the crime, the interrogator should capitalize on the fear that already exists in the subject's mind—the fear that his accomplice will "talk." The manner in which this can be done is as follows: "You know as well as I do, Joe, that in all these cases where two or more fellows pull off a job like this, sooner or later somebody talks, and in this case it might just as well be you. So let's get going before somebody leaves you holding the bag. Don't let the other fellow get his oars in first and splash all the blame on you. What you say now, before that happens, we can believe. Later on no one is likely to believe what you say even though at that time you may be telling the absolute truth."

By thus stirring up the already existing concern that the accomplice may talk, the interrogator may achieve either of two objectives: The initial and immediate one of perhaps persuading the subject to tell the truth *now*, and at the same time, the establishment of the groundwork for the application of the subsequently described technique (P) of "playing one against the other."

N. Point out to the Subject the Grave Consequences and Futility of a Continuation of His Criminal Behavior

During the course of their criminal careers, many offenders experience a fleeting desire or intention to reform. This is particularly true with regard to youthful offenders, or adults who are either first offenders or else in the early stages of their careers of crime. While in such a mood—which at times manifests itself during an offender's period of failure, that is, when he is accused or under arrest, and when thus brought face to face with the stark realities on the debit side of his activities—he becomes quite vulnerable to comments regarding the future consequences and futility of a continuation of his criminal behavior. This is particularly true when the offense is not of the most serious sort and when the offender is not too well-seasoned by a long series of offenses and police experiences. Under these circumstances he might be convinced (momentarily, anyway) that for his own sake it is a good thing that he was caught "early in the game," since this experience may serve to avoid much more trouble for him later on. In the course of his discussion—for instance in a larceny case—the interrogator may say, "You know what will happen to you if you keep this up, don't you? This time you've taken a relatively small amount of money; next time it will be more, and then you'll do it more often. You'll finally decide it's easier and more exciting to get what you're looking for at the point of a gun. You'll begin packing a rod. Then someday you'll get excited and pull the trigger when the muzzle's resting against somebody's belly. You'll run away and try to hide out from the police. You'll get caught. There'll be a trial, and when it's all over, despite the efforts of your parents and relatives, who in the meantime have probably spent their last dime in trying to save your neck, you'll either have to spend the rest of your life in the penitentiary or else sit down on the hot seat and have a lot of electricity shot through your body until your life's been snuffed out. Now's the time to put the brakes on—before it's too late."

It is also advisable, whenever possible, to point out the relative insignificance of the offense in terms of how much worse it might have been. For instance in a burglary case the interrogator may say to the subject, "Joe, all that happened the other night was the taking of some money. But if you keep this up, some night you'll crawl in a window thinking that no one is home. Someone is home, however, and he comes at you with a gun or a knife. Sure, you didn't intend to kill anybody; you didn't even carry a gun or a knife. But to save your own life you try to grab the gun or the knife and you have to use it on him. Joe, then it's the hot seat for you. Or, if you don't kill someone yourself, eventually someone may kill or cripple you for life. One of your intended victims, or perhaps a policeman, may do this to you. You may not realize it now, fellow, but getting caught early like this may be the best thing that could have happened to you. Joe, put the brakes on now, before it's too late."

Statements such as the one above tend to make the subject feel that he is indeed rather fortunate in having escaped more serious difficulty. Once in that frame of mind he becomes less reluctant co confess his crime.

Youthful offenders or adults who are not confirmed criminals, and who have not committed the most serious of crimes, may also be told, "Everyone makes mistakes, and we can all profit by such mistakes. A person with any brains at all can look upon them as lessons regarding his future conduct. And, after all, that's really what penitentiaries are for—to teach a fellow a lesson, in the hopes that he'll straighten himself out. Joe, if you don't own up to your present mistake and you think you've gotten away with something, you're bound to get yourself in worse trouble later on, and maybe then you won't have a chance to straighten yourself out. The police may do it for you when they catch you in a burglary or robbery; you may end up straightened out on a marble slab in the morgue."

The basic validity and effectiveness of the present technique may be explained by the fact that many offenders do have some awareness of the ultimate consequences of their continued criminal behavior. Moreover, when an offender vows that he will go straight he usually means it *at that time*. Perhaps that is the reason for the appealing effect of pointing out the grave consequences and futility of continuing with a criminal career.

O. Rather Than Seek a General Admission of Guilt, First Ask the Subject a Question as to Some Detail of the Offense, or Inquire as to the Reason for Its Commission

A properly conducted interrogation based upon the application of techniques such as the ones we have been discussing will ordinarily have the effect of producing in the subject moments of indecision, during which his struggle to avoid the consequences of his criminal act will be partially overcome by, or temporarily deadlocked with, his impulse to confess. He becomes pensive, he is no longer talkative, and he gives the impression of not even listening to what the interrogator is saying. He may turn his head aside; he may fiddle with his tie clasp or tie, or with a coin or other object; he may pick his fingernails or indulge in some other gesture such as dusting off his clothes with his hand; he may exhibit a wry smile; he may also display a "far away" look in his eyes as he ponders the question, "Shall I tell him the truth or keep on lying?"

When the subject is in this frame of mind, if the interrogator himself remains silent, or if he should leave the subject alone in the interrogation room, or if the interrogator at that point accedes to the subject's request for a cigarette or even a drink of water, or to go to the washroom (when there is every reason to believe it is merely a stall for time), the subject may quickly regain his composure and all of the interrogator's prior efforts will be lost. It is highly important, therefore, that this critical stage of the interrogation be recognized immediately, for then is the time for the interrogator to "move in" by asking a question regarding some detail of the offense—and preferably something preceding or following the occurrence itself. Or the interrogator may inquire as to the reason or excuse for the commission of the offense. In appropriate instances (as with most emotional offenders), such questions should be accompanied by one of the previously described friendly gestures such as a pat on the shoulder.

By a "detail" question we mean one based upon the where, the when, or the how of an act or event that is pertinent to the crime under investigation but yet removed in point of time or place from the main occurrence itself. As to questions regarding the reason or excuse for the subject's offense, we have in mind a question such as, "What is the reason for this, Joe?" Whenever a "what is the reason" question is asked, it should be coupled with a suggestion of the possible reason or excuse for what the subject did; in other words, the interrogator should offer a tentative answer to his own question.

An interrogator should always be mindful of the fact that when a criminal offender is asked to confess a crime, an awful lot is being asked of him. First of all, it is not easy to own up to any kind of wrongdoing. Furthermore, in a criminal case the subject may be well aware of the specific serious consequences of his telling the truth: it may be a long penitentiary sentence or even the electric chair. Therefore, the task of confessing should be made as easy as possible for the subject. That is done when the interrogator avoids a general admission of guilt question such as, "You did kill him, didn't you?"; "You did rape her, didn't you?"; "You did hit him with your car, didn't you?"; or "Tell us all about it, Joe." Any such questions will recall to the subject's mind a revolting picture of the crime itself—the scream of the victim, the blood spurting from a wound, or the pedestrian's body being thrown over the hood of an automobile or dragged along the street. It is much better, as a confession starter, to inquire about a detail of the offense by the asking of such questions as, "*Where* did you get the gun?"; "*When* did you get the gun?"; or, in a rape case, in which the subject has denied ever seeing the victim, "*How* did you happen to meet this girl?" The same desirable effect is presented when the question is asked, "What is *the reason* for this, Joe?"

As to the effectiveness of the "what is the reason" question, we all know from ordinary, everyday, non-criminal experiences that it is much easier to admit a mistake or any kind of wrongdoing if, at the time of the admission, we are permitted to explain why we did it. The same psychological factors prevail in a criminal case situation; it is much easier for a criminal offender to confess a crime if he is given an opportunity to couple his admission with an explanation or excuse for his conduct. This opportunity is afforded him when the interrogator inquires, "What is the reason for this, Joe?", especially when followed by the interrogator's suggestion of the possible reason or excuse, such as, "Was it because the loan shark had your back to the wall and your only way out was to take this money?"; or "Was it in self-defense?"; etc.

Questions of this type, asked at the proper psychological moment, possess a number of advantages which make them much more effective than inquiries or solicitations calling for an outright or general admission of guilt. In the first place, by delving into details of *where, when, how,* or of *the reason* for the offense, the interrogator effectively displays a greater certainty in the subject's guilt—for otherwise there would be no interest in details— and this, in itself, has a tendency to weaken the subject's resistance to telling the truth. Then there is the very desirable element of surprise in a question of this type. It catches the subject off guard at a very crucial time, and it stimulates to greater activity the already aroused impulse to confess. Also, a detail question with respect to the reason for the crime, when put to a subject who feels impelled to confess but who is thwarted by the task of bursting forth with the complete admission all at once, offers an opportunity for him to preface or combine his admission of guilt with whatever excuses or explanations he cares to make in an effort to ease his conscience, as well as to have the interrogator believe that the crime is less odious or less reprehensible than is actually the case. Moreover, an inquiry into a detail of the offense implies a rather sympathetic attitude on the part of the interrogator—it gives the impression that he is not particularly interested in a confession but rather in ascertaining and understanding the reasons for the offender's behavior, or in being informed of the circumstances or conditions which contributed to the consummation of the deed.

Occasionally, in the application of this detail question technique, the interrogator will encounter a subject who may grasp any one of the suggested explanations or excuses and persist thereafter in relying upon it for his legal defense, even though it may not represent the truth. Once the subject has admitted the act itself, however, the interrogator can almost always follow through successfully and obtain the accurate version by pointing out to the subject the flaws in the explanation or excuse given. Nevertheless, despite such eventualities, the tactical advantages to be gained from any admission which contradicts the subject's previous denials will sufficiently compensate for the risk involved in procuring the initial admission by the interrogator's suggestion of possible explanations or excuses.

The psychological principles involved in the foregoing situations of crime guilt are also applicable to other inquiries of a related nature. For example, when the interrogator has reason to believe that the subject possesses or knows the whereabouts of an instrument or article which might have some connection with the crime, instead of merely asking, "Do you have such-and-such?" or "Do you know where such-and-such is?", it is much better to assume in the question that the subject does have, or does know the location of, the object being sought. The effectiveness of this approach is well illustrated by the following case. In the course of an interrogation of a suspect in a rape-murder case, the interrogator received the impression that, regardless of the question as to the suspect's guilt or innocence, he was a sex deviate. The interrogator's previous experience in the interrogation of sex deviates of various sorts brought to mind the possibility that this suspect, like so many others of his class, may have been keeping a diary of his sex affairs and practices. Since such an instrument might be of some value in an interrogation, the interrogator was interested in finding out if one existed. Toward this end the interrogator asked the question, "Where is your diary?" The subject paused momentarily and then replied, "It's home—hidden underneath my desk." His permission was obtained to pick up the diary. Officers dispatched to the subject's home discovered a diary replete with records of numerous daily sexual experiences, running the gamut from "struggles" with girls he had picked up in his car to sexual stimulations and ejaculations provoked by reading his accounts of the past acts recorded in the diary. (His "struggles" in many instances actually were rapes which, unfortunately, had never been reported to the police.) When confronted with these diary entries the subject readily admitted a long series of rapes, and although no entry had been made in the diary of the most recent experience, the rape-murder, the interrogator became more and more convinced, as the interrogation continued, that the subject was guilty of the principal crime under investigation. The subject was constantly reminded of the significance attending his previous offenses and particularly as regards one of them in which the *modus operandi* was quite similar to many aspects of the principal offense. Eventually the subject admitted his guilt of the rape-murder, for which he was subsequently executed.

There is every reason to believe that in the foregoing case, if the issue of the diary had been brought up in any way other than by the question, "Where is your diary?" the subject probably would not have divulged its existence or its whereabouts, and the investigators would have been deprived of a very valuable means of eliciting the confession. Had the interrogator merely asked, "Do you have a diary?" the subject probably would have inferred that its existence was not already known and therefore denied that he had one. With the question phrased in such a way as to imply a certainty of its existence, however, it became difficult for the subject to make a denial—because for all he knew the interrogator or other investigators might already be aware of its existence or actually have it in their possession.[11]

Another possible application of this detail question technique is in cases in which the interrogator seeks to establish the identity of an accomplice or of another person who is in some way connected with the offense under investigation. Rather than confine the inquiry to, "Who is the person?" it is often much more effective to supplement the inquiry with, or perhaps use as a substitute, certain "piecemeal" questions, such as, "What part of the city does he live in?" or "What's his first name?" In this way the questions appear rather innocuous and render much less difficult the subject's task of giving the information. Once some piecemeal information is obtained, the complete identification usually follows immediately thereafter.

P. When Co-Offenders Are Being Interrogated and the Previously Described Techniques Have Been Ineffective, "Play One against the Other"

When two or more persons have collaborated in the commission of a criminal offense and are later apprehended for questioning, there is usually a constant fear on the part of each participant that one of them will "talk." Individually they all may feel confident of their own ability to evade detection and to stand up under the police interrogation, but no one seems to experience a comparable degree of confidence with regard to his co-offender's

[11] It is of interest to note that there was an entry in the subject's diary describing the rape of another one of his victims who had previously identified another man as her rapist.

ability or even willingness to do so. Uppermost in their minds is the possibility that one of them will confess in an effort to obtain special consideration for himself.

This fear and mutual distrust among co-offenders can be made the basis for a very effective interrogation technique known as "playing one against the other." Since it consists largely of a bluff on the part of the interrogator, however, it should be reserved as a last resort, to be used only after other possible techniques have failed to produce the desired result.

As previously stated with reference to the technique of pointing out the futility of resistance, the interrogator should always indicate to co-offenders, at the very outset of the interrogation, the strong probability that eventually some one of them is going to talk. The interrogator's early comments to this effect (as discussed in Technique *M*) constitute a desirable build-up for the subsequent utilization of this technique.

There are, in general, two principal methods which may be used in playing one offender against another. The interrogator may merely *intimate* to one offender that the other has confessed, or else he may actually *tell* him so.

In either event, there are two basic rules to follow: (1) keep the subjects separated from sight and sound of each other (except as regards the one variation subsequently to be discusssed); (2) use, as the one to play against the other, the less criminally hardened, or the follower rather than the leader of the two or more offenders, or the one who acted out the lesser role in the crime. (In such instances, of course, the *Miranda* warnings must be given.)

A simple form of intimation may consist of the practice of taking one subject into the interrogation room soon after the interrogation of the first one and then telling him, "This other fellow is trying to straighten himself out; how about you? Or do you want to let this thing stand as it is? I'm not going to tell you what I know now about your part in this job. I don't want to put the words in your mouth and then have you nod your head in agreement. I want to see if you have in you what it takes to tell the truth. I want to hear your story—straight from your own lips."

The following procedure has been successfully employed in intimating to one subject that his accomplice has confessed:

After subject No. 1 has been unsuccessfully interrogated, he is returned to the reception room occupied by a secretary who is engaged in carrying out her usual secretarial duties; then subject No. 2 is taken to the interrogation room. If likewise unsuccessful in this second interrogation, the interrogator returns to the receiving room and instructs the secretary, "Come in the back with your pencil and notebook." This instruction is given within hearing distance of subject No. 1, but in such a natural manner that it does not appear to be an act performed for his benefit. The secretary then proceeds to sharpen her pencils, turn back some pages of her stenographic notebook—all within the observation of subject No. 1—and then departs in the direction of the interrogation room. After thus absenting herself for the period of time that would ordinarily be required for the actual taking of a confession, she returns to the reception room and begins typing what might appear to be shorthand notes taken during the period of her absence. She uses legal size paper and provides for carbon copies also; and, again, this is all done within view of subject No. 1. After several minutes she pauses and inquires of an officer seated near subject No. 1, "How does this man [referring to subject No. 1] spell his last name?" (Or if the name is a simple one, then the inquiry is directed to his exact address, etc.) After receiving the information she continues with her typing. When finished, she takes the paper and carbons from the typewriter and, after sorting out the carbon sheets, she departs with the typewritten material in the direction of the interrogation room. Thereafter she returns to her desk without the papers, and resumes her usual secretarial duties.

After the lapse of fifteen or twenty minutes, the interrogator enters the receiving room and escorts subject No. 1 to the interrogation room (now vacated by subject No. 2 who has been taken to another room). After subject No. 1 is seated, the interrogator says, "Well, what have you got to say for yourself?" At this point the subject may confess, being under the impression that his co-offender has done so already.

Following is another way in which effective intimation may be employed, even before any interrogation has begun. Assume that two robbery suspects have been apprehended and that it is obvious that at least one, if not both, will be a difficult subject to interrogate, perhaps by reason of a prior penitentiary experience. Both may be placed in the same jail cell and shortly thereafter one of them (preferably the one who was perhaps the follower, rather than the leader, of the two) is taken from the cell and brought to an upstairs room in which he is then left alone, without anyone saying a word to him, for about an hour. Afterward he is returned to the cell and left with his accomplice, who, we may reasonably assume, will inquire, "What did they ask you?" to which, of course, the answer will be a truthful "Nothing." This, however, will appear to be untrue to the accomplice, because it will seem to him rather nonsensical that either one of them would be taken away for that long a time for "nothing." A doubt will thereby be created as to whether the cellmate has talked. Then the accomplice himself is taken from the cell and actually interrogated. He is not told that the other fellow has talked, but there is a strong intimation to that effect (e.g., "What have you got to say for yourself, Joe?"). The subject will therefore find himself in a position in which he is afraid to lie, because of his suspicion that his partner has already confessed; that suspicion may be further encouraged by the interrogator's looking at some typewritten sheets of paper as though he were reviewing some information in the other subject's "confession" before beginning the interrogation of the present one.

When two or more subjects are suspected of a series of offenses (e.g., a number of robberies), and the interrogator has been successful in obtaining a confession from one subject regarding perhaps only one or two of the offenses (which, in fact, may be all that particular subject committed, although he may know of the other offenses committed by his partner or partners), the interrogator may employ the following stratagem. Several sheets of paper, including the written confession obtained from the first subject, should be looked at within view of the present subject, before an interrogation of him is begun. Then the interrogator relates what the first subject told him about one of the offenses. If the present subject admits his implication he should then be told, "All right, now tell me about the others." If he balks at saying anything further, and this he might do on the assumption that the one case is all the interrogator knows about, then he may be told about the second offense. At this point the interrogator should then look at the papers again, as though they contained information about other additional offenses, and the subject should be told, in a tone of voice indicative of displeasure at the subject's attitude, "Let's hear from you about this one and all the others too."

Another kind of intimation that may be employed is illustrated by a case in which perhaps a father and son are involved in the commission of a crime, and they have consistently maintained that they were innocent, even when questioned separately. In such a case situation the interrogator may say to the father, "O.K., if you are both telling the truth, as you say you are, here's a piece of paper and a pencil. Write a note to your son; tell him that you have told the truth and that he too should tell the truth. You don't have to say anything else." As this is said, the actions and facial expressions of the subject should be carefully observed. If he delays in responding, or if he equivocates in his answer, this will be further assurance of deception, because if he and his son are telling the truth there should be no reluctance or unwillingness to write out such a message. The dilemma that is thereby presented to the subject may result in his writing and signing of the message to his son. Then, when the message is presented to the son, his actions, facial expressions, and verbal responses will be of helpful significance. If he questions the authenticity of the writing, or the signature, he will in effect be saying, "This is a trick; I won't fall for it," which, of course, will clearly indicate his guilt. On the other hand, if he is innocent, he will respond by saying something to the effect of, "I am telling the truth, and so is my father; so don't try to trick me into anything different."

If the son in the above described case is guilty and confesses, his subsequent written confession can then be shown to the father, or the interrogator may have the son orally relate what he has already stated in his signed confession.

The following case is an excellent illustration of the advisability of having some basis for any statement offered to one offender by way of proof that the co-offender has confessed. Several years ago one of the authors was interrogating two boys (brothers) who were suspected of committing a series of burglaries. Each one of them persisted in his denial of any of the offenses, including the particular offense which brought about their arrest and which was the chief object of the present interrogation. Finally the younger one of the boys made an admission concerning one burglary. He stated that he had assisted the other offender, his older brother, in throwing into a river some of the loot from a burglary. Equipped with this bit of information the interrogator resumed his interrogation of the other subject, this time with a view to making him believe that his younger brother had made a complete confession of all the burglaries. The subject was told, "Well, your kid brother has told us everything; now let's see if you can straighten yourself out." Since the subject seemed unimpressed and skeptical of what the interrogator had said, he was then told, "Just to show you I'm not kidding, how about that job when you and your younger brother unloaded the brass metal in the river when things got too hot for you?"

Thereupon the subject smiled and said, "You're bluffing; my brother didn't say that because it isn't true." Feeling quite confident that the younger boy was telling the truth about the brass disposal job, the interrogator decided to have him repeat the statement in the presence of the older boy. This was done, and the two boys then began to argue over who was telling the truth. However, soon thereafter the younger boy stated that he was mistaken about this particular job—adding that as regards this one particular offense he had his brother confused with another boy whom he named and identified as his confederate in the theft of the brass. Nevertheless, he did implicate his brother in several other burglaries. When confronted with such admissions the older boy also acknowledged his guilt.

In this case the boy to whom the interrogator had transmitted the incorrect information had every reason in the world to believe it was a bluff. Quite naturally he was not influenced by such a statement, and the same would be true in any case in which an interrogator was inaccurate in his guess as to some detail offered as proof of the fact that a co-offender had already confessed.

Whenever the more direct bluff is attempted—that is, whenever the subject is actually told that his co-offender has confessed —the interrogator must be careful not to make any statement, purporting to come from the co-offender, which the person to whom it is related will recognize as an inaccuracy and therefore as a wild guess and a bluff on the part of the interrogator. Once the interrogator makes such a mistake the entire bluff is exposed, and then it becomes useless to continue with the act of playing one against the other. Moreover, the interrogator himself is then exposed as a trickster and thereafter there is very little he can do to regain the confidence of his subject. Therefore, unless from his own independent knowledge the interrogator is quite certain of the accuracy of any detail of the offense which he intends to offer to one subject as representing a statement made by his co-offender, it is better to confine his remarks to generalities only.

An exception to the foregoing precautionary measure is to be made in a case where one of the offenders is definitely known to have played a secondary role in the commission of the offense. In such a case the subject may be told that the other offender has put the blame on him for the planning of the offense, or for the actual shooting, etc. At the same time the interrogator may add, "I don't think this is so, but that's what he says. If it's not the truth, then you let us have the truth." In this way the interrogator avoids any danger to his bluff, since he concedes the possibility of the statement being a falsehood.

In addition to its application to the "playing one against the other technique," there is a basic utility in emphasizing to an offender the fact that he performed the less offensive role in the commission of the offense. Moreover, he is the offender upon whom the interrogator should devote his principal efforts. For instance, in the investigation of a robbery-murder, of the two suspects who were to be interrogated, one was taller than the other, and a witness had reported that the taller of the two robbers was the one who struck the robbery victim the blow on the head that resulted in his death. In this situation, therefore, the offender who is generally easier to interrogate successfully is the shorter one who merely took the money and not the one who did the killing.

Such a subject may be told, "Joe, you're a thief, of course, but you're not a deliberate killer," and throughout the interrogation the idea should be emphasized that the other offender bears the primary responsibility for what occurred.

In a case such as the one above, after the offender who played the lesser role has confessed, it is usually a relatively easy matter to obtain the other offender's acknowledgement of guilt, even though he may not have admitted his guilt if his accomplice had not previously confessed.

TACTICS AND TECHNIQUES FOR THE INTERROGATION OF SUSPECTS WHOSE GUILT IS UNCERTAIN

The warnings as to the constitutional rights of a criminal suspect who is in police custody must be issued to him even though, in the opinion of the interrogator, the suspect's guilt is uncertain. Thereafter, there are, in general, three courses or approaches available to the interrogator: (1) from the very outset of the interrogation he may treat the subject as though he were actually considered guilty of the offense in question; (2) he may immediately treat the subject as though he were actually considered innocent of the offense; or (3) he may assume a neutral position and refrain from making any statement or implications one way or the other until the subject discloses some information or indications pointing either to his innocence or his guilt. What are the advantages and disadvantages attending each one of these three possible approaches?

The first approach, consisting of an implication or accusation of guilt, possesses the desirable element of surprise, and a guilty subject's consequent lack of composure may result in a disclosure of truth about certain pertinent information, or perhaps even an early confession of guilt. Another advantage is the significance of the general reaction of the subject when he is treated as though he were considered guilty. A guilty person will usually display no resentment to such treatment; on the other hand an innocent subject will usually express his resentment, to the extent of doing so very forcefully, or perhaps even in a highly insulting manner. A guilty subject is also more likely to react to the suggestion of guilt by fiddling with his tie clasp or tie, crossing his legs back and forth, squirming in his chair, dusting off his clothes with his hand, or turning his head away as the interrogator talks to him. These differences in reaction can be very helpful in determining whether or not the subject is guilty or innocent.

There are, however, two disadvantages to this first approach of an implication or accusation of guilt. If a guilty subject does not immediately make some incriminating "slip-up" or confess his guilt, he is thereby placed on his guard during the remainder of the interview, and if he eventually senses the fact that the approach is nothing more than a bluff, he is that much more fortified, psychologically, to continue with his lying and resistance to telling the truth. On the other hand, if he is innocent, he may become so disturbed and confused that it will be more difficult for the interrogator to ascertain the fact of the subject's innocence, or even to obtain possible clues or helpful information which might otherwise have been obtainable.

The second approach, consisting of an implication or statement of a belief in the subject's innocence, possesses two distinct advantages, but these are offset to some extent by an attending disadvantage. The advantages may be stated as follows: (a) the interrogator's statement or implication of a belief in the subject's innocence will undoubtedly place an innocent subject at greater ease, and, as a result, the fact of his innocence may become more readily apparent to the interrogator; moreover, under such circumstances the interrogator can more successfully elicit whatever pertinent information or clues the subject may be in a position to divulge; (b) if the subject is actually guilty, this approach may cause him to lower his guard: he may become less cautious or even careless in his answers and in his conversation, as a result of which he is more apt to make a remark or contradiction that will not only make evident the fact of his guilt but which also can be used as a wedge for eliciting a confession. On the other hand, there is a disadvantage attending this approach when used on a guilty subject. Once an interrogator has committed himself as a believer in the subject's innocence, he must more or less confine his in quiries to those based upon an assumption of innocence, for to do otherwise would tend to destroy the very relationship or rapport which he seeks to establish by this approach. In other words, he is handicapped to the extent that he cannot freely adjust his methods and questioning to meet the subject's changing attitudes or inconsistencies. This is not an insurmountable difficulty, of course, but it is nevertheless a possible disadvantage which the interrogator should consider before embarking upon this particular course.

The third approach, based upon a neutral position in which the interrogator refrains from making any commitments or implications as to the subject's innocence or guilt, obviously possesses neither the advantages nor the disadvantages of the other two. For this very reason, therefore, it may be considered the best approach to use in the average case where the interrogator's study and observation of his subject have given no encouraging indication that the subject might be particularly vulnerable to either one of the other two approaches.

Since the first approach is based upon an assumption of guilt, it calls for the immediate application of tactics and techniques designed to elicit an admission or confession. On the other hand, the second and third approaches require that the interrogator's efforts be directed immediately toward the detection of possible deception. As a matter of fact, if the first approach fails to produce the desired result, then even in that case the interrogator's problem becomes very much the same as that involved in the other two instances—the detection of deception.

It is not often possible to merely look at a person and determine whether or not he is lying (and guilty) or telling the truth (and innocent). Something more is necessary. The subject must be questioned and engaged in conversation in order to permit the interrogator to study his behavior and conduct, to search for significant remarks or contradictions in his statements, and to check his statements in the light of known facts and circumstances. The following techniques are submitted as useful aids toward the end of providing an interrogator with such an opportunity.

The alphabetical sequence of technique lettering has been continued from the previous group of techniques designed for subjects whose guilt is definite or reasonably certain. We have done this because of the fact that on occasion some of the following techniques may be of value in the interrogation of the former group of subjects, and vice versa. Moreover, an avoidance of letter duplication simplifies the identification of any one of the techniques, regardless of whether it falls within one general group or another.

Q. Ask the Subject if He Knows Why He is Being Questioned

(This technique is usable only on those subjects who are not in police custody or under some other form of police restraint, because, if they are, they must be warned of their constitutional rights, and this, of course, will require a disclosure of the matter under investigation. What follows, however, can be used on persons who come to the police voluntarily, or who are interviewed in the vicinity of the crime scene, and not under police restraint, or who may be interviewed in their own homes.)

If up to the time of his interview the subject has not been informed of its purpose (either by the investigators or by others), it is well for the interrogator to inquire of the subject. "Do you know why we have asked you to come here?", or "Do you know why we have come here to talk to you?"

A guilty person who is asked such a question as this is immediately placed in a vulnerable defensive position. If he professes ignorance when the circumstances clearly indicate his awareness of the purpose of the interrogation, that fact alone becomes of considerable importance to the interrogator, both for its diagnostic value as well as for its effect upon the subject's resistance when it is called to his attention as an indication of his guilt. On the other hand, if he admits knowing why he is being interrogated, he still may be kept on the defensive either by his own feeling of a necessity to offer an immediate explanation of his pretended innocence or, in the event he does not offer an unsolicited explanation, by an additional question such as, "Well, what do you know about it [the offense]?" By thus being required to immediately defend himself, a guilty person may at the very outset of the interrogation make some significant remark or exhibit certain symptoms of guilt which otherwise might not have been so readily provoked.

If the subject is innocent or ignorant of the particular offense under investigation, but guilty of another offense, or in possession of pertinent information concerning such other offense, a "do you know why you are here" question may result in a lead to the solution of the latter offense. For instance, a reply of, "Yes, you think I had something to do with the —— job." (referring to the unsuspected offense) would obviously prompt the interrogator to make further inquiries about it. Information gained in this unexpected manner has led to the solution of cases which otherwise might have escaped the interrogator's attention.

Since this technique provides the interrogator with the foregoing advantages when dealing with subjects who are either guilty or concealing information, and since no disadvantage is encountered in using it on an innocent person, it is recommended as an effective method for beginning an interview with a suspect whose guilt is doubtful or uncertain and who is not in custody or otherwise under police restraint.

R. Ask the Subject to Relate All He Knows about the Occurrence, the Victim, and Possible Suspects

In the early stages of the interrogation it is usually advisable to ask a few general questions regarding the subject's knowledge of the occurrence, the victim, possible suspects, etc. If the subject is innocent he is thereby given an opportunity to divulge possibly helpful information which otherwise might not be disclosed if his discussion were restricted to answering specific questions. On the other hand, if guilty, he is placed in a defensive position similar to that described with reference to Technique Q, whereupon he may make a remark signifying his guilt, or a comment suggestive of a certain line of specific questioning, which lead might not have manifested itself in the absence of this form of general questioning.

By asking a subject to reveal his suspicions as to who the guilty person may be, the interrogator may evoke a very significant and reliable indication of the subject's guilt or innocence. This is particularly true in a case where any one of several persons, who are all acquainted with each other, may have committed the offense. For example, in a case involving the burglary of a company office, where it appears that some one of six employees must have deliberately left a window or a door unlocked, or perhaps pinpointed the location of the stolen money, our experience has been that the guilty employee, when interrogated, will not reveal a suspicion about anyone else, no matter how much effort is made to have him do so. In other words, when asked, "From among your fellow employees, which one of them do you think might have gotten himself involved in this matter?" a guilty employee will say, "I don't know," or "I haven't the faintest idea." No matter what the interrogator says thereafter, a guilty person will usually remain adamant in his denial of harboring any suspicion. On the other hand, the innocent employee may, after some persuasion, tell of his suspicion, even though it has a very flimsy basis, or is based upon nothing more than a dislike or prejudice toward another employee. When asked the question regarding his suspicion he may first say, "I don't know," but then, in response to later questions, he will disclose his suspicion. For instance, after his initial, "I don't know," the following question may be put to him by the interrogator: "Joe, I'm not talking about actual knowledge or proof. Here's what I mean. There is no question but that some employee is involved in this affair. That being so, which one from among all of you do you think could or might have done such a thing? Now let me assure you that I will not tell anyone what you tell me. My primary purpose in asking the question is to give you an opportunity to relieve yourself of any thoughts along that line that you may have now in your mind, so that your holding back on that won't make it look like you're the one who's involved in this. If you had no part in it I want to know that, and without having any doubt about it. So let me now ask you, Joe, which one of the other fellows do you think might have done this?" The innocent person, after such persuasion as this, may disclose a suspicion about someone else. On the other hand, as previously stated, a guilty person will not reveal a suspicion, regardless of the interrogator's efforts to have him do so.

A subject who, after being questioned as above indicated, has not revealed a suspicion, should then be told: "Joe, there's no doubt but that some one of the six of you did this; you say you don't suspect anyone. Then tell me, which ones do you think *did not* do it?" The interrogator can then mention the names of the other five persons, and again the subject should be asked: "Which ones of them do you think *did not* do this?" An innocent subject will, in all probability, name one or more of them as being above suspicion, and perhaps add by saying something like, "The other fellows I don't know too well." On the other hand, a guilty person will not exclude any one individual; he will absolve them all and eliminate himself as well. He prefers that the investigative efforts be directed elsewhere.

S. **Obtain from the Subject Detailed Information about His Activities before, at the Time of, and after the Occurrence in Question**

Lawyers occasionally use a technique similar to this one in the cross examination of a witness whose testimony they seek to discredit by showing that although the witness' memory of his activities prior to and since the event in question is very bad (or very good, if such be the case), his memory of occurrences at the time when the offense was committed is, by comparison, unreasonably good (or unreasonably bad, as the case may be), and therefore an apparent indication of untruthful testimony. In like manner a criminal interrogator may obtain indications of a subject's guilt or innocence, but the technique also opens up a number of other opportunities as well.

In employing this technique some interrogators not only seek detailed information covering the time just before the offense in question, but also delve into the subject's past history, in order to get what may be termed "background" information; that is, information concerning the subject's place of birth, his education, work, etc., all of which afford the interrogator a better opportunity to study or "size up" his subject.

With respect to a subject's activities prior to the crime, it may not be necessary, in the average case, to go back much further than a few hours or days preceding the offense, but there are occasions when it is helpful to obtain information about his activities over a longer period of time. In any event, it is well for the interrogator to gradually lead his subject up to the day and time of the offense and then let him continue beyond that point, covering whatever subsequent period is deemed desirable.

Test the Validity of the Subject's Alibi

Unquestionably, the best way to check an alibi is by actual investigative methods. In other words, if a subject states that he was at a certain place during the time the offense was being committed elsewhere, the best way to determine whether or not he is telling the truth is to have an investigator check at the place cited by the subject and obtain information or evidence which will either substantiate or disprove his alibi. There are occasions, however, when this procedure is not feasible or even possible, and, therefore, reliance must sometimes be placed on interrogation methods alone.

As previously suggested, one way to test the validity of a subject's alibi is to consider it in the light of his account of activities prior to and since the offense. A recollection of considerable detail as to activities before and after the offense, in contrast to an absence of a similar quality of recollection for the period of the offense itself, may very well signify an effort to deceive, and calling this to the attention of the subject will have a desirable effect. Also of significance will be any contrast between a recollection of considerable detail at the time of the offense and the lack of it with regard to before and after occurrences. Moreover, a third situation might arise, to the ultimate advantage of the interrogator. A subject, while falsifying a detailed alibi, may realize the need for a comparable recollection of before and after activities and proceed to manufacture a set of details which may be easily recognized as false and proved to be such by known facts either already in the possession of the interrogator or discovered by subsequent investigation.

Whenever a subject submits an alibi couched in such general terms as, "I was out riding in my car the evening this crime was committed," it is advisable for the interrogator to have the subject relate all his activities during the period covered by the alibi, to name the places visited, to state the route traveled, and also to give the approximate time for each activity or when each place was visited or each route traveled. In other words, suppose the crime was committed at 8:00 p.m., and the subject states he was riding in his car from 7:00 to 9:00 p.m. He should then be asked to trace the route he took, name the places he visited, and give the time at which he arrived or left. In this manner, he may be placed in a position of being unable to account for the full period from 7:00 to 9:00, or else find it necessary to offer fictitious details easily detected and provable as false.

Another method for testing an alibi—particularly as regards juveniles or young adult offenders—consists in asking the subject if he observed a certain occurrence which supposedly happened at the place mentioned in his alibi and during the time the subject alleges he was present. Thinking that the interrogator is referring to an actual occurrence, the subject may acknowledge his observation of it and thereby expose his deceit and guilt. For instance, the subject may state as his alibi that he was taking a walk along the lake shore at the time of the offense. He then may be asked in a rather curious and forceful manner: "This is a coincidence. My wife and I happened to be driving by there at that time. Did you see all the excitement on the shore when the kid was saved from drowning by the lifeguard?" An admission that he observed such a fictitious occurrence certainly would constitute an indica tion of deception and guilt, to say nothing of its value to the in terrogator in his efforts to elicit a confession. On the other hand, if the subject says something like, "You must be thinking about some other time; there was no drowning while I was there," that response is indicative of truth-telling.

Some interrogators follow the practice of pausing at this stage of the interrogation to have a subject's detailed alibi statement reduced to writing and signed by him. Then, if the interrogator's subsequent efforts are unproductive of any specific indication of guilt or innocence, another statement regarding the alibi is obtained. This second statement is compared with the first one. If both statements agree in their various details, the fact is considered indicative of truth-telling, since few liars are able to remember all the details of a previous lie. On the other hand, however, if inconsistencies are present they can be called to the subject's attention and used as the basis for obtaining a confession.

Contrary to the generally prevailing notion, when two or more persons relate a bona fide alibi for themselves or give a truthful version of an occurrence, there *will be* some variations regarding the details, because two persons ordinarily do not observe an occurrence with equal accuracy, nor can they recall or describe the incident with the same degree of accuracy. Therefore, an interrogator should view with suspicion an alibi or an account of an occurrence given by two persons with a full coincidence of all details. For example, a husband and wife, who were suspected of a murder committed several weeks prior to their interrogation, related as an alibi their presence together at a dinner in a neighborhood restaurant. They each told in detail the time of arrival, the means used to get there, and what they had ordered for dinner that night. Their stories were the same with respect to all the details, but they were also too good to be true. It subsequently developed that the subjects were guilty of the murder and that they had decided upon the restaurant alibi for the following reason. They were frequent diners at this particular restaurant and were familiar with the menu served there on the various nights of the week; and they realized that the restaurant manager, waitresses, and others probably would not remember whether or not the subjects were there on the particular night in question.

Another illustration of the above mentioned point is a case involving the disappearance of a large sum of money from an armored money truck, to which four men had been assigned as guards. An investigation revealed that there had been no forced entry into the truck, and this fact cast suspicion on the four guards. At the outset of the investigation each one admitted that, in violaion of company orders, they had left the truck unguarded for a period of time while all had gone to a restaurant together for luncheon. The statements which were taken from the guards varied considerably with respect to some of the details about the events and activities during this lunch period, and that fact convinced the investigators that the guards were lying. However, when one of the authors was engaged to interrogate the guards he viewed the minor discrepancies in their statements as evidence suggestive of truth-telling rather than lying. Thereafter a recently discharged employee guard was interrogated and confessed that while still in the employ of the company he had managed to have a duplicate key made for the truck door and had awaited an appropriate time for using it to steal some money. He was, of course, familiar with the guards' habit of occasionally leaving the truck unguarded during the time they were eating together in this restaurant; this afforded him the timely opportunity for taking the money. Following his confession he led the interrogator and other investigators to the place where he had concealed the money, and the entire sum of money was recovered intact.

T. Where Certain Facts Suggestive of the Subject's Guilt Are Known, Ask Him about Them Rather Casually and as Though the Real Facts Were Not Already Known

The principal purpose of this technique is to afford the subject an opportunity to lie if he sees fit to do so. His answer will thus furnish a very good indication of his possible guilt or innocence, and if he is guilty, his position becomes very vulnerable when confronted with the facts possessed by the interrogator.

Rather than tell the subject a known fact and ask for an explanation, it is much more advantageous first to determine whether or not he will lie about the fact itself. Suppose, therefore, that in a robbery case the investigation disclosed that shortly after the robbery the subject made a substantial payment on his car, or paid off a large debt, or deposited money in a bank under a fictitious name. In such a case, instead of calling the occurrence to the subject's attention and asking for his explanation, the interrogator should casually inquire somewhat as follows: "Except for your salary [or other usual income] have you come into possession of any other money recently?" If he readily admits he has, and offers a satisfactory explanation of it, such a disclosure may serve to exonerate him from further suspicion. On the other hand, however, a lie to the question will be a strong indication of his possible guilt, and at the same time it will constitute a very valuable assist to the interrogator to use in his efforts toward obtaining a confession.

An additional illustration involves a case where a person is suspected of having set fire to his store about 10:00 o'clock one night. The investigation reveals that about 9:45 the store owner was seen leaving his house through the back door and walking down an alley in the direction of the rear exit of his store. In such a case situation nothing is apt to be gained by confronting him with this information, since he would immediately offer a false explanation for his actions. He may even say that he went to the store to get something he forgot to bring home when he locked the store at 6:00 o'clock. It is far better, therefore, to give him an opportunity to lie about his actions. For instance, the interrogator may ask him to state what time he arrived home after closing the store and to tell what he did thereafter, up until the time he was notified of the fire. Only after the subject has committed himself to having remained in his home all evening should he be confronted with the evidence of the walk down the alley at 9:45. Once caught in such a lie, a subject will have considerable difficulty avoiding a confession of guilt.

U. At Various Intervals Ask the Subject Certain Pertinent Questions in a Manner which Implies that the Correct Answers Are Already Known

This technique, the converse of the previous one, is designed to elicit truthful information from a subject by creating the impression that the correct answer to a question is already known and that the interrogator is only interested in determining whether or not the subject is willing to tell the truth.

The asking of questions which imply the expected answers is the most common method of applying this technique. For instance, "How long have you known John Jones?" rather than "Do you know John Jones?" Another method, and a very effective one, consists of the prefacing of a selected question (not bearing directly upon the issue of the subject's guilt or innocence) with the statement, "Think carefully before you answer this next question,"—an admonition which is apt to provoke a truthful reply even from a guilty subject, because of his concern that the truth is already known. The admonition can be rendered even more effective if the interrogator has some written papers in his hand or starts looking through some papers on a nearby table at the time he gives the admonition.

Whenever the desired acknowledgement does not result from the use of the "think carefully" warning, it is sometimes effective for the interrogator to express his skepticism about the reply given by asking, "Are you sure about that?" In this way an opportunity is afforded a lying subject to reconsider the possible risk he incurs by not telling the truth about a fact which seems to be already known to the interrogator.

In a case where the suspect's presence in the company of John Jones at a particular time would be of incriminating significance, but the interrogator does not know that the subject was, in fact, there, it is well to ask, "How long were you with John Jones that night?" This kind of question is more apt to produce a truthful answer such as, "Only for a few minutes," than if the question were phrased: "Were you with John Jones that night?" The latter question may draw a simple "no" answer.

Another excellent illustration of the application and effectiveness of the present technique has already been related under Technique O, where the question, "Where *is* your diary?" was asked of a sex deviate rape-murder suspect, even though the interrogator was unaware of the actual existence of the diary. An acknowledgement of the keeping of the diary and an examination of its incriminating entries regarding a series of rapes helped considerably in obtaining the subject's murder confession, and at the same time exonerated an innocent man accused of one of the subject's prior non-fatal rapes.

V. Refer to Some Non-Existing Incriminating Evidence to Determine whether the Subject Will Attempt to Explain It Away; if He Does, That Fact Is Suggestive of His Guilt

A guilty person is naturally concerned with "covering his tracks," and he is also understandably worried about the police discovery of evidence that will incriminate him. An innocent person has no tracks to cover, and he obviously does not have to do much speculation about incriminating evidence. In view of these considerations, much may be gained by the asking of questions such as these:

"Is there any reason, Joe, why there would be blood on your overcoat which laboratory tests show to be the same as that of this fellow who was stabbed?"

"Is there any reason why your fingerprints would be on a beer bottle in this fellow's home?"

"Is there any reason why the dirt on your shoes should match the dirt outside the window of that house?"

"Is there any reason why any of your belongings would be at this place where the money was taken?"

A guilty person will usually either try to offer a possible explanation or else he will ask for some further information about the matter mentioned by the interrogator. An innocent person will usually reply with some such statement as, "No, because I didn't do it," or "No, because I wasn't there."

While not proof of guilt or innocence, the nature of a subject's response or reaction may be very helpful, along with other factors, in determining whether or not the subject is the guilty person.

W. Ask the Subject whether He Ever "Thought" about Committing the Offense in Question or One Similar to It

If a subject will admit that he had "thought" about committing the offense in question, this fact is suggestive of his guilt. It is well, therefore, to inquire about such thoughts. For instance, the subject may be asked whether he ever thought about taking the missing money, or about holding-up the particular victim of a robbery, or of forcing himself upon a particular rape victim, or even about committing *any* offense of the type under investigation. A response of "No" is the characteristic answer of an innocent subject, for even though the idea may have flashed through his mind he would not have given it any further consideration. On the other hand, a guilty person is much more likely to say "Yes," although, to be sure, he is apt to add "but not seriously."

In utilizing this technique, if the interrogator does not receive an acknowledgement of having thought about committing the offense or one similar to it, he should then say: "The reason I'm asking you if you ever thought about doing this is because if you ever did, then that may account for the fact that your looks and appearances are giving the impression that you're not telling the truth." A guilty person is apt to try to explain away this impression by admitting that he had thought about doing the act in question or one similar to it. An innocent person will usually persist in his denial of any such thinking.

Once a subject admits having thought about the offense, or about a similar one, the interrogator should ask him to tell about the kind and frequency of such thoughts. If the thoughts went as far as plans or preparation, then the interrogator should become even more secure in his belief of the subject's guilt. The interrogator may then say: "Joe, this thinking finally got to a point where in one of your weakest moments (or when you were under the most pressure) you gave in. Right?"

In some case situations such as the investigation of a sex-motivated murder, a subject may be asked, "Have you ever dreamed about doing something like this?" Such a question was asked by one of us during the interrogation of a subject suspected of a sex-motivated murder in which the offender had decapitated the victim and taken further sexual liberties with the dead body. He admitted that he had dreamed about "placing naked women into a knife machine." Thereupon, the interrogator asked him to give the full details of the dream. Then, after further interrogation the subject admitted his guilt, and his confession was fully susbstantiated by such evidence as the finding of the girl's wrist watch at the place where the subject stated he had thrown it.

Although the foregoing case is a very unique one in our experience, perhaps further case situations of a similar nature may establish a relationship between the capacity to dream of such conduct and the doing of the act in question, which is comparable to the relationship we have found to exist in many cases between the thinking of certain criminal conduct and the actual commission of the act.

X. In Theft Cases, if a Suspect Offers to Make Restitution, That Fact Is Indicative of Guilt

Except for a most unusual case situation, no innocent person will agree to pay the victim the amount of his loss, or even any part of it. A guilty person, who is able, or who has the ultimate potential, to make any kind of restitution may be quite willing to do so. Consequently, an interrogator who is not certain whether his subject is guilty or innocent can derive considerable help from the response to a question such as this: "Joe, this fellow (or the company) is entitled to the return of that money. How about seeing that he gets it back?" An innocent person will respond by saying something like this: "I know he is, but I didn't take it!" On the other hand, the guilty person may ponder over his answer, or he may immediately say, "All right, I'll see that he is reimbursed, even though I didn't take it."

In instances where an ordinary thief or an embezzler agrees to make restitution for the loss of the missing sum (e.g., $300), the interrogator should then say, for the purpose of satisfying himself more completely regarding the conclusion of guilt, "Now what about paying back the other loss, the $200 one?" (Here the interrogator is referring to a fictitious loss, which should always be in a lesser sum or value than the actual loss.) In such a situation the subject will probably respond by saying, "No, I will not!" Then, when the interrogator says, "Why not?" the typical reply is, "Because I didn't take it!" Such a response will confirm the reasonable inference warranted by the subject's initial willingness to make restitution for the actual loss.

Y. Ask the Subject whether He Is Willing to Take a Lie-Detector Test. The Innocent Person Will Almost Always Steadfastly Agree to Take Practically Any Test to Prove His Innocence, whereas the Guilty Person Is More Prone to Refuse to Take the Test or to Find Excuses for not Taking It, or for Backing Out of His Commitment to Take It

Where facilities are available for a competently administered Polygraph ("lie-detector") test, it is always helpful, of course, to have such a test conducted on a subject whose guilt is uncertain. In only a relatively few communities, however, is such a service available, and the only remaining recourse is to a skillful, common sense interrogation without the aid of any instrumental assistance.

Regardless of the unavailability of Polygraph test facilities, much can be gained by telling a subject, "All right, if you're telling the truth, as you say you are, then you're willing to take a lie-detector test!" Without waiting for an answer, the interrogator should then say, "I'll immediately arrange for a test," and at the same time the interrogator should pick up a telephone directory or go to the door and direct someone to phone "the lie-detector laboratory." A guilty subject is likely to voice some objection or ask a question about the test or give an excuse for not wanting to be tested at that time. On the other hand, truthful subjects ordinarily will welcome the opportunity to take such a test. This customary difference in reactions to the suggestion of a Polygraph test provides a very helpful indication as to whether the interrogator has before him a guilty or innocent subject.

Whenever the above procedure is followed, it is important that the interrogator actually arrange for a test whenever circumstances permit his doing so, even for a subject who seems quite willing, because there are times when guilty persons will try to bluff their way through by agreeing to be tested. They feel that by expressing a willingness to take a test the interrogator will conclude they are innocent. This, of course, is a conclusion that should never be reached, even though the odds favor the assumption of possible innocence on the part of a willing subject.

Guilty subjects sometimes advance the objection that they have no confidence in Polygraph tests, that they are not infallible, and that the refusal of courts to admit test results in evidence is proof of lack of accuracy. Whenever this occurs, the interrogator should say, "All right, we can arrange for a truth-serum test!" A guilty subject will immediately offer an objection to such a test on the possible ground that he can not stand hypodermic needle shots or that his system cannot tolerate drugs. In any event he will either refuse to take a truth-serum test or resort to a delaying tactic of first checking with his physician.

If a subject does ultimately agree to take a truth-serum test, the interrogator can then resort to an impressive pretense of trying but failing to arrange for a test at that time.

Not only will the foregoing procedures furnish indications to the interrogator as to whether a subject is guilty or innocent, but the suggestions of a Polygraph or "truth-serum" test will frequently result in confessions from the guilty.

In all instances where suggestions are made about Polygraph or "truth-serum" tests, the interrogator should carefully avoid creating the impression that a subject is required to take the test. Indeed, it is essential that the proposal be presented in such a way that the subject knows it is only an invitation or an opportunity for him to establish his truthfulness.

Following a subject's refusal to take either a Polygraph or a "truth-serum" test, the interrogator can (at least for its effect upon the subject) point out the incriminating significance of a refusal.

Z. A Subject Who Tells the Interrogator, "All Right, I'll Tell You What You Want, but I Didn't Do It," Is, in All Probability, Guilty

An innocent person will remain steadfast in his denial of guilt, regardless of the attitude or statements of the interrogator (always assuming, of course, the absence of physical harm, threats, or promises of leniency). A guilty person, however, may try to placate his interrogator by expressing a willingness to admit the offense while at the same time denying that he committed it. An interrogator, therefore, may be materially assisted by an awareness that a statement of this type is characteristic of the guilty subject. The psychological factors that prevail are comparable to those involved when a subject in a theft case expresses a willingness to make restitution to the victim.

GENERAL SUGGESTIONS REGARDING THE INTERROGATION OF CRIMINAL SUSPECTS

1. Interview the Victim, the Accuser, or the Discoverer of the Crime before Interrogating the Suspect Himself

Whenever possible, the interrogator should interview the victim, the accuser, or the discoverer of the crime before he proceeds to interrogate the suspect himself. If he cannot personally attend to this phase of the case, it should be done by someone who will conduct a competent interview and make a full report to the interrogator.

Several basic reasons support this suggestion of a preliminary interview with the alleged victim, accuser, or discoverer of a reported crime:

(a) In the course of the preliminary interview the interrogator may determine that no crime at all has occurred. He may even be able to readily establish that as a fact; or perhaps he will obtain leads which will later provide proof that no crime was committed. For instance, an interview with the reporter of a larceny may disclose the fact or probability that the missing money or property has only been misplaced.

(b) The interview may result in proof, or in an investigative lead, that the reporter himself committed the crime. For instance, the person who reports a fire of incendiary origin may be the very one who started it, or the reporter of a murder may be the one who actually committed it. In such instances the reporter acts on the assumption that by taking the initiative of making the report he will divert suspicion from himself.

(c) If the crime report involves an accusation against someone with whom the accuser is acquainted or related, the interrogator should bear in mind the possibility that the accusation may be motivated by revenge or by some other base motive on the part of the accuser. A preliminary interview with the accuser might reveal such a motive, or perhaps even result in an admission of its existence. An example of this possibility is a case where a wife accuses her estranged husband of sexual liberties with one of their children.

(d) The interrogator may ascertain that a false crime report was made for the purpose of concealing the reporter's own criminal conduct or social indiscretion regarding some other related or unrelated matter. Instances of this type occur at times when a burglary or other theft is reported for the purpose of defrauding an insurance company, or for covering up an embezzlement. Also to be considered is the possibility that a fictitious robbery or other theft may have been reported in order to account for money lost in a gambling venture, or as a result of the reporter's indulgence in some other indiscretion which he seeks to conceal from his wife or others.

(e) A preliminary interview with the alleged victim, the accuser, or the discoverer of the crime will also serve the purpose of adequately informing the interrogator of all the pertinent facts and details of the offense. He will thereby be better prepared to conduct an effective interrogation of the suspected or accused person. Moreover, as regards a truth-telling accuser, the interview will serve the additional purpose of fortifying the interrogator psychologically for his subsequent interrogation efforts. In other words, once he completely satisfies himself that the accuser is telling the truth, the interrogator will be able to more convincingly display an air of confidence in the subject's guilt. He will also have a stronger incentive for being persistent in his interrogation of the accused.

The Nature of the Interview

A crime victim should be asked to relate the details of the occurrence and to give, whenever possible, a detailed description of the offender or of the place where the offense occurred.

If the report of the offense is couched in generalities only, it should be viewed with skepticism, since it is characteristic of a false report to be lacking in the kind of details that are almost always present in a genuine report. For instance, if an employee has falsely reported a robbery in which company money was involved, he will ordinarily be very vague as to a description of the robber, or as to when, or how, or where the incident occurred. A genuine robbery report will ordinarily reveal such details.

A child victim of a sex offense should be asked to describe the scene of the occurrence. For instance, if the crime is alleged to have occurred in the home of a particular individual, the child should be asked to describe the room, as to curtains, wall paper, decorations on the wall, the rug on the floor, the bed, and other such objects. If her description is an accurate one, that fact will corroborate her accusation, and when disclosed to the subject, the child's accurate information will have a very desirable effect.

Of incidental interest at this point is the fact that it is exceedingly rare for a child to falsify a sex report. The exceptions to guard against are situations in which there is a reasonable likelihood that some adult induced her to make the accusation. An illustration of this possibility is a situation (to which we have already referred) where the accused is the estranged husband of the child's mother, or where there may be some motive on the part of the mother or other member of the child's family to embarrass or otherwise hurt the accused or damage his reputation.

Female sex victims generally are very reluctant to reveal the details of the offense. They encounter difficulty in relating precisely what the offender did and said. The interrogator can ease their burden by telling the victim that she should consider the interrogator very much in the same light as a doctor whom she might consult regarding a sexual organ problem. This tends to relieve the victim of much of her embarrassment. Also, in some instances the interrogator may find it helpful to have the victim write out, rather than relate orally, the details of what the offender said to her.

An interrogator should view with suspicion any anonymous reports implicating a person in a criminal offense, and particularly in instances where it appears that the reporter is a woman. There are many known instances of jilted or deserted women who have sent the police an anonymous letter suggesting that the man who offended them committed a certain crime. They may do this out of spite, or for the purpose of getting the man into a situation where he may need their help, or be required to delay a planned departure from the city or country—all for the purpose of "getting him back again." It is always a good practice, therefore, for an interrogator to view with suspicion a "tip" or accusation based upon an anonymous report. To be sure, there are occasions when the report is well-founded, but in the vast majority of instances it stems from some ulterior motive.

2. Be Patient

An interrogator should never lose sight of the fact that when a criminal offender is asked to confess his crime, a great deal is requested of him. A confession may mean the loss of his liberty, or even his life. Moreover, it is ordinarily difficult for anyone to admit even a simple mistake that involves no possible penal consequences, or perhaps not even any social stigma. There is no reason, therefore, why an interrogator should expect a subject to confess without hesitation and reluctance, and particularly when the case is one in which there is little or no provable evidence of guilt at the time of the interrogation. It is necessary, therefore, that the interrogator be possessed with the quality of patience. The lack of it, or a driving urge to "get the job done quickly," may be an asset insofar as certain other types of police work are concerned (e.g., field investigations), but such characteristics in an interrogator are definitely undesirable.

Once a subject senses the fact that his interrogator is impatient, he is thereby encouraged to persist in his deception. He develops the attitude that if he holds out the interrogator will soon give up. Then, too, the emotional factor of impatience will interfere with the interrogator's exercise of sound judgment and reasoning that the task at hand demands of him. Moreover, his impatience may lead to anger and he will then become personally involved in what should be strictly a professional undertaking. His anger may produce threats or the use of physical force. He will thereby endanger the welfare and security of the innocent or else elicit from the guilty a confession that is legally valueless as evidence.

Not only must the interrogator have patience, but he must also display it. It is well, therefore, to get the idea across, in most case situations, that the interrogator has "all the time in the world." He may even express himself in those exact words. (In some cases of a minor nature, however, the opposite impression should be given: that the case is not deserving of a lot of time and effort and that the interrogator has more important tasks to perform.)

It is generally advisable for an interrogator to avoid any "rapid fire" talking. His statements should be expressed in normal language speed.

It is not necessary for the interrogator to be talking always about something new. In fact, it is usually effective to go back over and over again to the salient points that were made earlier. This serves to emphasize their importance. Moreover, a certain amount of repetition is required in order to be sure that the subject actually hears and gives consideration to what is being said.

Whenever a subject is resentful of the fact that he is under suspicion—and again attention is called to the fact that as a rule the innocent are much more prone than the guilty to express resentment—the interrogator should let the subject vent his feelings. The interrogator should "hear him out," and in so doing the impression may be given that the interrogator is really weighing and considering what the subject is saying. Also, if the interrogator knows or finds out about any hobbies or special interests the subject has, the latter should be engaged in a conversation about such matters. Without too much delay the interrogator can thereafter bring the subject back to the realities of the case itself. Meanwhile, however, the interrogator will have established a better rapport with the subject. If he is innocent, that fact may be readily ascertainable; if guilty, he is brought much closer to a disclosure of the truth.

If a subject adopts an attitude of despair and resignation and says something like, "I don't care whether you believe me or not; I'd just as soon go to jail; there's nothing for me to look forward to anyway," invite him to talk about his general troubles and misfortunes. The interrogator should then listen and console him with sympathetic understanding. The interrogator may say, "Joe, I guess life has treated you rather roughly, hasn't it?" Such a question will very likely "open up" the subject. He will probably begin with a simple "yes" answer, after which the interrogator can delve into the matter with specific questions regarding childhood difficulties, etc. After a relatively brief period of attentive listening the interrogator can shift the discussion toward the offense itself and then proceed with other appropriate interrogation techniques.

Another prime requisite for a successful interrogation, in addition to patience, is persistence. In this respect the following rule of thumb is a helpful one for an interrogator to follow: *Never conclude an interrogation at the time when you feel discouraged and ready to give up, but continue for a little while longer—if only for ten or fifteen minutes.* The authors have observed many instances in which the subject confessed, or later said he had decided to confess, just at the very time when the interrogator was ready to abandon, or did abandon, his efforts. The reason for this occurrence is the fact that ordinarily the time when the interrogator becomes discouraged coincides with the time when the subject fully realizes the futility of his continued lying.

During the above suggested "overtime" periods, the interrogator should devote his attention to the main aspects of the case. Aimless, irrelevant talking at this point will prove fruitless.

When the interrogator feels that he has expended all his techniques, it is helpful, in many instances, to leave the subject alone in the interrogation room for awhile, but only after saying to him before departing, "Think it over, Joe; I'll be back in a few minutes." Upon returning to the interrogation room the interrogator should be seated, and then he should resume his interrogation by first saying something like, "Well, Joe, what about it?". During the period when the subject is left alone, he will probably do a lot of thinking and may conclude that the time is at hand for telling the truth.

With respect to persistence, it is well for the interrogator to bear in mind that on many occasions the subject who appears tough and not likely to confess is actually more vulnerable to an effective interrogation than some subjects who give the impression of being rather easy.

In considering the foregoing suggestions the interrogator should bear in mind that he is not privileged to conduct unreasonably long interrogations. If he does, that fact, according to the Supreme Court, may be considered as evidence that a suspect in custody, or under other police restraint, did not actually waive his rights in the first instance.

3. Make No Promises When Asked, "What Will Happen to Me if I Tell the Truth?"

Whenever a subject under interrogation makes an inquiry such as, "What will happen to me if I tell you the truth?", or "Do you think I'll go to jail if I confess?", under no circumstances should the interrogator point out any of the possible consequences of a confession, nor should he hold out any inducement whatsoever. Any such reply would nullify the legal validity of the confession that may follow, and rightly so, because a promise of leniency or immunity may induce an innocent man to confess. Moreover, the interrogator should realize that whenever a subject raises a question of that sort, he is beginning his confession. For these two reasons, therefore, the interrogator's reply should be somewhat as follows: "Joe, I can't tell you what will happen. I'm in no position to say; I don't have the authority, and it wouldn't be fair to you if I made any commitment to you. Joe, my advice to you is to tell the truth—and to tell it now. Then if you think you have a break coming, talk it over with the district attorney or the judge." Immediately therafter, the interrogator should ask a detail question such as where, how, when, or why the subject did the act in question.

By responding to the subject's "what will happen to me" question in the above suggested way, the interrogator displays an attitude of fair play, which is quite impressive. Moreover, if later on the offender retracts his confession on the ground that it was obtained as a result of promises and inducements, the interrogator can in all sincerity relate the foregoing comments to good advantage.

4. View with Skepticism the So-called "Conscience-Stricken" Confession

Criminal offenders whose guilt is unknown to the police will rarely surrender themselves and confess their guilt. The instinct for self-preservation stands in the way. Consequently, an interrogator should view with considerable skepticism any conscience-stricken confession. Such a confession is very likely to be false. It may be the product of a mentally ill person, or it may stem from an otherwise normal person's effort to incur a temporary police detention in order to gain some other deliberately conceived objective. Among the latter possibilities are instances where an individual may merely be seeking free transportation back to the state or community where the crime was committed. In other instances the purpose may be that of being incarcerated, either for a brief or even a relatively long period, in order to evade police consideration of him as a suspect for a much more serious crime. Then, too, there are times when the only motive of a conscience-stricken confession is the publicity the confessor seeks to achieve.

A genuine conscience-stricken confessor will give the appearance of a person who has been broken in health and spirit as a result of his troubled conscience. On the other hand, with the exception of the mentally ill person, the false confessor is apt to be rather light-hearted in his appearance and conduct. He recognizes that if and when the prosecution stage is reached, he will retract his confession and offer convincing evidence to support his claim of innocence.

One method for checking the authenticity of a conscience-stricken confession, or one that appears to be the result of mental illness, is to refer to some fictitious aspects of the crime and test whether the subject will accept them as actual facts relating to the occurrence. This tactic presupposes, of course, that all the true facts of the case have not already been disclosed to the subject. As the reader will recall, in Technique B we urged a withholding of such disclosures for this very reason, as well as for other considerations.

5. When a Subject Has Made Repeated Denials of Guilt to Previous Interrogators, First Question Him, Whenever Circumstances Permit, about Some Other, Unrelated Offense of a Similar Nature of Which He Is Also Considered to Be Guilty

As already suggested, an interrogator should make every possible effort to keep the suspect from uttering repeated denials of guilt, since such denials make it all the more difficult for the subject to tell the truth later on, even when he feels impelled to do so. In other words, the subject will find it hard to then tell the interrogator, in effect, "I've been lying to you, and to the other investigators, but now I'll tell the truth." With this consideration in mind, an interrogator, when called upon to interrogate someone who has repeatedly denied his guilt to other investigators, should, whenever circumstances permit, first try to obtain an admission from him regarding another similar, though unrelated, offense for which he is also guilty, and regarding which he is presently under suspicion. For instance, if a person has committed a theft such as stealing a purse in a school, office, or hospital, and he has made repeated denials of guilt, it is far easier for him to tell about other purse stealings he committed, than to admit the one regarding which he has made repeated denials of guilt. For this reason the interrogator should first concentrate his efforts on an admission about some other similar, unrelated offense that was committed either in the same or in some other school, office, or hospital. Then, after obtaining an admission for such other offense or offenses, the interrogator can proceed with an interrogation about the main offense in question.

The above stated procedure is particularly helpful with female subjects. A woman is much more reluctant than a man to confess a crime about which she has previously made repeated denials of guilt.

6. An Unintelligent, Uneducated Criminal Suspect, with a Low Cultural Background, Should Be Interrogated on a Psychological Level Comparable to That Usually Employed in the Questioning of a Child Respecting an Act of Wrongdoing

An unintelligent, uneducated offender, with a low cultural background, presents a different interrogation problem than that encountered with other types of subjects. In some essential respects he must be dealt with on a psychological level comparable to tnat usually invoked during the questioning of a child who has committed a wrongful act.

A guilty subject of this general type is ordinarily able to indulge in some very effective acting. He has the capacity with such acting to deceive an inexperienced interrogator into believing he is telling the truth. Another common characteristic of this particular group of offenders is that they ordinarily do not exhibit the observable symptoms of deception that are so helpful to the interrogator with respect to other types of subjects. Moreover, the unintelligent, uneducated offender from a low cultural environment is usually able to sit and listen very calmly to what the interrogator says, and he may even nod his head as though in agreement with what he hears—but then he may eventually comment, with perhaps a smile on his face, "I don't know anything about this thing."

It is necessary, with a person of the type now under consideration, to speak to him in very simple terms. However, care must be exercised as to tone of voice, because a very soft voice seems to lull the subject into a state of tranquility to such an extent that he becomes unmindful of what the interrogator is saying to him. In fact, the interrogator may have to resort to dramatic tones and gestures. At times it may become necessary to even invoke some feigned displays of impatience.

In instances where a subject of the type under consideration happens to be a member of a minority race or group, the interrogator must never make a derogatory remark about that race or group. (Nor should he assume that a person's attitude, conduct, or even his criminality are the result of the color of his skin or his nationality!) To the contrary, the interrogator should (and in good conscience he always can) eulogize some outstanding member of that race or group and suggest that the subject try to measure up to the conduct exemplified by that particular individual. Moreover, where the interrogator is personally acquainted with the individual example to whom he refers, he should make that fact known to the subject by way of further emphasizing his commendable qualities.

Throughout the interrogation of an unintelligent, uneducated offender with a low cultural background, the interrogator must maintain a very positive attitude, without ever relenting in his display of a position of certainty regarding the subject's guilt. It is only a matter of how, when, where, or why the offender did the act in question. With a subject of this type, considerable emphasis should be placed upon the possible *excuses* for his conduct. In other words, in a theft case, the possibility should be emphatically stressed that he took the missing article "by mistake," or without knowing he had it in his possession. (Thereafter, of course, the interrogator should seek the truthful explanation, as was suggested earlier.)

THE INTERROGATION OF WITNESSES AND OTHER
PROSPECTIVE INFORMANTS

The basic principles underlying the previously described techniques for interrogating suspects and offenders are, in general, equally applicable to cases involving the interrogation of witnesses and other prospective informants.

This search for and the interview of witnesses at the actual crime scene calls for the employment of proper psychological techniques in much the same way as does the interrogation of witnesses or informants who are located later and questioned at a place other than the scene of the crime. An excellent illustration of the proper method for interrogating witnesses at a crime scene is the one appearing below from an *Accident Investigation Manual* published by the Northwestern University Traffic Institute.[12] Although it describes an automobile accident investigation, the principles there developed are equally applicable to a murder case or any other type of offense.

"Some officers seem never to be able to find witnesses; others have little difficulty. One officer in the former category would shoulder his way through a crowd. 'Did anybody see this accident?' he would shout. 'How about you?' 'How about you?' He would all but push the people about. Naturally, he found very few witnesses. In reporting back to his partner he would say, 'There weren't any witnesses. I went through the crowd four times asking everybody, but nobody saw the accident.' An adroit officer uses his head rather than his lung power. He goes about the job quietly. Perhaps he spots a talkative woman—at least one such person is to be found at most accidents. 'How do you do, madam,' he says. 'Did I understand you to say that you saw this accident?' 'Why, no, officer,' she replies, probably feeling flattered that he singled her out, 'I didn't see it, but that man in the straw hat over there was telling me all about it. He was right here when it happened.' In approaching the man, the officer is very courteous but just a little

[12] Pp. 171–172.

more brisk and businesslike. He plans his question carefully. He does not say, 'Did you see this accident?' but rather, 'Pardon me, sir, would you mind telling me what you saw in connection with this accident?' This officer seldom has difficulty in finding witnesses.

"He listens carefully to their accounts of the accident. Then, if they are willing to write out a statement, he provides them with notebook and pencil and asks them to sign what they write. If they will not write the statement, he writes it, reads it to them aloud, then has them sign it. If they refuse to sign, he does not insist; they are still his witnesses and he wants their good will when they appear on the stand in the trial, if a trial follows.

"In brief, the good investigator usually seeks his witnesses indirectly. He finds somebody who knows that somebody else saw the accident. Getting the witness' name if possible, he addresses him by it. He is quiet and courteous. In requesting the witness to write and sign a statement or merely to sign it, he puts his question positively, not negatively. Instead of saying, 'Won't you sign this, please?' he hands the pencil to the person and says, 'Sign here, if you don't mind. It will make our investigation complete.' If the witness does not want to sign, the officer is cheerful, not resentful."

Although a criminal interrogator ordinarily will experience very little difficulty in obtaining information from witnesses to a crime or from persons in possession of information derived from some other source, there are instances when a witness or other prospective informant will attempt to withhold whatever information he may have concerning another's guilt. In the interrogation of such subjects the following suggestions should assist the interrogator in obtaining the desired information.

1. **Assure the Willing but Fearful Witness or Other Prospective Informant That He Will Not Be Harmed by the Offender or His Relatives or Friends, and That He Will Receive Police Protection in the Event Such Protection Becomes Necessary**

It is quite natural that under certain conditions and circumstances a witness or other prospective informant might be desirous of assisting the police but yet be restrained from doing so because of his fear of retaliation at the hands of the offender or his relatives or friends. In such instances it is advisable to give the subject the following assurances:

(a) That retaliation is an extremely rare occurrence when the witness or informant is acting in good faith and without any selfish motive, such as receiving pay for his information, seeking personal revenge on the offender, etc. In this connection it is well to ask the subject if he knows of any case where an honest court witness, or an honest policeman or prosecuting attorney, was ever subsequently harmed by the offender or by someone else acting in the offender's behalf.

(b) That (where circumstances permit—e.g., where court testimony from the subject may not be necessary) the information he gives will be kept confidential and that therefore the offender and others will never know of the subject's cooperation with the police.

(c) That if it becomes necessary for him to testify in court, his previous cooperation will not be disclosed by the police, and since he will be subpoenaed as a witness he can always justify his act of testifying on the ground that he was ordered to do so by the court.

(d) That an adequate police guard will be assigned to the subject if he so desires, or if such protection is deemed necessary.

Along with the foregoing attempts to secure the proper degree of cooperation from a subject of this type, it is advisable to point out to him the fact that the interrogator is asking no more of him than he himself would expect of another person in the event that the subject or some member of his family were the one against whom the offense had been committed. Moreover, it is well to impress upon the subject his obligations, as a citizen of the community, to render such cooperation to the police.

In the event that none of the foregoing suggestions suffice to elicit the desired information, the willing but fearful witness or other prospective informant may be treated as an actual suspect, in the manner described below. Ordinarily, however, resort to the latter method is unnecessary.

2. Whenever a Witness or Other Prospective Informant Refuses to Cooperate Because He Is Deliberately Protecting the Offender's Interests, or Because He Is Anti-Social or Anti-Police in His Attitude, Seek to Break the Bond of Loyalty between the Subject and the Offender, or Accuse Him of the Offense and Proceed to Interrogate Him as Though He Were Actually Considered to Be the Offender Himself

Occasionally it is possible to break the bond of loyalty between a subject and the offender he is attempting to protect, by convincing the subject of disloyalty on the part of the offender. For instance, in the interrogation of a subject who is the mistress of the offender, she may be told that the offender was unfaithful to her and in love with another woman (whose true or fictitious name should be given). By this method the subject may be induced to change her attitude toward the interrogator's request for helpful information. It is also possible, on occasion, to change a subject's anti-social or anti-police attitude by patiently pointing out to him the unreasonableness and unsoundness of his views. Ordinarily, however, some more effective measures are necessary.

There is one consideration which a subject of this type is likely to place above all others, and that is the protection of his own interest and welfare. When all other methods have failed, therefore, the interrogator should accuse the subject himself of committing the crime (or of being implicated in it in some way) and proceed to interrogate him as though he were, in fact, considered to be the guilty individual. A witness or other prospective informant, thus faced with the possibility of a trial or conviction for a crime he did not commit, will sooner or later be impelled to abandon his efforts in the offender's behalf or in support of his anti-social or anti-police attitudes.

As previously stated, it is well to bear in mind that occasionally the reporter of a crime—a "witness," for instance—is actually the offender himself. In certain instances, therefore, or even as a rather routine procedure, the statements of important witnesses should be checked out for their accuracy and truthfulness. For instance, if such a witness states that someone was with him shortly before the offense, or that he was at a certain place immediately before the offense, a check should be made on the truthfulness of his statement. Otherwise an offender who is seeking to conceal his guilt by representing himself as a witness may well succeed in his efforts to evade detection.

THE WRITTEN CONFESSION

Most confessed criminal offenders will subsequently deny their guilt and allege that they either did not confess or that they were forced or induced to do so by physical abuse, threats, promises of leniency, or other illegal means. Occasionally the defendant in a criminal case will even go so far as to say that he was compelled to sign the statement without reading it, or without it being read to him, or that he was forced to place his signature on a blank sheet of paper and all that appears above it was inserted later.

In a community or jurisdiction where the police enjoy the respect and confidence of the public, such denials and charges, if false, are rather easily overcome, and the prosecution may even secure a conviction on the basis of an oral, unwritten, or unrecorded confession. In most cases, however, the problem is much more difficult, and an oral confession is considered less desirable than a written or recorded one. When it is in a written or recorded form, the controversy between the prosecution and the defense becomes more than merely a matter of whether or not the court or jury is to believe the oral testimony of the police or the accused; the written or recorded statement lends considerable support to the prosecution's contention that the accused did in fact confess.

With regard to a written or sound-recorded confession, the preference among prosecuting attorneys is for the former, even though, as will be subsequently discussed, sound-recorded or video-taped confessions are also admissible in evidence. Among the various practical disadvantages attending the use of sound-recorded or video-taped confessions is the one whereby a law enforcement agency that uses this means of preserving a confession may find it necessary to do so in all cases, despite the fact that in some cases it is not feasible to make a recording, for one reason or another. A failure to follow the practice in a particular case will afford defense counsel an opportunity to effectively contend that the reason no recording was made is due to the fact that the investigators in this instance employed interrogation methods which they did not want to have revealed by a sound or video-taped recording. Another point to consider is the fact that since sound-recorded confessions are subject to undetectable tampering, they do not constitute the kind of unassailable evidence that is sometimes attributed to them.

Assuming that the established practice within any particular law enforcement agency is to reduce confessions to writing and to have them signed, it is highly desirable that this be done as soon as possible after the subject has made his oral confession. The next morning or even a few hours after the oral confession may be too late. During such an interval the subject may reflect upon the legal consequences of his confession and then claim that he neither committed the crime nor confessed to it. This is most likely to occur if he is placed in the company of another prisoner or prisoners during the period between the oral confession and the attempt to reduce it to writing. No time should be lost, therefore, in preparing for and obtaining a written, signed confession. If time and circumstances do not afford the opportunity for a stenographic transcription or even for writing out a detailed statement, the interrogator should write or type a brief statement of what the subject orally related—even if it be only two or three sentences long—and present it to the subject for his signature. Once an offender has committed himself in writing—regardless of its brevity—he is far less likely to refuse later on to make and sign a more detailed version of the crime. Many good cases have been lost because an interrogator assumed that the next morning, or a few hours later, would be time enough to have a confession written up and signed, only to find that in the meantime the offender had changed his mind about admitting his guilt. It is a safe practice, therefore, to lose no more time than is absolutely necessary in obtaining some kind of signed statement. It may even be in the form of a suggested note or letter addressed to a relative, a friend, or an employer, explaining why the writer committed the offense. Such a document will serve as security against a change of mind or a denial during the period before the taking of a formal, detailed statement.

In addition to the avoidance of a time delay with respect to a written admission, it is also advisable to obtain such a statement, or the complete written confession itself, in the same room where the interrogation was conducted. A change to another place, or even to another room close by, may result in the subject's change of mind.

1. Warning of Constitutional Rights

Even though the required warnings have been issued before the interrogation began, it is well, nevertheless, to repeat and record the warnings at the start of the written or sound recorded confession. The primary reason for this is the fact that the suspect's initial waiver of his right to remain silent and his right to counsel may be revoked at any time he wishes to do so. By incorporating the warnings in the confession itself the interrogator will thereby preserve evidence of the fact that the waiver was a continuing one.

If the confession is to be in question and answer form, or sound recorded, the interrogator should say:

"Again I want to advise you: (a) that you are not required to give this recorded statement; (b) that anything you say can be used against you; (c) that you still have a right to have a lawyer present here; and (d) that you are entitled to have one provided for you if you are unable to afford one. Knowing this, are you still willing to give this recorded statement here and now?"

If the confession is to be written out, either by the confessor himself, or by the interrogator for subsequent signing by the confessor, the written confession should begin by reciting something as follows:

"I have been advised that I am not required to make this statement, that it can be used against me, that I have a right to have a lawyer present and to be provided for me if I am unable to pay for one. But I am willing to make this statement anyway."

In the event the subject informs the interrogator he does not wish to make the statement, or that he wants a lawyer, the interrogator must cease any further questioning or recording.

If the oral confession has been made to the police by a person who was not in custody when the interrogation began, and to whom, therefore, the warnings did not have to be issued initially, they should be given now, at the start of the written or sound recorded confession, in the way and manner we have just described.

2. Form of Confession

A written confession may be prepared in the form of questions by the interrogator and answers by the confessor, or in the form of a narration by the confessor. Such confessions may be written out by hand, typed by the interrogator, or taken down by a stenographer and transcribed into typewritten form.

Almost all interrogators and prosecuting attorneys prefer to have a stenographer record the confession in shorthand or stenotype for later transcription into a typewritten document that will be read to, or by, the confessor, and then signed by him. Moreover, some interrogators, including the authors, prefer that the stenographer be a woman rather than a man, and that she also sign the confession as a witness. A women stenographer is an excellent safeguard against fake claims of brutality or other improper conduct on the part of the interrogator. A jury is not apt to believe that she would be a participant in any such impropriety. In fact, defense counsel may even be completely dissuaded from making the claim, once he knows that the stenographer was a woman rather than a man. In other words, a confession that is taken down and transcribed by a woman is a much more unassailable piece of evidence than one taken by a male stenographer or typist.

The stenographer who has a confession assignment should be briefed about the case and given the subject's name and other such information before she enters the interrogation room. She should also be instructed that once inside the interrogation room she should sit off to the side of the subject rather than in front of him, and refrain from talking to the interrogator or asking him any questions other than perhaps to have him or the subject speak louder or more slowly, or to repeat something that was not sufficiently audible for recording purposes.

If the case involves a sex offense the subject may experience some embarrassment in talking in the presence of a woman, but this can be readily overcome by telling him to ignore the fact that the stenographer is a female because she has heard hundreds of statements equal to or far worse than anything the subject will relate.

During the taking of a confession no one should be in the interrogation room other than the subject, the interrogator, and the stenographer. In addition to the previously discussed psychological reasons for such privacy, there is a persuasive legal factor. In some jurisdictions, each person present during the interrogation or the taking of a confession will have to be produced as a witness at the trial whenever the defendant contends that improper methods were used to obtain his confession. This obviously imposes a burden upon the prosecution that can and should be avoided.

Some prosecutors prefer the question and answer form of confession; others have a preference for the narrative form. Perhaps the best procedure is to effect a compromise whereby the preliminary and concluding aspects of the offense are elicited by means of specific questions from the interrogator, but the details of the actual occurrence are given by the confessor in narrative form. For instance, the subject may be asked specific questions as to his name, address, age, place of employment, the time he arrived at the scene of the crime, the names of persons who were with him up to that time, and then, after the interrogator's questions have brought the suspect right up to the time and place of the crime, he may be asked, "What happened then?" Thereafter, as long as the subject confines himself to an orderly recitation of the occurrence, he should be permitted to continue to narrate what happened. If he hesitates or seems to be relating events out of sequence, the interrogator can interpose a specific question in order to have the subject continue in an orderly fashion. At the same time, however, some irrelevant talking should be permitted, because its very irrelevancy may be considered as evidence of the voluntariness of the confession.

After the main occurrence has been covered in the confession, the interrogator may return to the use of specific questions, such as "Where did you go then?"; "What time did you get there?"; etc. Specific questions may also be used, of course, to bring out previously revealed facts which were omitted from the subject's narrative statement.

In addition to the above mentioned advantages of a question and answer form confession, it also lends itself more readily to the deletion of certain parts, if the trial court should consider any deletion necessary, before the confession is read to the jury.

All of the interrogator's questions should be short and also very simply worded. The use of lengthy, complicated questions and the kind of answers that are likely to follow renders the document much less impressive than one with short, simple, and "to the point" questions and answers.

Under no circumstances should a confessor be put under oath by a notary public or by a justice of the peace or by anyone else before the taking of his confession. Such a practice is viewed as a coercive influence, and it may serve to nullify the legal validity of the confession.[13]

3. Readability and Understandability

Throughout the taking of the confession the interrogator must always be on guard to see that its contents will be readily understood and easily followed by a reader or subsequent listener who has no other independent knowledge as to what occurred. All too often the interrogator neglects to realize that although what is going into the confession is perfectly clear to him, in view of his extensive knowledge of the occurrence, its contents may be vague and indefinite to others, such as the judge or jury that will try the case. For instance, when a subject has orally confessed to a rape, the interrogator who takes the written confession knows full well what the subject means when he admits he did "it," but "it" may be rather meaningless to someone else. Also, when a confessor says he set fire to "the place," and that it was on "that night," the person who does not have the benefit of other independent knowledge

[13] See *infra* p. 203.

about "the place" or "that night" is at a loss to comprehend the confession. Moreover, when a confession is that vague and indefinite, a trial judge may refuse to let it be used at all.

The way to clarify indefinite words or phrases is to interrupt the confessor and ask him a question that will explain away the uncertainty. For instance, in a rape case, if the subject speaks in terms of "it," he may be asked, "What do you mean by 'it'?", or "By 'it', you mean sexual intercourse?" In an arson case he may be asked, "What do you mean by 'place'?", or "By 'the place' you mean the house at the corner of First and Main Streets in this city?", or "What do you mean by 'that night' "?, or "By 'that night,' you mean the night of July 9 of this year?"

For the psychological effect on the jury when the written confession is read to them, it is advisable to ask the confessor, very early in the confession, a question which will call for an acknowledgement from him that he committed the crime. This can be done after the first three or four questions about his name, address, age, etc. (For example, "As regards the fire in the store at First and Main Streets, do you know how it started?" Answer: "I started it.") Then, after that acknowledgement, the interrogator can continue with further preliminary questions as he leads up to the main event and asks the subject to narrate the details of what occurred.

The early acknowledgement of guilt in a confession will serve to arouse an immediate interest in the document by the jury as it is read to them. It makes clear to them at the very outset that what is being read is a confession of guilt, and they will then follow more closely the details which are subsequently disclosed.

An additional advantage of the early acknowledgement of guilt is the effect it has on the confessor himself. Once he has thus committed himself he is far less likely to balk at continuing with the details.

The details of a confession should not only include the details of the offense itself, such as the date, time, place, purpose, and manner of its commission, but also such things as the places where the confessor had been before the crime, where he went after the crime, and the names of people he saw and talked to before and after the event. In some instances, the confessor should also be asked to describe the clothing he wore at the time, since this may be an important factor with respect to his identification by the victim or witnesses.

4. Avoidance of Leading Questions

A confession in which the interrogator has done most of the talking, and the subject has confessed largely through "yes" or "no" answers, is not nearly so convincing and effective as one in which the interrogator plays the minor part and the subject plays the leading role of both informer and confessor. It is highly important, therefore, that the interrogator let the subject supply his own details of the occurrence, and to this end the interrogator should avoid or at least minimize the use of leading questions.

To illustrate the point, suppose a subject is in the process of confessing a murder in which it is a known fact that the gun involved in the crime was thrown away under a certain house. The confessor has been giving various details of the crime and the interrogator is about to inquire regarding the disposal of the gun. At this stage some interrogators say, "Then you threw the gun under the house, didn't you?"—a question calling merely for a "yes" answer. It is far more convincing to a court or jury to have the gun details appear in answer to a non-leading question such as "Then what did you do with the gun?"—a question calling for detailed information from the confessor himself.[14]

In addition to the foregoing advantages attending non-leading questions, there is another factor to be considered. An interrogator may encounter a situation—although its occurrence will be *rare*—where subsequent to the confession he may become skeptical as to its validity, particularly where there is some suspicion that the confessor is a pathological liar and may be absolutely innocent of the

[14] The practical importance of avoiding leading questions is well-illustrated by the United States Supreme Court case of Lyons v. Oklahoma, 322 U.S. 596 (1943), in which the Court, in sustaining the admissibility of a confession, placed considerable significance upon the fact that "The answers to the questions, as transcribed by a stenographer, contain statements correcting and supplementing the questioner's information and do not appear to be mere supine attempts to give the desired response to leading questions." (p. 605.)

crime to which he has confessed. In such instances the interrogator will find considerable comfort in being able to evaluate the confession in the light of certain known facts, and this he can ordinarily do unless during the interrogation he discloses such facts to the subject in the form of leading questions. In other words, in the above stated hypothetical case situation regarding the gun under the house, an interrogator who had asked the subject what he did with the gun, and was told, "I threw it under the house," (where the gun was actually found) is in a far more desirable position than the now skeptical interrogator who had told the subject, "Then you threw the gun under the house, didn't you?" and merely received a "yes" answer.

5. Use of the Confessor's Own Language

In the preparation of the written confession no attempt should be made to improve the language used by the subject himself. It should represent his confession *as he tells it*, and unless it does, a judge or jury may be reluctant to believe that a defendant whose education may have ended at the third grade spoke the language of a college graduate.

6. Personal History Questions

At his trial the offender may attack the validity of a confession by alleging that he only stated what he was told to say—that the interrogator "put the words into my mouth." An excellent precautionary measure to effectively meet such a defense is the practice of incorporating in the confession a number of more or less irrelevent questions calling for answers that only the offender himself would know. For instance he may be asked the name of the grade school he attended, the name of the school principal, or for other similar information. Care must be exercised, however, in avoiding questions that call for answers about which the confessor himself may not be sure (e.g., place or hospital in which he was born).

When accurate personal information is included in a confession, the prosecutor may point to it as evidence that the accused actually gave the information contained in his confession and was not merely accommodating the interrogator by repeating what he was told to say.

7. Intentional Errors for Correction by the Confessor Himself

For much the same reasons that personal history data are incorporated into the confession, it is a good practice to purposely arrange for the presence, on each page of the confession, of one or two errors, such as an incorrect name of a person or street which will be subject to later correction by the confessor when the document is read by or to him. Any such corrections, of course, should be in the confessor's own handwriting, accompanied by his initials or signature in the margin alongside the corrections. When confronted at his trial with a confession bearing corrections of this nature, the confessor will encounter considerable difficulty in denying that he read the document before signing it.

8. Reading and Signing of Confession

It is advisable for the interrogator to read aloud a carbon copy of the confession as the confessor follows the original copy word for word. When the previously described intentional errors are reached, the subject himself will usually call them to the interrogator's attention; to play safe, however, the interrogator should keep the errors in mind and raise a question about them in the event the subject neglects to do so.

In addition to the placing of initials or signatures alongside corrections, the subject should be requested to place his "O.K.," followed by his initials or signature, at the bottom of each page after the contents have been read by or to him. Then, at the end of the confession, it is well to have the offender write out, in his own hand, some such statement as the following: "I have read this statement of mine and it is the truth. I made it of my own free will, without any threats or promises having been made to me by anyone." After this should appear his signature.

The person who types the confession should avoid placing a signature line at the end of it. First of all, the line connotes too much legalism and may discourage the confessor from affixing his signature to the document. Secondly, in the event that a confessor refuses to sign the confession, the document will look far better without the unused signature line on it. (In some jurisdictions an unsigned confession is usable as evidence as long as the interrogator can testify that it accurately represents what the defendant said.[15])

When the time comes for the signing of a confession, the interrogator should never say, "Sign here." It is much better, psychologically, to say, "Put your name here," while pointing out the place for the signature.

In the event that the confessor is illiterate, there is very little purpose to be served by having him sign, or even place his mark (an X) on a typewritten confession. Nevertheless, an unsigned typewritten copy may be helpful at the trial. The interrogator should be permitted to testify that it accurately represents not only what the accused said, but also that after it was read to him he acknowledged it to be the truth. In such instances, it is advisable for the prosecutor to offer as a witness the stenographer who recorded the confession; she could testify directly from her shorthand notes.

Another possibility in cases involving illiterate subjects is to make a sound recording of their confessions, even though, as previously stated, written confessions are generally more suitable.

9. Witnesses

In most instances where the offender does not object to the oral confession being reduced to writing he will readily sign it in the presence of one or more witnesses in addition to the interrogator himself. There are some occasions, however, when a hesitating and wavering confessor may balk at the signing if other persons, and particularly uniformed police officers, enter the room for the obvious purpose of witnessing the signature. In such instances it may be advisable to have the confession signed in the interrogator's presence only. Then, a few minutes later, in the presence of other witnesses, the interrogator may elicit an identification of the signature and an acknowledgement of the validity of the confession itself.

[15] See *infra* p. 206.

A written confession need not be signed by any witnesses. All that is required is to have some one person authenticate it—someone to testify he saw the defendant sign it. For greater effectiveness, of course, the authenticating witness should also be the one to establish the fact that the accused made the confession and that the written document was read to him as he himself followed the written contents. All this testimony can best be supplied by the interrogator.

As regards all of these various considerations regarding written confessions, the fact should be borne in mind that an oral confession is as admissible in evidence as a written one, the only difference being the greater weight and credibility usually given to the written, signed confession.

10. Only One Written Confession

An interrogator should always seek to take as full and complete a confession as may be necessary for use as evidence at the trial. This does not necessarily mean that it must be lengthy; as a matter of fact the ordinary crime can be—and should be—adequately related within a relatively few pages, if the interrogator is aware of the essential requirements of a confession. A relatively short, though complete written confession is a much more persuasive document than one that is cluttered with unnecessary verbiage and a lot of irrelevant facts.

If the interrogator's written confession is inadequate, the prosecuting attorney may have to take a second one. This duplication may add to the prosecutor's trial court difficulties, because defense counsel may demand an inspection of the first one, and an attempt will be made to capitalize on whatever differences there may be between the two. In fact, unfavorable inferences may be drawn by the jury itself, without any aid from defense counsel.

Whenever an interrogator is unskilled in the taking of written confessions, perhaps the best thing for him to do is merely to write out for the subject's signature, or else have the subject himself write out, a very brief statement acknowledging the commission of the offense, and then leave to the prosecuting attorney the preparation of one which will incorporate the full details.

On those occasions when a written confession is later considered inadequate, as lacking in some essential details, an entirely new confession should be prepared rather than one that merely supplements the first. This will serve to minimize the controversies and legal difficulties that would otherwise be presented by each document's dependence upon the other for completeness.

In the evaluation of a written confession, either by the interrogator himself or by a prosecuting attorney, consideration should be given to the fact that it is a rather common occurrence for the confessor to a major crime to lie about some incidental aspect(s) of the offense. For instance, a murderer may deny that he indulged in a certain sex activity prior to the killing of a woman victim, when the circumstantial evidence clearly established that sexual conduct preceded the killing. The reason for this is that in the subject's own mind the killing is not nearly so revolting as the sexual act itself. Therefore, a discrepancy of this kind between the confessor's statement and circumstantial evidence of this type should not serve to discredit an acknowledgement of guilt.[16]

In an effort to minimize the possibility or the extent of a confessor's lying about some incidental aspect of the occurrence, the interrogator should follow a practice of having the confessor relate *all* the details of the crime *before* any effort is made to reduce the confession to writing; and if there appear to be any false statements or any withholding of pertinent information, then is the time to try to gather in the truth rather than during the taking of the written confession.

In instances where the written confession is to be taken by someone other than the interrogator who obtained the oral confession, or where the taking of a second confession is considered necessary because of some shortcoming or defect in the original one, the second interrogator (e.g., a prosecuting attorney) should first familiarize himself very thoroughly with the case and also with whatever is known about the subject himself. Following this, he should, as a rule, talk to the subject alone and listen to his confession before any attempt is made to reduce it to writing. In this way the interrogator will become acquainted with the subject

---

[16] See *supra* note 10.

and therefore be better prepared to question him at the time when the confession is to be reduced to writing. Then, after this preliminary visit, the interrogator should leave the interrogation room in order to get the stenographer who is to reduce the confession to writing. The procedure from this point on has already been described.

11. Confine Confession to One Crime

If a subject has confessed to two or more crimes, separate confessions should be taken of each one, unless the crimes are so closely related in point of time, place, or other circumstance that the account of one crime cannot be related without referring to the others. For instance, if a subject confesses to several robberies or to several burglaries, or to a robbery and a burglary, a separate confession should, as a rule, be taken of each offense. The exceptions occur when several persons are robbed at the same time, or when the occupant of a burglarized home is also robbed by the burglar, or when a kidnapped person is also murdered. In such instances the crimes are so closely related that it is practically impossible to describe what occurred without referring to the other offense or offenses. The situation is different, of course, as regards the robbery of "John Jones" on a Monday night and a robbery of "Frank Smith" on Wednesday night. Either of such offenses can be described without a reference to the other one. Moreover, the courts hold that it is improper, because of the inherent prejudicial effect, to offer evidence to a jury about any other crime than the one for which the defendant is on trial.

For similar reasons a confession should never contain any reference to the fact that the subject had previously been arrested or convicted. Any such statement would have to be deleted from the confession before it could be accepted in evidence at the trial.

12. Physical Evidence, Photographs, and Sketches

When a crime weapon is referred to in a confession, and the weapon has been recovered and is available (either at the time of the written confession or subsequent thereto), a separate, supplemental statement may be taken from the subject about the weapon and the use to which he put it. He should be shown the weapon and asked if it is the weapon he used. Following an affirmative answer, he should be asked to put an identifying mark on it—his initials, for instance. Then a written statement should be prepared, for his signature, in which he merely states something to this effect: "This 38 caliber (Colt) revolver (or knife) with my initials (J. B.) on the handle is the gun I used in the robbery and shooting (or in the stabbing) of John Jones last Monday, September 4, 1961, at First and Main Streets in this city of Hamlet." Such a statement may be put on a card and actually tied on to the weapon.

A separate statement of this type may be more effective than a similar statement incorporated in the confession itself, since the latter would break the continuity of the account of what occurred. Then, too, if the weapon is a bloody knife or other such instrument, and it is shown to the subject during the taking of the written confession, it may cause him to balk at continuing with his confession. Moreover, in the reading of a confession to the jury, the pause for the weapon identification may interfere with an otherwise orderly recitation of the facts of the occurrence.

Where photographs of the crime scene are available, they may also serve as the basis for a supplemental statement. For instance, if a photograph shows the location of the place where the fire started, and it also shows the container in which the flammable fluid was transported, the subject may be asked to point them out on the photograph and to place a number alongside each one. Then, on the back of the photograph, or on a separate sheet of paper which can be attached to the photograph, he should be asked to write out, "On this photograph of the interior of the house at First and Main Street, A is where I started the fire; B is the can in which I carried the gasoline." Such a statement should then be signed, of course.

If no photographs are available, there may be occasions when it will be advisable to have the subject make a sketch of the crime scene and to point out thereon the location of certain objects, or the place where something of significance occurred. Accompanying the sketch should be a signed statement such as has been suggested for use with a photograph.

The value of having a subject make a sketch of the crime scene is well illustrated by the following case. An elderly recluse was murdered and his cabin was burned in an effort to conceal the murder. Six years later one of the authors interrogated a suspect and obtained a confession from him. He was then asked to make a sketch of the cabin—locating the bed, the stove, and other such objects. His sketch located these various objects just as they appeared in a photograph which investigators had made immediately after the crime. It proved to be of considerable value as further evidence of the confessor's guilt.

GENERAL SUGGESTIONS REGARDING CONFESSIONS

1. Preservation of Stenographic Notes

Although a confession written and signed as previously outlined will be difficult to attack in crurt, there may be occasions when it will become necessary to refute certain objections to it by calling as a witness the stenographer who prepared the typewritten copy from her shorthand notes. The only way this can be done, of course, is to have the stenographer read to the court and jury the original shorthand notes. It is advisable, therefore, that these notes be preserved until the case has been finally disposed of in court.[17]

2. Notes Regarding Conditions and Circumstances under Which Confession Was Obtained

At the time of trial, usually several months after the confession, an interrogator may be cross-examined at considerable length re garding the conditions and circumstances under which the confession was obtained. To meet such a contingency, he should never rely solely upon his memory. It is desirable, therefore, to keep notes regarding such matters as the issuance of the *Miranda* warnings, the time when the interrogation was begun and ended, the

---

[17] The procedure usually followed at the trial is for the prosecutor to hand the stenographer the confession and ask her if she has compared it with her notes (which, of course, should have been done before trial). Following a "yes" response she will then be asked if the typewritten copy is an accurate reproduction of what transpired. Her "yes" answer will usually serve to dispel any further doubts abuut the accuracy of the typewritten document.

time when the confession was signed, the names of the persons who witnessed the signing, and also information as to the general condition of the interrogation room, particularly with reference to its lighting arrangements and approximate temperature.

3. Photograph and Medical Examination of Confessor

In communities where defense counsel indulge in a rather routine practice of attempting to show that the police interrogators employ "third degree" methods to obtain confessions, much can be gained, if time and circumstances permit, by photographing the confessor after he has given his confession. The photographs should include not only a front view but also both side views of him. However, the photographs should not be taken of him in a posed position; it is much better to take them while he is talking to someone and perhaps while also smoking.

Moreover, whenever such defense tactics are anticipated, it may be well, in important cases, to have a physician examine the confessor so as to be able to establish at his trial the lack of bruises or other alleged evidence of the "third degree." [18]

4. Confession Not the End of the Investigation

Many investigators have the impression that once a confession has been obtained the investigation is ended, but seldom, if ever, is this true.

A confession that is unsubstantiated by other evidence is far less effective at the trial than one which has been investigated and subjected to verification or supporting evidence. For instance, assume that a confessed murderer has told when and where he purchased the knife he used in the killing, identified a gas station where he washed his bloody hands, and told of a chance meeting he had with an acquaintance as he left the gas station. There should then be an immediate investigation regarding the purchase of the knife. If the seller remembers the transaction, he should be asked to give a signed statement about it. This will serve to insure his coopera-

[18] For an example of the advantages of taking photographs of a confessor, see People v. Perez, 300 N. Y. 208, 90 N. E. 2d 40 (1950).

tion at the time of the trial and minimize the risk of his possible appearance as a witness for the defense to deny any such transaction. For similar reasons interviews should be had with, and statements obtained from, the gas station attendants and the defendant's acquaintances. A confession thus supported and substantiated will be far more valuable than the bare document itself. Moreover, there will be many occasions when a thorough post-confession investigation will produce enough incriminating evidence to render unnecessary the use of the confession itself.

In the case where a post-confession investigation has resulted in the discovery and procurement of overwhelming physical and circumstantial evidence of guilt, it is well tor the prosecuting attorney of the jurisdiction to anticipate a possible plea of insanity. It is advisable, therefore, for him to arrange for the immediate taking of signed statements from the subject's relatives and friends, in which they express themselves as to the subject's mental condition (i.e., whether he was normal, whether he had ever sustained a head injury, etc.). At this stage of the case the truth will be more prevalent than at the time of trial.

Another matter that deserves a prosecutor's serious consideration is the advisability of trying the case without even using the confession. Many prosecutors are of the view that if there is sufficient other evidence of guilt, which has been procured either before or after the confession, it is better to rely upon such evidence and not use the confession as part of the prosecution's case in chief. The confession will be available, of course, for rebuttal purposes or the impeachment of the confessor if he takes the stand and testifies.

The principal reason for the foregoing practice of omitting the confession from the prosecution's proof of guilt is the fact that an attack on the confession and on the interrogator who obtained it—however unfounded the attack may be—might divert the jury's attention from the significance and weight of all the physical or circumstantial evidence presented by the prosecution. Each case, of course, will present its own separate problem, and, consequently, a prosecutor should not follow any set rule about the use or non-use of a confession as evidence.

5. Post-Confession Interview

After a person confesses a crime he usually is very willing, or perhaps even anxious, to talk further with the interrogator—to talk about his troubles generally. He is also usually willing to discuss the reasons why he confessed, even to the extent of answering the interrogator's specific questions as to the impact of particular techniques that the interrogator employed to obtain the confession. Here, then, is an excellent opportunity for an interrogator to improve his knowledge and skill. We suggest, therefore, that whenever time and circumstances permit, the interrogator should conduct a post-confession interview. It will be a highly rewarding experience in several respects.

First of all, what the interrogator learns from one confessed offender can be employed to good advantage in the interrogation of others, and particularly those who have committed similar offenses. Secondly, and of even greater importance, such post-confession interviews will permit the interrogator to obtain an insight into human nature that he cannot possibly obtain in any other way or from any other source. Moreover, the greater his insight, the more understanding and sympathetic he will become regarding all criminal behavior and all criminal offenders. Eventually he will develop an attitude that will prevent him from ever "hating" anyone—regardless of the kind of crime a person may have committed. This attitude, in our opinion, is a prime requisite for effective interrogation. Criminal offenders will intuitively recognize whether or not an interrogator has such an attitude, and they find it easier to talk and confess to an understanding, sympathetic interrogator than to one who lacks these qualities.

A person who aspires to become a skillful interrogator need not be concerned over the possibility that the development of an understanding, sympathetic attitude will make a "softy" of him and thereby ultimately destroy the very skill he seeks to achieve. That will not happen, at least not as a consequence of an understanding, sympathetic attitude. Not one of the effective interrogators we know has ever sustained a diminution of effectiveness by reason of the development of such an attitude. To the contrary, it has always produced a higher degree of interrogation skill than that previ ously possessed.

The authors have conducted post-confession interviews on numerous occasions over the years. In fact, post-confession interviews are the source of much of the information upon which many of the foregoing techniques are based. We even followed the practice to the extent that on one occasion, a rapist-murderer was interviewed in his death cell a few days before his execution—for the sole purpose of ascertaining why he confessed. In that death cell one of the authors obtained the most valuable lesson in criminal interrogation that he has ever received from any single source. His "instructor" was well qualified. He had committed a series of rapes which had culminated in the murder of his last victim. The night he confessed there was no opportunity for a post-confession interview, but the opportunity eventually presented itself after the subject's trial and conviction, and after he had become reconciled to the fate that awaited him. He not only talked freely, but also frankly specified and discussed the various interrogation techniques that were most effective in persuading him to confess. He also supplied the interviewer with information that permitted the formulation of a new technique which has been used effectively ever since on other similar subjects.

The post-confession interview may be conducted during the time when the stenographer is typing up the confession from her shorthand notes. In addition to the factor of time conservation, it is well to keep the confessor occupied during this period, as a safeguard against a change of attitude and a possible retraction or a refusal to sign the typewritten confession.

THE LAW GOVERNING CONFESSION
ADMISSIBILITY

1

HISTORICAL REVIEW OF THE TESTS OF CONFESSION ADMISSIBILITY

The cruelty and injustice that were involved in the early practices of extorting confessions from accused persons by tearing their
bodies apart on a rack, or by inflicting other forms of torture,
eventually led to the development of certain precautionary rules
regarding the admissibility of confessions.[1] The basic rules declared that before a confession could be used against an accused
person it must be shown to represent a *voluntary* acknowledgement of guilt, or else it must have been obtained under conditions or circumstances which could not reasonably be considered
as rendering it *untrustworthy*.

Although legal scholars differ somewhat as to which is the historically accurate test—the test of voluntariness or the test of trustworthiness—as a practical matter it seemed to make little difference which of these two tests was applied. In other words, the
type of force, threats, or promises that would be considered sufficient to render a confession involuntary (by a court applying the
test of voluntariness) would in all probability be declared sufficient to render a confession untrustworthy (by a court applying
the test of trustworthiness); likewise, an untrustworthy confession would seldom be a voluntary one.[2]

[1] WIGMORE, EVIDENCE §§822, 865, 2266 (1940).
[2] The late Dean Wigmore, in his treatise on EVIDENCE, condemned the test
of voluntariness as historically incorrect as well as inadequate. He contended
that those who sponsor the test of voluntariness do so under the erroneous impression that there is an association between the confession rule and the privilege against self-incrimination, whereas the fact is that in point of time the
origin of the confession rule and the privilege are widely separated. (The confession rule was enunciated about one hundred years after the recognition of
the privilege against self-incrimination.) Moreover, the privilege against self-
incrimination was designed to cover only statements in court under process

The voluntary-trustworthy test of confession admissibility prevailed in both federal and state courts until 1943–1944, at which time the United States Supreme Court laid down a much more restrictive test in federal cases, and it also modified the conventional test in state cases.[3]

A. The General Test in Federal Cases

By reason of its supervisory power over lower federal courts, the United States Supreme Court has always had the privilege of imposing whatever standards it desired regarding confession admissibility in federal cases. It exercised this power in the 1943 case of *McNabb v. United States*,[4] in which the Court held that

as a witness, whereas the confession rule was intended to cover statements both in court and out. See WIGMORE, EVIDENCE §§823–827, 2266 (1940).

On the other hand, Professor McCormick and others find a kinship between the confession rule and the privilege against self-incrimination, and they see in the test of voluntariness an indication that the rules restricting the use of confessions are prompted by a desire to protect the subject against torture as well as by a desire to safeguard the trustworthiness of the evidence. For an excellent discussion of the relative merits of these two views, see McCormick, *The Scope of Privilege in the Law of Evidence*, 16 TEX. L. REV. 447 at pp. 452–457 (1938). Also see McCormick, *Some Problems and Developments in the Admissibility of Confessions*, 24 TEX. L. REV. 239 (1946); and Morgan, *The Privilege Against Self-Incrimination*, 34 MINN. L. REV. 1 (1949). Also see Culombe v. Connecticut, 367 U.S. 568 (1961), note 25, and compare State v. Bronston, 7 Wis. 2d 627, 97 N.W.2d 504 (1959).

For a concise discussion of the history and policy of the privilege against self-incrimination and of its relationship to the confession rule, see INBAU, SELF-INCRIMINATION: WHAT CAN AN ACCUSED PERSON BE COMPELLED TO DO? 3–9 (1950).

[3] Prior to 1943 the practice of the Supreme Court in both federal and state cases was to determine from the trial court record whether the judge acted reasonably in holding that the defendant's confession had not been "forced" out of him, or, stated somewhat differently, "had not been obtained in a manner which rendered it untrustworthy." If the Supreme Court decided that the evidence clearly indicated force, and therefore untrustworthiness, the due process clause of either the Fifth Amendment (in federal cases) or the Fourteenth Amendment (in state cases) would be invoked and the case reversed. On the other hand, if the record did not clearly disclose coercion or untrustworthiness, the court would accept as final the trial court's finding that the confession was voluntary or trustworthy. Wilson v. United States, 162, U.S. 613 (1896); and Brown v. Mississippi, 297 U.S. 278 (1936)—the first state court confession case to be decided by the United States Supreme Court.

[4] 318 U.S. 332 (1943).

not only must a confession be voluntary and trustworthy but it must also have been obtained by "civilized" interrogation procedures. Specifically, the Court held that where federal officers interrogated an arrested person instead of taking him, without unnecessary delay, before a United States commissioner or a federal judge, as required by law, any confession obtained during the period of delay was inadmissible in evidence, regardless of its voluntariness or trustworthiness.

The *McNabb* case reached the United States Supreme Court shortly after the Court had reversed several state court convictions based on confessions obtained by interrogation procedures which could well have induced confessions from innocent persons.[5] Unfortunately, the Court apparently assumed that such practices were universally employed by all or most law enforcement officers, federal as well as state; and in the *McNabb* case the Court embarked upon its crusade to end such practices.

[5] Chambers v. Florida, 309 U.S. 227 (1940); White v. Texas, 310 U.S. 530 (1940); Ward v. Texas, 316 U.S. 547 (1942).

In the Chambers case, the defendants were kept in jail for a week and interrogated every day for many hours—to such an extent that the sheriff, according to his own testimony, was too tired to continue at night—and then an all-night session was finally held, during which time the subjects were interrogated in the presence of a number of persons, including police officers and several private citizens. The first written confession obtained that night was rejected by the prosecuting attorney who thereupon informed the interrogators not to call him from his home again until they had secured "something worthwhile." Subsequently the interrogators obtained confessions which were considered satisfactory. At their trial the defendants were convicted, and the convictions were sustained by the Supreme Court of Florida. When the case reached the United States Supreme Court, however, it was reversed on the ground that the use of the confessions thus obtained had deprived the defendants of due process of law.

In the White case, a farm hand who had been arrested on a rape charge was confined to jail for about a week and taken into the woods on several nights and interrogated there "because the jail was too crowded," and then just prior to his confession he had been interrogated in a locked elevator for four hours. On the basis of these facts the United States Supreme Court held that the defendant had been deprived of the due process of law guaranteed by the Constitution of the United States, and therefore the Texas Court of Criminal Appeals was held to be in error in upholding the admissibility of the confession.

Similar physical and psychological abuses were involved in the Ward case.

The *McNabb* case involved an investigation into the killing of an agent of the Alcohol Tax Unit of the Bureau of Internal Revenue. Five members of the McNabb family were arrested as suspects and questioned regarding the killing. Several hours after the last McNabb was arrested he confessed, upon being told that his brothers accused him of firing the fatal shot. Later on two others confessed their implication in the crime. A federal court trial resulted in a verdict of guilty, and the defendants ultimately appealed to the United States Supreme Court, alleging that the confessions were improperly admitted into evidence. The government contended that the confessions were voluntarily given and therefore properly admitted.

Ordinarily an issue of the sort raised in the *McNabb* appeal would have been resolved on the basis of a "due process" inquiry as to whether the confessions were voluntary or trustworthy. Here, however, the Court conceded that since the defendants had not been threatened, abused, or otherwise coerced, there was no problem of constitutional law respecting the confessions and their admissibility; but the Court then stated that its reviewing power in federal cases was not confined to the ascertainment of constitutional validity. Justice Frankfurter, speaking for the majority of the Court, said that "judicial supervision of the administration of criminal justice in the federal courts implies the duty of establishing and maintaining civilized standards of procedure and evidence," and that such standards "are not satisfied merely by observance of those minimal historic safeguards . . . summarized as 'due process of law.' "[6] Justice Frankfurter then proceeded to state that the McNabb brothers had been put in "barren cells" and kept there for many hours of "unremittting questioning," instead of being taken "before a United States commissioner or a judicial officer, as the law requires, in order to determine the sufficiency of the justification for their detention."[7] Because of this supposed infraction of the law by the federal agents, the Court held that the confessions obtained during the delay in arraignment (i.e., "preliminary hearing") should not have been admitted

[6] 318 U.S. 332 at p. 340 (1943).
[7] 318 U.S. 332 at pp. 344–345 (1943).

in evidence, and accordingly the convictions were set aside. The Court considered the interrogators' conduct a "flagrant disregard" of federal laws and expressed the view that if the convictions were upheld, the Court would become an accomplice to the wilful disobedience of the law; and that although Congress had not explicitly forbidden the use of evidence so procured, if the courts permitted such evidence to stand they would stultify the policy which Congress enacted into law. In opposition to this view, Justice Reed objected to "broadening the possibilities of defendants escaping punishment by these more vigorous technical requirements in the administration of justice." "If these confessions are otherwise voluntary," said Justice Reed, "civilized standards . . . are not advanced by setting aside these judgments because of acts of omission which are not shown to have tended toward coercing the admission."[8]

A rather amazing feature of the McNabb case is the fact that the defendants actually had been arraigned promptly, but the trial court record did not disclose the arraignment and the Supreme Court erroneously assumed that no arraignment had occurred until after the confessions had been obtained.[9] Moreover, the fact of actual arraignment was even called to the Court's attention in the government's petition for a rehearing, but to no avail.[10] A retrial of the case resulted in a second conviction which was affirmed by the Circuit Court of Appeals and the case ended there.[11]

In addition to the Court's mistaken interpretation of the factual situation in the McNabb case, the federal statute, relied upon by the Court as embodying a policy which it thought an affirmance of the case would "stultify," was actually enacted for entirely different reasons than the one mentioned by the Court. Its legislative history reveals that the sole purpose of the legislation (passed in 1893 as an amendment to an appropriation bill) was to suppress

---

[8] 318 U.S. 332 at p. 349 (1943).
[9] See Circuit Court of Appeals' decision affirming the conviction of the McNabbs upon their second trial· 142 F 2d 904 (6th Cir. 1944).
[10] 319 U.S. 784 (1942); also, *supra* note 9, and 90 Cong. Rec. 9199 (1944.
[11] *Supra* note 9

a widespread practice whereby federal commissioners and marshals were cheating the government in the matter of fees and mileage expense charges. The issue of interrogation practices and confessions was entirely without congressional consideration.[12]

Regardless of the Court's misinterpretation in the *McNabb* case of the pertinent statutory provisions and of the case facts themselves, there is no doubt but that the Supreme Court does possess the inherent power to establish such a test of confession admissibility for use in federal cases. The Court did not need the *McNabb* case, nor even the breach of any federal statute; it could have prescribed a similar rule in any other federal confession case where federal law enforcement officers had employed what the Court considered to be "uncivilized" interrogation procedures. Nevertheless, the rule itself has been severely criticized ever since it was announced.[13] It even had a close call in the Supreme Court in a subsequent confession case, *Upshaw v. United States,*[14] decided in 1948. In the *Upshaw* case the rule survived by the narrow margin of a five to four decision. Moreover, immediately after the decision in *McNabb,* Congress embarked upon a series of attempts to nullify it. It almost succeeded in 1966, but a presidential veto nullified its efforts.[15] Congress ultimately prevailed, with the enact-

[12] For a detailed discussion of the legislative history of this act as well as of similar federal legislation, see Inbau, *The Confession Dilemma in the United States Supreme Court,* 43 ILL. L. REV. 442, 455–459 (1948).

[13] At a meeting of the American Bar Association soon after the McNabb decision, the Association voted overwhelmingly against the incorporation in the Federal Rules of Criminal Procedure of a proposed rule which in effect would have perpetuated the McNabb case decision as a rule of court. The proposed rule was deleted from the draft of rules finally presented to the Supreme Court by the drafting committee. (The Supreme Court's apparent tacit approval of the rejection did not, of course, remove the effect of the McNabb decision itself.)

For further evidence of the general disapproval of the McNabb case rule, see: Hearings Before Subcommittee 2 of the Committee on the Judiciary, House of Representatives, 78 Cong., 1st Sess., on H.R. 3690, 11–17 (1944). A Statement by the Committee on Bill of Rights of the American Bar Association on H.R. 3690, 42 (1944); 90 Cong. Rec. 9366, 9368 (1944). Also see Waite, *Police Regulation by Rules of Evidence,* 42 MICH. L. REV. 679, 688–692 (1944); Inbau, *supra* note 12.

[14] 335 U.S. 410 (1948).

[15] Soon after the McNabb decision, a bill known as the Hobbs Bill was introduced in Congress to nullify the rule laid down in that case. It passed the House at three different sessions and was voted upon favorably by the Senate

ment of the Omnibus Crime Act of 1968. Meanwhile, however, in 1957 the Supreme Court had unanimously re-affirmed the *McNabb*

Judiciary Committee. The bill progressed no further, however, because some of its supporters thought that legislation was no longer necessary after the Supreme Court's decision in Mitchell v. United States, 322 U.S. 65 (1944), which was erroneously interpreted as representing a substantial modification of the extreme position taken in the McNabb case. Subsequent efforts in Congress have also been unsuccessful. The 1958 attempt was the introduction of a bill (H.R. 11477, 85 Cong., 2nd Sess.) which provided essentially that no statement or confession would be inadmissible as evidence solely because of delay in taking the arrested person before a commissioner or judge. The bill passed the House by a substantial majority. The Senate, by a forty-one to thirty-nine vote, amended it by the addition of one word, but a very crucial one. Whereas the House bill provided that no confession was to be excluded "solely because of delay" in arraignment, the Senate amendment inserted the word "reasonable" in front of the word "delay," so that the Senate version would have required that no confession was to be excluded "solely because of *reasonable* delay." The bill, as thus amended, was referred to a House-Senate conference committee. The House conferees, apparently realizing that the word "reasonable" just about emasculated the bill, resorted to the ingenious device of adding a rather cumbersome proviso, which appears in the italicized portion of the bill as it was reported out by the committee: "Evidence, including statements and confessions otherwise admissible, shall not be inadmissible solely because of reasonable delay in taking an arrested person before a commissioner or other officer empowered to commit persons charged with offenses against the laws of the United States; *Provided, that such delay is to be considered as an element in determining the voluntary or involuntary nature of such statements or confessions.*"

Congress was in its last day of session when the bill reached the Senate floor. A strong supporter of the McNabb case rule raised a point of order, claiming that the conference committee had added "new matter" to the bill, in violation of Senate rules. His point of order was sustained and no vote was taken on the bill. (For a detailed account of the congressional activities regarding the above mentioned bill, as well as a report on other bills dealing with the same subject, see Hogan and Snee, *The McNabb-Mallory Rule: Its Rise, Rationale and Rescue*, 47 GEO. L. J. 1 (1958).)

In 1963 the House of Representatives passed an anti McNabb-Mallory bill which provided as follows, but failed of passage in the Senate:

(a) In the courts of the District of Columbia, evidence, including, but not limited to, statements and confessions, otherwise admissible, shall not be inadmissible solely because of delay in taking an arrested person before a commissioner or other officer empowered to commit persons charged with offenses against the laws of the United States.

(b) No statement, including a confession, made by any person during an interrogation by a law-inforcement officer made while such person is under arrest shall be admissible unless prior to such interrogation the arrested person had been advised that he is not required to make a statement and that any statement made by him may be used against him.

rule in *Mallory v. United States*.[16] Thereafter the reference to it became known as the *McNabb-Mallory* rule.

Since the *McNabb-Mallory* rule was established by the Supreme Court in the exercise of its supervisory power over lower federal courts, rather than as a constitutionally mandated decision, Congress was at full liberty to abolish it. This, as previously stated, is what Congress did, in the following provision of the Omnibus Crime Act of 1968:

"(c) . . . In any criminal prosecution by the United States or by the District of Columbia, a confession made or given by a person who is a defendant therein, while such person was under arrest or other detention in the custody of any law-enforcement officer or law-enforcement agency, shall not be inadmissible solely because of delay in bringing such person before a magistrate or other officer empowered to commit persons charged with offenses against the laws of the United States or of the District of Columbia if such confession is found by the trial judge to have been made voluntarily and if the weight to be given the confession is left to the jury and if such confession was made or given by such person within six hours immediately following his arrest or other detention: *Provided,* That the time limitation contained in this subsection shall not apply in any case in which the delay in bringing such person before such magistrates or other officer beyond such six-hour period is found by the trial judge to be reasonable considering the means of transportation and the distance to be traveled to the nearest available such magistrate or other officer.[17]

Another provision of the same Act purports to abolish the rules laid down in *Miranda v. Arizona*. It will be subsequently discussed (pp. 183–184).

The foregoing bill was finally enacted by congress in 1966 (as **H. B. 5688**), but it was vetoed by President Johnson, on the grounds of "unconstitutionality".

[16] 354 U.S. 449 (1957).

[17] 18 U. S. C. § 3501.

Until the foregoing enactment, if federal law enforcement officers delayed in bringing an arrested person before a federal commissioner or judge for arraignment (i.e., the equivalent of a "preliminary hearing" in state courts), and the delay was for the purpose of obtaining a confession of guilt, the resulting confession was inadmissible in evidence. This was true on the local federal level (e.g., the Washington, D. C., police) as well as on the national level (e.g., the F.B.I.).[18] The exclusion applied regardless of the confession's independent quality of voluntariness or trustworthiness.

B. The General Test in State Cases

Over the past twenty years the task of seeking to find a "general test" of confession admissibility from the Supreme Court decisions has been an exceedingly difficult one. Although in federal cases

[18] For an interesting case that illustrates the extent to which the Court of Appeals for the District of Columbia has been willing to go in applying the McNabb-Mallory rule, see Killough v. United States, 315 F. 2d 241 (1962). In this case the police were investigating the disappearance of the defendant's wife, who disappeared under suspicious circumstances, following an argument between the two. The defendant was questioned, while in police custody, and he admitted killing his wife. He led the police to the garbage dump in which he had buried her body. He was tried and convicted, but the Court of Appeals, in a 5 to 4 decision of the full court, held the confession inadmissible and reversed the conviction, because the police had neglected to take the defendant before a commissioner or judge "without unnecessary delay."

It has been said many times that if the F.B.I. can "live" with the McNabb-Mallory rule, so can other law enforcement agencies. But consider what happened in the following case when the F.B.I. was involved in a typical "local" crime case rather than one of the usual "national" crime cases which generally lend themselves to solutions without the use of an interrogation of the suspect. In the case of Greenwell v. United States, 336 F. 2d 962 (D.C. Cir. 1964), F.B.I. agents, assisted by two local Washington, D. C., police officers, arrested a bank robbery suspect about nine o'clock at night, pursuant to a federal arrest warrant. The arrestee was placed in a police car, and a few blocks away the driver of the car parked it under a street lamp. The agents then advised the arrestee of his legal rights and proceeded to interview him concerning the robbery. Within a few minutes he confessed. He told where he had hidden the loot ($2,083.00) and the pistol he had used in the robbery. He took them to his parents' home, where he retrieved the money and the pistol from their hiding place. The arrestee was then taken to police headquarters, where he signed a confession. The conviction was reversed because the arrestee had not been brought before a magistrate "as quickly as possible." The delay rendered invalid the seized evidence and the confession.

the Court could, in the exercise of its supervisory power over lower federal courts, establish whatever test it desired, in state cases it was required to operate within the framework of the "due process" clause of the Fourteenth Amendment. Consequently, those members of the Court who felt impelled to exercise supervisory power over state courts (and indirectly, therefore, over state law enforcement officers) were constantly confronted with the basic restriction of a lack of authority beyond the "due process" check. In consequence of this inhibition, the Court has vacillated very considerably as to which interrogation practices do or do not comply with the requirements of "due process." Only recently has there been some clarification.

In order for anyone to achieve an adequate understanding of the confession problem that currently confronts the police, lawyers, and lower courts, it is advisable to present a chronological analysis of the most important Supreme Court decisions since 1943, the year the Court embarked upon its crusade to "police the police":

One year after the United States Supreme Court promulgated its "civilized standards" doctrine for federal cases, a somewhat similar attempt was made to impose a higher ("civilized") standard of investigative practices on state law enforcement officers. Lacking the supervisory power that it could exercise in federal matters, the Supreme Court invoked the seemingly simple expedient of enlarging its concept of the "due process" requirement of the Fourteenth Amendment. Instead of merely requiring that confessions be voluntary or trustworthy, the Court now insisted that they should be free of any "inherent coercion." It laid down that rule in the 1944 case of *Ashcraft v. Tennessee*.[19]

In the *Ashcraft* case the defendant had been taken late one afternoon to a morgue where he identified as his wife the body of a woman who had been beaten to death. From the morgue Ashcraft was escorted to the county jail and questioned for several hours, after which he was released without having been placed under formal arrest. Nine days later he was arrested and taken to

[19] 322 U.S. 143 (1944).

jail for further questioning. He was interrogated intermittently for 28 hours, whereupon he told the officers that a man named Ware had killed his wife. Ware, who had not been suspected previously, was arrested and promptly admitted the killing, stating further that Ashcraft had hired him to do it. Ashcraft was confronted with Ware's confession and the interrogation continued for another 8 hours, at the end of which time Ashcraft admitted his guilt but refused to sign a written confession. He repeated his admission of guilt to two business men and to his own family physician, who were called in to witness the confession. The doctor also examined Ashcraft and found him free from any signs of physical abuse. His oral confession was admitted in evidence, and his conviction in the trial court was affirmed by the Supreme Court of Tennessee. Upon appeal to the United States Supreme Court, however, that Court, in a six to three decision, reversed the conviction on the ground that the holding of Ashcraft incommunicado, without sleep or rest, for thirty-six hours of interrogation, was "inherently coercive" and a violation of "due process."

In its consideration of the *Ashcraft* case, the majority of the Court made what appears to be an abstract psychological appraisal of a thirty-six hour interrogation and decided that an interrogation of that duration was "inherently coercive," for which reason the confession would be held inadmissible regardless of the effect of the police practices upon the particular defendant and regardless of the otherwise trustworthiness of the confession.

The principal objection to the *Ashcraft* case has been directed not so much to the result reached in the case itself, but rather to the general rule laid down in the majority opinion. For instance, in his dissenting opinion, Justice Jackson severely criticized the majority opinion for excluding a confession "on an irrebuttable presumption that custody and examination 'are inherently coercive' if of some unspecified duration within thirty-six hours." In his analysis of the case, Justice Jackson expressed the view that "despite the 'inherent coerciveness' of the circumstances of Ashcraft's examination, the confesssion when made was delivered free, and voluntary in the sense in which that term is used in criminal law."

In further criticism of the majority opinion in the *Ashcraft* case, Justice Jackson said, "The Court bases its decision on the premise that custody and examination of a prisoner for thirty-six hours is 'inherently coercive.' Of course it is. And so is custody and examination for one hour. Arrest itself is inherently coercive, and so is detention. When not justified, infliction of such indignities upon the person is actionable as a tort. Of course such acts put pressure upon the prisoner to answer questions, to answer them truthfully, and to confess if guilty.... If the constitutional admissibility of a confession is no longer to be measured by the mental state of the individual confessor but by a general doctrine dependent on the clock, it should be capable of statement in definite terms. If thirty-six hours is more than is permissible, what about 24?; or 12?; or 6?; or 1? All are 'inherently coercive.' "

For several years following the *Ashcraft* case it appeared that the growing restrictions on state interrogation practices would soon eliminate the opportunity for effective interrogation of criminal suspects. This possibility seemed quite imminent after the Supreme Court's five to four decision in *Haley v. Ohio*,[20] a 1948 case in which a reversal was ordered of the conviction of a 15-year-old boy who had been questioned, without the use of force, threats, or promises, for five hours by several police officers "in relays of one or two each." His interrogation was considered "inherently coercive." The majority opinion stated that in any case where the undisputed evidence "*suggested*" that coercion was used the conviction would be reversed "*even though without the confession there might have been sufficient evidence for submission to the jury.*"

The author of the majority opinion in the *Haley* case, Justice Douglas, soon thereafter expressed himself as favoring the outlawing of any confession, however freely given, if it was obtained during the period between the arrest and the preliminary hearing before a judicial officer.[21] In answer to this suggestion, another

[20] 332 U.S. 596 (1948).
[21] Watts v. Indiana, 338 U.S. 49 at p. 57 (1949). Also see Justice Jackson's reference to Justice Douglas' concurring opinion. Justice Jackson said: "A concurring opinion ... goes to the very limit and seems to declare for outlawing

member of the Court, Justice Jackson, pointed out that an opportunity to interrogate criminal suspects was an absolute necessity, since many crimes are solvable only by that process. He also added that there were only two alternatives regarding this issue of whether or not police interrogations should be permitted: "to close the books on crime and forget it," or "to take suspects into custody for questioning. . . ." He further commented that if the Constitution required the Supreme Court to hold that a state may not take into custody and question one suspected reasonably of an unwitnessed murder, "the people of this country must discipline themselves to seeing their police stand by helplessly while those suspected of murder prowl about unmolested."[22]

Four of the Supreme Court Justices who dissented in the *Haley* case rather clearly committed themselves, in three state cases that were decided in 1949, to abandoning the *Ashcraft* case "inherent coercion" test in favor of the original voluntary-trustworthy test of state court confession admissibility.[23] Within a couple of years thereafter, a majority of the Court did revert to the voluntary-trustworthy test. This was done in the 1951–1952 cases of *Gallegos v. Nebraska*[24] and *Stroble v. California*,[25] in both of which there were only two dissenters (Justices Douglas and Black). The majority of the Court in the *Gallegos* case said that, "So far as due process affects admissions before trial. . . ., the accepted test is their voluntariness." The opinion further stated that the voluntariness issue in any case requires an appraisal of the particular

---

any confession, however freely given, if obtained during a period of custody between arrest and arraignment—which, in practice, means all of them." (338 U.S. at p. 58.)

Justice Douglas reiterated this same view in his dissenting opinion in Stroble v. California, 343 U.S. 181 (1952), when he stated: "The practice of obtaining confessions prior to arraignment breeds the third degree and the inquisition. As long as it remains lawful for the police to hold persons incommunicado, coerced confessions will infect criminal trials in violation of the commands of due process of law."

[22] 338 U.S. 49 at pp. 58 and 61 (1949).
[23] Watts v. Indiana, 338 U.S. 49 (1949); Turner v. Pennsylvania, 338 U.S. 62 (1949); and Harris v. South Carolina, 338 U.S. 68 (1949).
[24] 342 U.S. 55 (1951).
[25] 343 U.S. 181 (1952).

facts of that case. In other words, the inherent coercion test of the *Ashcraft* case was no longer applicable.

The majority of the Court in the foregoing cases of *Gallegos v. Nebraska* and *Stroble v. California* also unequivocally rejected defense counsel proposals to categorically outlaw confessions obtained by state law enforcement officers during a period of "unnecessary delay" in taking an arrested person before a committing magistrate for a preliminary hearing. The Court held that in state cases such a delay was only one factor to be considered along with all the other evidence in determining the voluntariness of the confession.

In addition to its return in the *Gallegos* and *Stroble* cases to the voluntary-trustworthy test of state court confession admissibility, a majority of the Supreme Court soon thereafter also repudiated what it had said in the *Haley* case, and in several other cases, about the inherent invalidity of any conviction in which a coerced confession had been used as evidence. In a six to three decision in the 1953 case of *Stein v. New York*,[26] the Court held that a state court conviction which was supportable by other evidence would stand even though a coerced confession had been used as evidence in the trial. The majority opinion pointed out that in confession cases, the Fourteenth Amendment is not a rigid exclusionary rule of evidence but only a guarantee against convictions based upon untrustworthy evidence. The opinion also clearly revealed, as did the opinions in the *Gallegos* and *Stroble* cases, that in determining a confession's admissibility in state cases the Court would no longer make a psychological appraisal of the facts and circumstances involved in the interrogation of the accused (as was done in the *Ashcraft* case), but that it would examine the confession and events leading up to it and determine whether or not the interrogation had a coercive effect on the particular person making the confession. In utilizing that test of admissibility, the Court, in a six to three decision in the 1957 case of *Fikes v. Alabama*,[27] held inadmissible a confession made by an uneducated man of low mentality, who had been questioned intermittently

[26] 346 U.S. 156 (1953).
[27] 352 U.S. 191 (1957).

over a ten-day period of detention, during which time he was isolated from other prisoners and denied visits from his father and a lawyer who tried to see him. The majority of the Court held that the "totality of these circumstances" went beyond allowable limits. The three dissenting justices were of the view that the interrogation did not involve police brutality or psychological coercion, which are usually associated with a due process violation. They also expressed the opinion that the Court should have "due regard for the division between state and federal functions in the administration of criminal justice."

The "totality of circumstances" approach in the foregoing case of *Fikes v. Alabama* was also utilized in the 1958 case of *Payne v. Arkansas*[28] to reverse the conviction of a 19-year-old boy accused of robbery-murder. He had been held incommunicado for three days, had been denied food "for long periods of time," and was told that a mob was outside the jail to "get him." The Court decided that even though there was other evidence of guilt, "no one can say what credit and weight the jury gave the confession," and consequently the conviction would have to be reversed because of a violation of due process. Justice Clark, however, dissented on the ground that there was sufficient other evidence, apart from the confession, to sustain the conviction on the authority of the Court's 1953 decision on this point in *Stein v. New York*.

In the 1959 case of *Spano v. New York*,[29] the Supreme Court appears to have brushed aside all that it had been saying and holding in several of its cases during the preceding eight years, for now the Court began to talk once more about other factors than than voluntariness or trustworthiness in determining a confession's admissibility in the state courts. It expressed itself as though it was about ready to impose upon the states, as a due process requirement, the same kind of "civilized standards" rule it had imposed on lower federal courts and federal officers in the *McNabb* and *Mallory* cases. Here is what the Court said in *Spano*: "The abhorrence of society to the use of involuntary confessions does not turn alone on their inherent trustworthiness. It also turns on

[28] 356 U.S. 560 (1958).
[29] 360 U.S. 315 (1959).

the deep rooted feeling that the police must obey the law while enforcing the law; that in the end life and liberty can be as much endangered from illegal methods used to convict those thought to be criminals as from the actual criminals themselves." The Court found fault with the fact that the defendant, a foreign born man, 25 years of age, with only one-half year of high school, was questioned by a number of persons for about eight hours. It also mentioned that the interrogation was not conducted "during normal business hours." Emphasis was also placed upon the fact that the defendant had been denied the right to contact his attorney. This denial was considered all the more serious by reason of its coming after the defendant had been indicted—in other words, after the criminal prosecution had been initiated.

Perhaps because the "totality of circumstances" may have been considered sufficient to warrant a reversal anyway, there was no dissent in the *Spano* case. On the other hand, four of the justices (Warren, Black, Brennan, and Douglas) made it perfectly clear that they viewed the denial of counsel factor sufficient, in itself, to constitute a violation of due process, and in their opinion, it mattered not whether the denial came before or after the judicial process had begun. In two earlier five to four decisions, however, the Court had held that a denial of counsel prior to the beginning of the judicial process (e.g., indictment) did not constitute a due process violation, and consequently a confession obtained thereafter was admissible as evidence.[30]

Until very recently, the clearest expression to come from the United States Supreme Court regarding a "general test" of state court confession admissibility is to be found in the six to two majority opinion in the 1961 case of *Rogers v. Richmond*.[31] In this case the Court said that a confession's admissibility in a state court should be determined on the basis of "whether the behavior of the State's law enforcement officials was such as to overbear [the accused person's] will to resist and bring about confessions not freely de-

---

[30] See Crooker v. California, 357 U.S. 433 (1958); and Cicenia v. La Gay, 357 U.S. 504 (1958). For a detailed discussion of the issue as to an arrestee's right to counsel, see *infra* pp. 173–181.

[31] 365 U.S. 534 (1961).

termined." The Court also stated that this question was to be answered "with complete disregard of whether or not [the accused] in fact spoke the truth."

Three months after the *Rogers* case, the Supreme Court decided another state court confession case, *Culombe v. Connecticut*,[32] in which the majority opinion stated that "the ultimate test" of confession admissibility in the state courts "remains that which has been the only clearly established test in Anglo-American courts for two hundred years: the test of voluntariness." The majority opinion then went on to outline the following criteria in determining voluntariness: "Is the confession the product of an essentially free and unconstrained choice by its maker? If it is, if he has willed to confess, it may be used against him. If it is not, if his will has been overborne and his capacity for self-determination critically impaired, the use of the confession offends due process. . . . The line of distinction is that at which governing self-direction is lost and compulsion, of whatever nature or however infused, propels or helps to propel the confession."[33]

Even assuming that the above stated general test is clear and understandable, the various concurring opinions of Justices Warren, Black, Brennan, and Douglas cast considerable doubt as to the qualifications that would be attached to this test in future cases.

[32] 367 U.S. 568 (1961). Between the Rogers and the Culombe decisions the Court had reversed, 7 to 2, the case of Reck v. Pate, 367 U.S. 433 (1961), because the majority found that a "totality of coercive circumstances" surrounded the defendant's confession. The minority of the Court was of the view that the Supreme Court should not set aside the trial court findings of facts which had been accepted by the previous reviewing courts.

[33] 367 U.S. 568 at p. 602. Justice Frankfurter, who authored the test offered an explanation of it in the following terms, but the reader may well wonder whether it helps much: "The inquiry whether, in a particular case, a confession was voluntarily or involuntarily made involves, at the least, a three-phased process. First, there is the business of finding the crude historical facts, the external, 'phenomenological' occurrences and events surrounding the confession. Second, because the concept of 'voluntariness' is one which concerns a mental state, there is the imaginative recreation, largely inferential, of internal, 'psychological' fact. Third, there is the application to this psychological fact of standards for judgment informed by the larger legal conceptions ordinarily characterized as rules of law but which, also, comprehend both induction from, and anticipation of, factual circumstances." (p. 603.)

Indeed, Chief Justice Warren actually castigated Justice Frankfurter, who authored the *Culombe* case opinion, for speaking out in such general terms. Chief Justice Warren said that although Justice Frankfurter's opinion was unquestionably written with the intention of clarifying the law regarding confession admissibility, "it is doubtful that such will be the result, for while three members of the Court agree to the general principles enunciated by the opinion, they construe those principles as requiring a result in this case exactly the opposite from that reached by the author of the opinion." The Chief Justice said he "would prefer not to write on many of the difficult questions which the opinion discusses until the facts of a particular case make such writing necessary." But in the *Miranda v. Arizona*[34] decision of June, 1966, Chief Justice Warren did precisely what he so severely criticized Justice Frankfurter for doing in the *Culombe* case.

Evidence of the fact that the *Culombe* opinion did not represent much of a clarification of a general test of confession admissibility is to be found in the following excerpt from the majority opinion of the Court:

"It is impossible for this Court, in enforcing the Fourteenth Amendment, to attempt precisely to delimit, or to surround with specific, all-inclusive restrictions, the power of interrogation allowed to state law enforcement officers in obtaining confessions. No single litmus paper test for constitutionally impermissible interrogation has been evolved: neither extensive cross-questioning—deprecated by the English judges; nor undue delay in arraignment—proscribed by McNabb; nor failure to caution a prisoner—enjoined by the Judges' Rules; nor refusal to permit communication with friends and legal counsel at stages in the proceeding when the prisoner is still only a suspect—prohibited by several state statutes."

The next confession case decided by the Supreme Court was *Gallegos v. Colorado*,[35] which reversed (in a four to three decision involving only seven of the nine Justices) the murder conviction

[34] 384 U.S. 436 (1966).
[35] 370 U.S. 49 (1962).

of a 14-year-old boy because the trial court had admitted a confession that had been obtained while the boy was being questioned alone. According to the majority of the Court, he had "no way of knowing what the consequences of his confession were without advice regarding his constitutional rights from someone concerned with securing him those rights—and without the aid of more mature judgment as to the steps he should take in the predicament in which he found himself." "Adult advice," said the majority, "would have put him on a less unequal footing with his interrogators."

The language of the majority opinion seemed to lay down a general rule protecting persons of the approximate age of the defendant from any interrogation conducted outside the presence of counsel or other "friendly adult advisor." The dissenting Justices were very critical of the majority view. They referred to "the hop, skip, and jump fashion" in which the majority concluded that "the totality of circumstances" of this case constituted a violation of due process, and they expressed their "regret" that the conviction was reversed "without support from prior cases and on the basis of inference and conjecture not supported in the record." They found no significant factors of coercion or even impropriety in the questioning of the defendant. To them, the written confession, and more particularly the one made by the defendant immediately after he was apprehended, was completely voluntary.

In the 1963 case of *Lynumn v. Illinois*,[36] the Court, in a unanimous opinion, reversed a woman's conviction for the possession and sale of marijuana because of the use of a confession obtained after the police interrogators had told her that if she did not "cooperate" she would be deprived of state financial aid and her children would be taken away from her. Quite understandably, the Court considered the confession to have been obtained by coercion.

The unanimity of the Court in the *Lynumn* case was only a fleeting one. Two months later the Court split five to four in *Haynes v. Washington*,[37] which involved the following facts: The defendant had been observed walking along the street near the place of a

[36] 372 U.S. 528 (1963).
[37] 373 U.S. 503 (1963).

nighttime gas station robbery shortly after its commission. As the police car approached him the defendant went into the yard of a home. When questioned he told the police he lived there. He then walked onto the porch of the home and began fumbling with the screen door as if to unlock it. An officer remained at the sidewalk curb observing the defendant. Within a few moments the defendant came down from the porch and told the officers "you got me, let's go." He was placed in a police car and he then admitted the robbery and, as the police drove to the scene of the robbery, the defendant identified the filling station where the robbery occurred. He was then taken to the police station, where he arrived twenty minutes after his arrest, and there he made a second oral confession to a police lieutenant. Both confessions were within one hour and twenty minutes after arrest. On the following morning a written confession was obtained by the police, and later on he made another confession to a deputy prosecutor, but this one he refused to sign. Thereafter the defendant was held incommunicado for a week.

The defendant (who had a prior criminal record as a burglar) challenged the admissibility of the written confession on the ground that it was obtained after he had requested and was denied permission to call his wife and an attorney, and after he had been told that he could call after a written confession was obtained. The police testimony, according to the majority of the Court, did not refute the defendant's claims. The majority reversed because they found that what the police did amounted to coercion.

Four members of the Court (Justices Clark, Harlan, Stewart, and White) considered the issue of what had actually occurred to be a disputed one, and they also referred to the Court's previous decisions in which the Court found no coercion or inducement in confessions obtained after the arrestees had actually been denied counsel and not just merely the opportunity to contact one.

Over the years, since 1943, the vacillations of the Court and the sharp differences of viewpoint among the Justices themselves made it practically impossible for anyone to advise criminal interrogators, in any accurate, understandable way, as to the general test of confession admissibility in state cases. Although, as will be subsequently discussed, the Court recently spelled out what it wanted done by way of warnings as to constitutional rights, there still remains considerable uncertainty as to what interrogators may or may not say or do in the course of their post-warning interrogation of suspects who have waived their right to remain silent and their right to a lawyer. And until the matter is clarified we continue to recommend that the interrogator should use the "rule of thumb" of asking himself:

"Is what I am about to do, or say, apt to make an innocent person confess?"

If the answer to the above question is "no" the interrogator should go ahead and do or say what was contemplated; on the other hand, if the answer is "yes," the interrogator should refrain from doing or saying what he had in mind.

In our judgment this was and still is the only understandable test for interrogators to follow. It is also the only one of any practical value and utility. Moreover, it is the only test that is fair both to the public and to the accused or suspected individual.

2

ADMISSIBILITY IN STATE COURTS OF CONFESSIONS OBTAINED DURING A PERIOD OF "UNNECESSARY DELAY" IN TAKING AN ARRESTEE BEFORE A COMMITTING MAGISTRATE

Practically every state has a statute which requires arresting officers to take arrested persons before a committing magistrate "without unnecessary delay," or "immediately," or "forthwith"; Rule 5(a) of the Federal Rules of Criminal Procedure requires federal officers to take the arrestee before the nearest available commissioner or other committing officer "without unnecessary delay." [38]

Although originally the statutory provisions in England regard-

[38] See listings of state statutes in McNabb v. United States, 318 U.S. 332 (1943), note 7, and in Culombe v. Connecticut, 367 U.S. 568 (1961), note 26. For a discussion of the earlier federal statutes and their legislative history, see Inbau, *The Confession Dilemma in the United States Supreme Court*, 43 ILL. L. REV 442, 455–459 (1948).

ing the preliminary examination of arrested persons by justices of the peace were for the benefit of the prosecution (as a means of obtaining further evidence against the accused), the primary purpose of present day statutory provisions regarding preliminary hearings is to determine whether the known evidence against the accused is sufficient to justify further proceedings against him.[39] It is intended to obviate the annoyance and expense of a defense in any further proceeding unless there is sufficient evidence to indicate at least the probability that the accused is guilty. If the examining magistrate concludes that there is insufficient evidence to justify further proceedings, he discharges the accused from custody. On the other hand, if the evidence disclosed by the prosecution indicates that a conviction might reasonably result, the accused is held in jail for trial or temporarily released on bond.

Until the United States Supreme Court decision in *McNabb v. United States*,[40] there was no doubt of the validity of a confession which had been obtained during a period of delay in taking the accused before a committing magistrate for a preliminary hearing.[41] At most, the delay, in violation of a statutory provision regarding an early hearing before a committing magistrate, was only one factor to be considered in determining the voluntariness or trustworthiness of the confession.[42] The only direct consequence of the violation was a possible civil action against the arresting officer or perhaps disciplinary action against him by his commanding officer.[43] As previously stated, however, in the *McNabb* case the United States Supreme Court held that a confession obtained by federal officers during a period of "unnecessary delay" in arraignment (i.e., "a preliminary hearing") was inadmissible as

[39] ORFIELD, CRIMINAL PROCEDURE FROM ARREST TO APPEAL 53–59, 72–75 (1947).

[40] *Supra* note 4.

[41] State v. Alex, 265 N.Y. 192, 192 N.E. 289 (1934). Also see Cahill v. People, 111 Colo. 29, 137 P.2d 673 (1943), which was decided a few days after the McNabb case, but apparently without knowledge of the Supreme Court decision; and People v. Devine, 46 Cal. 46 (1873).

[42] People v. Mummiani, 258 N.Y. 394, 180 N.E. 94 (1932). As will be subsequently shown, this is still true in state cases, despite the McNabb case rule in federal cases.

[43] Madsen v. Hutchison, 49 Idaho 358, 290 Pac. 208 (1930).

evidence in a federal case, regardless of its voluntariness or trust-worthiness; but the Court specifically stated that it was establish-ing this rule in the exercise of its supervisory power over lower federal courts and federal officers, rather than by reason of its constitutional power to safeguard "due process." Since no such supervisory power exists as regards state courts or state officers, the states have been at liberty, *thus far,* to accept or reject the *McNabb-Mallory* principle.

In one of the early state cases in which defense counsel urged the application of the *McNabb* case principle, the Supreme Court of Oregon expressed the view that "adherence to such a rule would place unnecessary obstacles in the way of the detection of crime and result in the acquittal of many a guilty man." [44] In another case the Supreme Court of Connecticut[45] said it was not unmind-ful of the judicial and ethical standards involved in the *McNabb* case, but considered that "society, as well as the defendant, is en-titled to equal protection of the law and to due process of law." Similar views have been expressed, or are implicit, in the many state decisions rejecting the *McNabb* case principle.[46]

[44] State v. Folkes, 174 Ore. 568, 150 P.2d 17 (1944).
[45] State v. Zukanskas, 132 Conn. 450, 45 A.2d 289 (1945).
[46] The decisions, listed in state alphabetical order, are: *Alabama:* Ingram v. State, 252 Ala. 497, 42 So.2d 36 (1949); Myhand v. State, 259 Ala. 415, 66 So.2d 544 (1953). *Arizona:* Hightower v. State, 62 Ariz. 351, 158 P.2d 156 (1945); State v. Jordan, 83 Ariz. 248, 320 P.2d 446 (1958). *Arkansas:* State v. Browning, 206 Ark. 791, 178 S.W.2d 77 (1944); Moore v. State, 229 Ark. 335, 315 S.W.2d 907 (1958). *California:* Rogers v. Supreme Court, 46 Cal. 2d 3, 291 P.2d 929 (1955) (but see dissent urging adoption of the McNabb-Mallory rule); People v. Bashor, 48 Cal. 2d 763, 312 P.2d 255 (1957). *Colorado:* Downey v. People, 121 Colo. 307, 215 P.2d 892 (1950); Leick v. People, 136 Colo. 535, 322 P.2d 674 (1958). *Connecticut:* State v. Zukanskas, 132 Conn. 450, 45 A.2d 289 (1945); State v. Guastamachio, 137 Conn. 179, 75 A.2d 429 (1950). *Florida:* Finley v. State, 153 Fla. 394, 14 So.2d 844 (1943). *Georgia:* Russell v. State, 196 Ga. 275, 26 S.E.2d 528 (1943). *Hawaii:* Territory of Hawaii v. Young, 37 Haw. 189 (1945); Territory of Hawaii v. Aquino, 43 Haw. 347 (1959). *Illi-nois:* People v. McFarland, 386 Ill. 122, 53 N.E.2d 884 (1944); People v. Lazenby, 403 Ill. 95, 85 N.E.2d 660 (1949); People v. Miller, 13 Ill. 2d 84, 148 N.E.2d 455 (1958); People v. Jackson, 23 Ill. 2d 270, 178 N.E.2d 299 (1961). *Indiana:* Krauss v. State, 229 Ind. 625, 100 N.E.2d 824 (1951). *Iowa:* State v. Williams, 245 Iowa 494, 62 N.W.2d 742 (1954). *Kansas:* State v. Smith, 158 Kans. 645, 149 P.2d 600 (1944). *Kentucky:* See Commonwealth v. Mayhew, 297 Ky. 172, 178 S.W.2d 928 (1944). *Louisiana:* State v. Solomon, 222 La. 270, 62

Of all the states, only Michigan has adopted (or appears to have adopted) the *McNabb-Mallory* rule. In the 1960 case of *People v. Hamilton*,[47] the Michigan Supreme Court's opinion contains lan-

So.2d 481 (1953) (but the court also found that the defendant was not illegally detained during the murder investigation, since he was under a charge of vagrancy at that time). *Maryland:* Cox v. State, 192 Md. 525, 64 A.2d 732 (1949); James v. State, 193 Md. 31, 65 A.2d 888 (1949). *Massachusetts:* Commonwealth v. Banuchi, 355 Mass. 649, 141 N.E.2d 835 (1957) (dicta). *Mississippi:* Winston v. State, 209 Miss. 799, 48 So.2d 513 (1950). *Missouri:* State v. Sanford, 354 Mo. 1012, 193 S.W.2d 35 (1946); State v. Lee, 361 Mo. 163, 233 S.W.2d 666 (1950); State v. Smith, 310 S.W.2d 845 (Mo. 1958). *Nevada:* State v. Boudreau, 67 Nev. 36, 214 P.2d 135 (1950); State v. Williams, 67 Nev. 373, 219 P.2d 184 (1950). *New Jersey:* State v. Pierce, 4 N.J. 252, 72 A.2d 305 (1950); State v. Bunk, 4 N.J. 461, 73 A.2d 249 (1950); State v. Wise, 19 N.J. 59, 115 A.2d 62 (1955); State v. Smith, 32 N.J. 501, 161 A.2d 520 (1960); *New York:* People v. Perez, 300 N.Y. 208, 90 N.E.2d 40 (1949). *North Carolina:* State v. Brown, 233 N.C. 202, 63 S.E.2d 99 (1951); State v. Davis, 253 N.C. 86, 116 S.E.2d 365 (1960). *North Dakota:* State v. Nagel, 75 N.D. 495, 28 N.W.2d 665 (1947). *Ohio:* State v. Lawder, 147 Ohio 530, 72 N.E.2d 785 (1946); *Oklahoma:* Fry v. State, 78 Okla. Cr. R. 299, 147 P.2d 803 (1944); Hendrickson v. State, 97 Okla. Cr. R. 379, 229 P. 2d 196 (1951); Thacker v. State, 309 P.2d 306 (Okla. Cr. 1957). *Oregon:* State v. Folkes, 174 Ore. 568, 150 P.2d 17 (1944); State v. Munn, 212 Ore. 546, 321 P.2d 356 (1958). *Pennsylvania:* Commonwealth v. Agoston, 364 Pa. 464, 72 A.2d 575 (1950); Commonwealth *ex rel* Sleighter v. Banmiller, 392 Pa. 133, 139 A.2d 918 (1958). *Rhode Island:* State v. Andrews, 86 R.I. 341, 134 A.2d 425 (1957). *Tennessee:* McGhee v. State, 183 Tenn. 20, 189 S.W.2d 826 (1945). *Texas:* Dimery v. State, 156 Tex. Cr. R. 197, 240 S.W.2d 293 (1951); Childness v. State, 166 Tex. Cr. 95, 312 S.W.2d 247 (1958). *Utah:* Meres v. Hill, 118 Utah 484, 222 P.2d 811 (1950); State v. Gardner, 119 Utah 579, 230 P.2d 559 (1951). *Vermont:* State v. Goyet, 120 Vt. 12, 132 A.2d 623 (1957). *Virginia.* Campbell v. Commonwealth, 194 Va. 825, 75 S.E.2d 468 (1953). *Washington:* State v. Winters, 39 Wash. 2d 545, 236 P.2d 1038 (1951). *Wisconsin:* State v. Babich, 258 Wis. 290, 45 N.W.2d 660 (1951). In addition to the New York case of People v. Perez, *supra*, see People v. Everett, 10 N.Y.2d 500, 180 N.E.2d 556 (1962).

In addition to the obvious implications of the Supreme Court's opinion in the McNabb case to the effect that the states were at liberty to accept or reject the rule of that case, the Court has since then specifically sanctioned state court rejections. Stroble v. California, 343 U.S. 181 (1952).

Advocates of the McNabb-Mallory rule often say that if the Federal Bureau of Investigation can operate effectively with it there is no reason why state law enforcement agencies cannot function under a similar rule. This argument overlooks the fact that local law enforcement agencies are confronted with entirely different case problems—cases which can usually be solved *only* by interrogating criminal suspects. For case illustrations see *infra* p. 213.

[47] 359 Mich. 410, 102 N.W. 2d 738 (1960).

guage suggestive of adoption, but there were other factors, such as denial of counsel, that may have warranted a reversal on the basis of the "totality of circumstances." Nevertheless, in the 1962 case of *People v. Harper*[48] the Michigan court refused to hold a confession inadmissible because of the arraignment (i.e., preliminary hearing) delay factor alone. The court said: "None of the circumstances which so strongly compelled on finding Hamilton's confession was involuntary is present in the case at bar." But in another 1962 case, *People v. McCager*,[49] the court stated that in the Hamilton case Michigan became "the first State to adopt the exclusionary rule principle announced in *McNabb v. United States.* (In *McCager* the confession was made four days after the defendant's arrest.)

Despite the unequivocal statement in *McCager* that Michigan had adopted the *McNabb-Mallory* rule, four of its eight justices declined to rely upon it in their "remand" of the 1965 case of *People v. Ubbes.*[50] They, or at least three of them anyway (since one of the four concurred "in result" only), were of the view that "time of detention alone, without arraignment is not the test of confession admissibility"; in their view "the lapse of 16½ hours *per se* is not conclusive." The other four justices wanted to "reverse and remand" solely because of the delay in arraignment.

An analysis of the Michigan cases gives rise to the impression that the status of the *McNabb-Mallory* rule there rests upon a rather shaky foundation.

The only other state that has ventured along a similar path has been Wisconsin, and there only with respect to delays incurred in *arrest warrant* situations. In the 1966 decision of *Phillips v. State*,[51] which involved a 3½ hour delay for the purpose of interrogating a person arrested *without warrant* the court upheld the admissibility of the confession, but it went on to say that "an arrest *upon warrant* would seem to presuppose sufficient evidence and its purpose is to cause the arrested person to be brought before a magistrate, . . . so that the criminal process of determining guilt or in-

[48] 365 Mich. 494, 113 N.W. 2d 808 (1962).
[49] 367 Mich. 116, 116 N.W. 2d 205 (1962).
[50] 374 Mich. 571, 132 N.W. 669 (1965).
[51] 29 Wis. 2d 521, 139 N.W. 2d 41 (1966).

nocence can commence. A detention for a period longer than is reasonably necessary for such limited purpose violates due process and renders inadmissible any confession obtained during the unreasonable period of the detention." [52]

The Wisconsin viewpoint with respect to arrest warrant case situations is one that is likely to be shared by other state courts. In anticipation of this possibility criminal investigators may prefer to rely upon "reasonable grounds" arrests without warrant in those cases where they deem an interrogation to be essential. If the arrest is upon a warrant they may be precluded from an interrogation opportunity.

Although the previously discussed Congressional abolition of the *McNabb-Mallory* rule affected only federal cases, it will probably dissuade the state courts or legislatures from any further experimentation with it.

3

THE PRIVILEGE AGAINST SELF-INCRIMINATION, THE RIGHT TO COUNSEL, AND THE REQUIRED WARNINGS WITH RESPECT TO BOTH

The Privilege Against Self-Incrimination

The constitutional provision that no person shall be compelled to be a witness against himself always has been considered of such force and effect as to require a *judicial tribunal* to advise an accused person, who is unrepresented by counsel, of his privilege against

---

[52] Emphasis added.

Also consider, with respect to another, qualified attempt at state adoption of the McNabb-Mallory rule, the Delaware case of Vorhauer v. State, 212 A. 2d 886 (Del. 1965). Following his arrest, upon a warrant for burglary, the arrestee was held for about 36 hours before being taken to a magistrate. This exceeded the prescribed 24 hour statutory limit. The Delaware Supreme Court excluded the confession obtained after the delay past the 24 hour limitation. The court said it was adopting the McNabb-Mallory rule "within the framework of the case before us". It then went on to state: "Our ruling is expressly limited, however, to a detention in excess of the 24 hour period [specified by statute] ... Consideration of the standards of reasonableness of the detention of less than 24 hours must await another case".

self-incrimination before his testimony could be heard; and the rule had been considered applicable not only to trial court proceedings but also to preliminary hearings and coroner's inquests.[53] However, in the absence of a statutory provision, police interrogators, until recently, were not obligated to warn a suspect that he had a right to remain silent. Decisions to that effect had been rendered by the highest courts of more than thirty different states.[54]

[53] Maki v. State, 18 Wyo. 481, 112 Pac. 334 (1911); McDonald v. State, 70 Fla. 250, 70 So. 24 (1915); State v. Meyer, 181 Iowa 440, 164 N.W. 794 (1917); Wood v. United States, 128 F.2d 265 (D.C. 1942). Also see cases collected and discussed at 79 A.L.R.2d 643 (1961), and People v. Jackson, 23 Ill.2d 263, 178 N.E.2d 310 (1962). As to grand jury hearings, however, see United States v. Scully, 225 F. 2d 113 (1955).

As regards the reasons behind the requirement for the warning in judicial proceedings, see State v. Gilman, 51 Me. 206 at p. 223 (1862): "The impressiveness of obligation and the solemnity of the occasion would have a tendency to wring from the party thus situated facts and circumstances which he is not bound to disclose, and therefore can in no just sense be said to be voluntary. As a general proposition this may be true, especially if the party is uninformed with regard to his rights"; and Bram v. United States, 168 U.S. 532 at p. 550 (1897): "The reason upon which this rule rested undoubtedly was that the mere fact of the magistrate's taking the statement, even though unaccompanied with an oath, might, unless he was cautioned, operate upon the mind of the prisoner to impel him involuntarily to speak." Also see Hickson v. State, 196 Tenn. 659, 270 S.W.2d 313 (1954).

Some state statutes specifically require the warning at preliminary examinations. See §4561 of the North Carolina Code (1939): "The magistrate shall then proceed to examine the prisoner in relation to the offense charged. Such examination shall not be on oath; and before it is commenced, the prisoner shall be informed by the magistrate of the charge made against him, and that he is at liberty to refuse to answer any question that may be put to him, and that his refusal to answer shall not be used to his prejudice in any state of the proceedings."

[54] *Alabama:* Trimble v. State, 40 Ala. App. 354, 114 So.2d 164 (1959). *Arizona:* Wagner v. State, 43 Ariz. 560, 33 P.2d 602 (1934). *Arkansas:* Greenwood v. State, 107 Ark. 568, 156 S.W. 427 (1913); Smith v. State, 230 Ark. 634, 324 S.W.2d 341 (1959). *California:* People v. Chan Chaun, 41 Cal. App. 2d 586, 107 P.2d 455 (1940); People v. Triplett, 70 Cal. App. 2d 534, 161 P.2d 397 (1945); People v. Tipton, 48 Cal.2d 389, 309 P.2d 813 (1957). *Colorado:* Reagan v. People, 49 Colo. 316, 112 Pac. 785 (1911); Cahill v. People, 111 Colo. 29, 137 P.2d 673 (1943); Leick v. People, 136 Colo. 535, 322 P.2d 674 (1958); Castro v. People, 140 Colo. 493, 346 P.2d 1020 (1959). *Connecticut:* State v. Guastamachio, 137 Conn. 179, 75 A.2d 429 (1950). *Florida:* Kearson v. State, 123 Fla. 324, 166 So. 832 (1936); Rollins v. State, 41 So.2d 885 (Fla. 1949); Jennings v. State, 106 So.2d 99 (Fla. 1958). *Georgia:* McDonnell v. State, 78

And a similar conclusion had been reached by the Supreme Court
of the United States many years ago.[55]

Ga. App. 116, 50 S.E.2d 633 (1948). *Idaho:* State v. Johnson, 74 Idaho 269,
261 P.2d 638 (1953). *Illinois:* People v. Fahrner, 330 Ill. 516, 162 N.E. 133
(1928); People v. Shelton, 388 Ill. 56, 57 N.E.2d 473 (1944); People v. Weber,
401 Ill. 584, 83 N.E.2d 297 (1949). *Indiana:* Hawkins v. State, 219 Ind. 116,
37 N.E.2d 79 (1941); Marshall v. State, 227 Ind. 1, 83 N.E.2d 763 (1949);
but see Johnson v. State, 226 Ind. 179, 78 N.E.2d 158 (1948), where a warning
was considered necessary because of prior abusive treatment. *Iowa:* State v.
Mikesh, 227 Iowa 640, 288 N.W. 606 (1939); State v. Harriott, 248 Iowa 25, 79
N.W.2d 332 (1956). *Kansas:* State v. Criger, 151 Kans. 176, 98 P.2d 133 (1940),
but see State v. Seward, 163 Kans. 136, 181 P.2d 478 (1947), where the court
expressed the view that a 17-year-old defendant should have been advised of
his constitutional rights before handwriting specimens were obtained from
him. In this case, however, the court was apparently greatly affected by the
youthfulness of the accused, and the court's view regarding the warning in
this case should be considered in the light of its previous Criger case decision.
Louisiana: State v. Burks, 196 La. 374, 199 So. 220 (1940); State v. Holmes,
205 La. 730, 18 So.2d 40 (1944); State v. Alleman, 218 La. 821, 51 So.2d 83
(1950). *Massachusetts:* Commonwealth v. Mabey, 299 Mass. 96, 12 N.E.2d 61
(1938); Commonwealth v. Lundin, 326 Mass. 551, 95 N.E.2d 661 (1950); Commonwealth v. Valcourt, 333 Mass. 706, 133 N.E.2d 217 (1956). *Mississippi:*
Newell v. State, 209 Miss. 653, 48 So.2d 332 (1950); Lewis v. State, 222 Miss. 140,
75 So.2d 448 (1954). *Missouri:* State v. Hoskins, 327 Mo. 313, 36 S.W.2d 909
(1931); State v. Tillett, 233 S.W.2d 690 (Mo. 1950). *Nebraska:* Bush v. State,
112 Neb. 384, 199 N.W. 792 (1924). *Nevada:* State v. Gambetta, 66 Nev. 317,
208 P.2d 1059 (1949). *New Jersey:* State v. Pierce, 4 N.J. 252, 72 A.2d 305 (1950);
State v. Bunk, 4 N.J. 461, 73 A.2d 249 (1950). *New Mexico:* State v. Archuleta,
29 N.M. 25, 217 Pac. 619 (1923); State v. Caro, 55 N.M. 176, 228 P.2d 957 (1950).
New York: People v. Randazzio, 194 N.Y. 147, 87 N.E. 112 (1909); but see People
v. Leyra, 302 N.Y. 353, 98 N.E.2d 553 (1951) to the effect that if a privileged
communication between a doctor and a patient is used to obtain a confession,
then the accused must be warned of his self-incrimination privilege; and People v. Noble, at end of this footnote. *North Carolina:* State v. Grier, 203 N.C.
586, 166 S.E. 595 (1932); State v. Lord, 225 N.C. 354, 34 S.E.2d 205 (1945), and
also see State v. Matthews, 231 N.C. 617, 58 S.E.2d 625 (1950). *Oklahoma:* Tark-
ington v. State, 41 Okla. Cr. 423, 273 Pac. 1015 (1929); Wininegar v. State, 97
Okla. Cr. 64, 257 P.2d 526 (1953). But compare Fields v. State, 77 Okla. Cr. 1,
138 P.2d 124 (1943), in which the court said: "The fact that the defendant, 17
years of age, under arrest on a felony charge, in the absence of parent, guardian
or counsel, was not advised of his constitutional right to refuse to answer questions that might incriminate him, should be considered as affecting the admissibility of any statement made by him purporting to be a confession of
guilt." Also compare Sholes v. State, 97 Okla. Cr. 158, 260 P.2d 440 (1953), in
which the Court said: "The county attorney, as we have often stated, should always caution a prisoner that any statement he might make could be used

The Code of Military Justice has always required that an interrogator in the armed forces must warn a suspected or accused person

against him." Also compare Clark v. State, 95 Okla. Cr. 375, 246 P.2d 422 (1952)
Oregon: State v. Wilder, 98 Ore. 130, 193 Pac. 444 (1920); State v. Folkes, 174
Ore. 568, 150 P.2d 17 (1944); State v. Henderson, 182 Ore. 147, 184 P.2d 392
(1947); State v. Nunn, 212 Ore. 546, 321 P.2d 356 (1958). *Pennsylvania:* Commonwealth v. Dilsworth, 289 Pa. 498, 137 Atl. 683 (1927), but see Commonwealth v. Woong New, 354 Pa. 188, 47 A.2d 450 (1946), where the court condemned several police practices involved in the case, including the failure to
warn the defendant, a Chinese, of his constitutional rights. *Rhode Island:* State
v. Gancarelli, 43 R.I. 374, 113 Atl. 5 (1921). *South Carolina:* State v. Green, 227
S.C. 1, 86 S.E.2d 598 (1955). *Tennessee:* Hickson v. State, 196 Tenn. 659, 270
S.W.2d 313 (1954). *Utah:* State v. Karumai, 101 Utah 592, 126 P.2d 1047 (1942).
Vermont: State v. Watson, 114 Vt. 543, 49 A.2d 174 (1946); State v. Goyet, 120
Vt. 12, 132 Atl. 623 (1957). *Virginia:* Mendoza v. Commonwealth, 199 Va. 961,
103 S.E. 2d 1 (1958), but the court said: "We think the better and safer course
for an officer to pursue, when a prisoner is about to make a statement, is to
warn him that it may be used against him." *West Virginia:* State v. Digman, 121
W. Va. 499, 5 S.E.2d 113 (1939). *Wisconsin:* Link v. State, 217 Wis. 582, 259
N.W. 428 (1935), State v. Storlecky, 273 Wis. 362, 77 N.W.2d 721 (1956); State
v. Bronston, 7 Wis. 2d 627, 97 N.W.2d 504 (1959).

An exception to the general rule regarding warnings was made in cases
where prior threats, force, or objectionable promises have been made, or where
a previous improper confession has been obtained. In such instances a warning may be required, in order to indicate to the subject that the previous improper conditions and circumstances no longer exist. See Van Buren v. State,
24 Miss. 512 (1852), and the above cited Indiana case of Johnson v. State. Another exception is the case where the police interrogate someone *after* he has
been formally charged with a crime; in other words, after the judicial process
has begun. In such instances the warning should be given. See Griffith v. Rhay,
infra note 72.

A distinction had been made by the New York Court of Appeals between
a failure to warn a suspect or an accused and the refusal to do so after he has
asked whether he is under compulsion to talk. In People v. Noble, 9 N.Y. 2d
571, 175 N.E.2d 451 (1961), the murder confession of the accused was about to
be taken by an assistant district attorney when the accused inquired if he was
compelled to answer questions before he consulted legal counsel. His inquiry
was ignored, and that fact was the basis for the reviewing court's ruling that
"the confession should not have been admitted in evidence by the trial court."
The appellate court viewed the refusal as a violation of the defendant's privilege against self-incrimination. The court said: "When a person under suspicion of crime is being questioned, there is a vast difference between a mere
failure to warn and a *flat refusal* to answer a proper inquiry as to his
rights. . . . It offends against our concept of fairness. The defendant was entitled to an answer . . . receiving none the defendant could reasonably have
believed that he had no choice and was bound to answer."

of his right to remain silent and that any statement made by him may be used against him in a court-martial trial.[56] In civilian criminal investigations, however, apparently Texas was the only state which, by statute, made a warning necessary.[57]

---

[55] Wilson v. United States, 162 U.S. 613 (1896). Also see Powers v. United States, 223 U.S. 303 (1912).

[56] Article 31. It provides, in full, as follows:

Compulsory self-incrimination prohibited.

(a) No person subject to this code shall compel any person to incriminate himself or to answer any question the answer to which may tend to incriminate him.

(b) No person subject to this code shall interrogate, or request any statement from, an accused or a person suspected of an offense without first informing him of the nature of the accusation and advising him that he does not have to make any statement regarding the offense of which he is accused or suspected and that any statement made by him may be used as evidence against him in a trial by court-martial.

(c) No person subject to this code shall compel any person to make a statement or produce evidence before any military tribunal if the statement or evidence is not material to the issue and may tend to degrade him.

(d) No statement obtained from any person in violation of this article, or through the use of coercion, unlawful influence, or unlawful inducement shall be received in evidence against him in a trial by court-martial.

The reason usually given in justification for the warning requirement prescribed in the Code of Military Justice is the aura of compulsion that prevails in any military organization—the duty to obey commands, follow orders, etc. In other words, a military man, under suspicion of committing a crime, may feel that his very status as a military man compels him to talk; consequently he should be advised of his right to remain silent.

The fact that a suspect or an accused person is in military service does not require non-military investigating officers to issue a warning to him, as military interrogators are required to do. Commonwealth v. Beaulieu, 333 Mass. 640, 133 N.E.2d 226 (1956); United States v. Holder, 10 USCMA 448 (1959).

[57] Art. 727, CODE CRIM. PROC.: "The confession shall not be used if, at the time it was made, the defendant was in jail or other place of confinement, nor while he is in the custody of an officer, unless made in the voluntary statement of the accused, taken before an examining court in accordance with law, or be made in writing and signed by him; which written statement shall show that he has been warned by the person to whom the same is made: First, that he does not have to make any statement at all. Second, that any statement made may be used in evidence against him on his trial for the offense concerning which the confession is therein made; or, unless in connection with said confession, he makes statements of facts or circumstances that are found to be true, which conduce to establish his guilt, such as the finding of secreted or stolen property, or the instrument with which he states the offense was committed. If the defendant is unable to write his name, and signs the statement

Criminal interrogators generally have viewed any warning requirement as an unnecessary and undesirable practice. That a warning hampers the interrogator is readily apparent to anyone who has observed the natural reluctance on the part of criminal offenders to confess their guilt. A warning offers fortification to that basic reluctance. Criminal interrogators, therefore, were obviously in sympathy with the following viewpoint which had been expressed by a federal court of appeals in answer to the contention of a narcotics peddler that the lack of a warning to him before he confessed violated his privilege against self-incrimination:

"We feel no urge to elevate to the dignity of a Constitutional right a practice which, perhaps even as a matter of etiquette, may, in the present condition of society, be an unwarranted extravagance." [58]

Whether the warning about the self-incrimination privilege is or is not an "unwarranted extravagance" is now a dead issue. The *Miranda v. Arizona*[59] Supreme Court decision of June, 1966, labeled it a constitutional requirement. And in anticipation of that holding, several state supreme courts (e.g., California and Oregon)[60] had already changed their decision law to that which is now constitutionally required of all the states.

The Right to Counsel

The Constitution of the United States and the constitutions of the various states refer only to the right of counsel for an accused

---

by making his mark, such statement shall not be admitted in evidence, unless it be witnessed by some person other than a peace officer, who shall sign the same as a witness," (an act of 1907). (Replaced by Art. 38.22 of the 1965 Code of Criminal Procedure.)

[58] United States v. Wilson, 264 F.2d 104 (2d Cir. 1959). (Opinion written by Judge Madden.)

For other federal circuit court cases holding that a warning is not required see United States v. Block, 88 F.2d 618 (2d Cir. 1937), cert. den. 301 U.S. 690 (1937); Heitner v. United States, 149 F.2d 105 (2d Cir. 1954), cert. den. 326 U.S. 727 (1945).

[59] 384 U.S. 436 (1966).

[60] People v. Dorado, 42 Cal. Rptr. 169, 398 P.2d 361 (1965); State v. Neely, 239 Ore. 487, 398 P.2d 482 (1965); *Cf*. People v. Hartgraves, 31 Ill. 2d 375, 202

person in "criminal prosecutions" and "for his defense." [61] They make no reference to any right to counsel during the investigative stages of a case. But even prior to the recent *Miranda* decision, several states, by statute, had provided that a person under arrest is entitled to communicate and confer with counsel if he makes such a request, and the statutes even prescribed penalties to be imposed upon anyone who denies an arrestee the privilege to do so. [62]

In years past there was no legal requirement that a police interrogator advise a suspect of any right to counsel. The simplest and most direct explanation for such holdings is to be found in a New Jersey Supreme Court opinion, in which the court said:

"A person is only entitled to counsel to aid him in his defense, not to save him from his own voluntary act." [63]

The New York Court of Appeals had made a distinction, how-

N.E. 2d 33 (1964), *cert. den.* 380 U.S. 961; People v. Gunner, 15 N. Y. 2d 226, 205 N.E. 2d 852 (1965).

[61] Art. VI, UNITED STATES CONSTITUTION: "In all criminal prosecutions, the accused shall enjoy the right ... to have the Assistance of Counsel for his defence." Illustrative of the state constitutions, the Illinois Constitution, for example, provides: "In all criminal prosecutions the accused shall have the right to appear and defend in person and by counsel"; (Art. II, §9).

[62] See, for example, §825 of the California Penal Code, which provides that after arrest any attorney may, at the request of the prisoner or any relative of the prisoner, visit the person so arrested. It is further provided that "any officer having charge of the prisoner so arrested who wilfully refuses or neglects to allow such attorney to visit a prisoner is guilty of a misdemeanor." Moreover, "any officer having a prisoner in charge, who refuses to allow any attorney to visit the prisoner when proper application is made therefor, shall forfeit and pay to the party aggrieved the sum of five hundred dollars, to be recovered by action in any court of competent jurisdiction." Kansas has a statute, §62-1304a of KANS. GEN. STAT., which provides "that any person held in restraint of his liberty pending trial or held for investigation in any jail or other place of confinement in this state shall be permitted upon request to immediately confer privately with an attorney of his choice in the same room with such attorney and without any barriers between such person and his attorney, and without any listening in or recording devices." Also see COLO. REV. STAT., 1953 (Cum. Supp., 1960), ch. 39-1-1; ILL. REV. STAT., 1961, ch. 38, §736b; IOWA CODE ANN. (1960 Supp.) §755.17; MO. STAT. (Vernon's 1953), §544.170; MONT. REV. CODE, 1947, §93-2117; N. H. REV. STAT., 1955, ch. 594.16; N. C. GEN. STAT., 1953 (Cum. Supp. 1959), §15-47; OHIO REV. CODE, §2935.16.

[63] State v. Bunk, 4 N.J. 461, 73 A.2d 249 (1950). The above language was quoted with approval in Leick v. People, 136 Colo. 535, 322 P.2d 674 (1958).

ever, between a mere failure to advise a person as to counsel and a "flat refusal" to do so when the subject made an inquiry about it. In this case, during the taking of the defendant's murder confession by an assistant district attorney, the defendant asked if he was compelled to speak before consulting counsel. His question was ignored, and the prosecutor's flat refusal to answer was considered offensive to the court's concept of fairness. It held that the accused was entitled to an answer, and a refusal to give him one invalidated the ensuing confession.[64]

The most critical issue of all was presented by those cases in which there had been an outright refusal to permit an arrestee to contact or confer with counsel. In two 1958 state court confession cases, *Crooker v. California*[65] and *Cicenia v. La Gay*,[66] the United States Supreme Court, by the narrow margin of five to four decisions, upheld the admissibility of a confession obtained after the arrestee had been denied counsel.

It is of interest to note the consideration which the majority of the Court gave to the contention of defense counsel in these two cases. ". . . it can hardly be denied," states the majority opinion, "that adoption of petitioner's position would constrict state police activities in a manner that in many instances might impair their ability to solve difficult cases." [67] Also, according to the majority, "the doctrine suggested by petitioner would have a . . . devastating effect on enforcement of criminal law, for it would effectively preclude police questioning—*fair as well as unfair*—until the accused was afforded opportunity to call his attorney." [68] The Court may well have added, "who would tell him to keep his mouth shut."

Also, in accord with the holding that a cautionary instruction regarding counsel is not an essential step in the establishment of a confession's voluntariness: Mares v. Hill, 118 Utah 484, 222 P.2d 811 (1950); Commonwealth v. McNeil, 328 Mass. 436, 104 N.E.2d 153 (1952); People v. Tipton, 48 Cal.2d 389, 309 P.2d 813 (1957). Also see United States v. Moore, 290 F.2d 436 (2d Cir. 1961). But see Griffith v. Rhay, *infra* note 72.

[64] People v. Noble, 9 N.Y. 2d 571, 175 N.E.2d 451 (1961).
[65] 357 U.S. 433 (1958).
[66] 357 U.S. 504 (1958).
[67] 357 U.S. 504 at p. 509.
[68] 357 U.S. 433 at p. 441.

The minority of the justices were of the view that "the right to have counsel at the pre-trial stage is often necessary to give meaning and protection to the right to be heard at the trial itself." They also felt that the right to counsel "may also be necessary as a restraint on the coercive power of the police." The minority of the Court assumed at the outset that the constitutional right to counsel extended to the investigative stage of a criminal case. They even stated that the majority of the Court conceded this, although no such concession appears in the majority opinion itself. In fact, the very language of the majority opinion—as well as the result reached—is indicative of no such concession. In any event, the point was not specifically discussed.[69]

In addition to the foregoing United States Supreme Court decisions upholding the admissibility of confessions obtained after the police had deprived the arrestee of an opportunity to contact and confer with counsel, there were a number of state court decisions to the same effect.[70]

An important limitation had been placed, however, upon the denial of counsel practices which were involved in the *Crooker* and *Cicenia* cases. It is with respect to case situations in which the police have denied counsel to persons against whom the judicial process has begun to operate—for example, after indictment. At that point, the "criminal prosecution" has begun, and from then on there may be a constitutional right to counsel. The practical effect of this, of course, is the termination of the police interrogation opportunity in such cases. In fact, the New York Court of

[69] Over the years, the case law has been to the effect that the right to counsel arises only in a proceeding that adjudicates guilt or innocence; in other words, it arises at the trial itself, and not at any pre-trial hearing. See Comment, 107 U. PA. L. REV. 286 (1958), and cases cited therein.

[70] Day v. State, 196 Md. 384, 76 A.2d 729 (1950) and Audler v. Kriss, 197 Md. 362, 79 A.2d 391 (1951); State v. Braasch, 119 Utah 450, 229 P.2d 289 (1951); State v. Haynes, 364 P.2d 935 (Wash. 1961). Also see the following federal circuit court of appeals decision in a habeas corpus hearing of a Puerto Rican case, Escute v. Dalgado, 282 F.2d 335 (1st Cir. 1960), in which the court said that due process would be violated only when a deprivation of counsel on the investigative level infects the subsequent trial with an absence of "that fundamental fairness essential to the very concept of justice."

Appeals, in the 1961 case of *People v. Waterman*,[71] actually held that "any secret interrogation of the defendant, from and after the finding of the indictment, without the protection afforded by the presence of counsel, contravenes the basic dictates of fairness in the conduct of criminal causes and the fundamental rights of persons charged with crime." The court also reasoned that "since the finding of the indictment presumably imports that the People have legally sufficient evidence of the defendant's guilt ... the necessities of appropriate police investigation 'to solve a crime, or even to absolve a suspect' cannot be urged as justification for any subsequent questioning of the defendant." [72]

The New York Court of Appeals' decision in the foregoing *Waterman* case was referred to with approval in the 1964 decision of the Supreme Court of the United States in *Massiah v. United States*,[73] which seemed to portend (as later proved to be so) an even greater extension of the right to counsel concept. The defendant Massiah and certain other persons had been indicted for possession of narcotics aboard a United States vessel. After indictment the defendant retained a lawyer, pleaded not guilty, and was released on bail, along with his co-defendants. A few days later, and without the defendant Massiah's knowledge, one of his co-defendants decided to cooperate with the government agents in their continued investigation of the narcotics activities of the group. The co-defendant permitted an agent to "wire him for sound" so as to record

[71] 9 N.Y. 2d 561, 175 N.E.2d 445 (1961).
[72] To this same general effect is the United States Supreme Court decision and the various opinions in Spano v. New York, 360 U.S. 315 (1959). Note particularly the concurring opinion at pp. 324–326. Also consider Griffith v. Rhay, 282 F.2d 711 (9th Cir. 1960), in which a 19-year-old boy, accused of murder, was questioned after he had been formally charged with the crime. The federal court of appeals held, in a habeas corpus hearing after a state court conviction, that the failure to advise the accused of his right to counsel, as well as of his right to remain silent, "infected his subsequent trial with an absence of 'that fundamental fairness essential to the very concept of justice.'" The court did not rest its holding on the fact that the judicial process had started; it merely assumed that the accused had the right, and since he was not advised about it, the failure to do so was a violation of due process. Also, with regard to the limitations upon the interrogation of youthful suspects, consider the previously discussed decision in Gallegos v. Colorado, *supra* note 35.
[73] 377 U.S. 201 (1964).

a conversation between him and Massiah. In the course of the conversation Massiah made several incriminating statements, which were admitted into evidence at his trial, over the objection of defense counsel.

The Supreme Court, six to three, reversed Massiah's conviction because of the use of this evidence against him. The majority held that while the Government was privileged to continue its investigation after indictment, it could not indulge in any interrogation of the indicted defendant outside the presence of counsel, a right to which he was entitled under the Sixth Amendment.

Until recently, the problem presented by the denial of counsel during the investigative stage of a criminal case was considered to be rather similar to that encountered with respect to the failure of police investigators to comply with state statutory provisions requiring that arrestees be taken before committing magistrates "without unnecessary delay." Neither situation was thought to constitute a *constitutional* violation. At most they involved a breach of a directive from the legislature. Moreover, as regards the matter of counsel, in many states there were no statutory provisions at all regarding an arrestee's access to counsel.

Another similarity between police denial of counsel and the practice of delaying the taking of an arrestee before a magistrate was, and still is, the impracticability of compliance by law enforcement officers who seek to give the law-abiding public the protection it demands of them. Both requirements, in effect, deprive police investigators of an interrogation opportunity, whereas interrogations under conditions of privacy and for a reasonable period of time are indispensable to effective criminal investigation.

The late Justice Jackson of the United States Supreme Court pointed to the core of the problem respecting the right to counsel during the investigative stage of a case, when he said:

"To subject one without counsel to questioning, which may and is intended to convict him, is a real peril to individual freedom. To bring in a lawyer means a real peril to solution of the crime, because, under our adversary system, he deems that his sole duty is to protect his client—guilty or innocent—

and that in such capacity he owes no duty whatever to help society solve its crime problem. Under this conception of criminal procedure, any lawyer worth his salt will tell the suspect in no uncertain terms to make no statement to police under any circumstances." [74]

The above admonition, as well as those which had been given by many other persons with a similar viewpoint, had no persuasive effect on five of the Justices who were on the Court when it had before it, in June of 1964, the case of *Escobedo v. Illinois*.[75] The facts in that case were as follows: Escobedo and several others were arrested and questioned concerning the murder of Escobedo's brother-in-law. Escobedo asked to be allowed to confer with a lawyer, but the request was refused. Moreover, his lawyer appeared at the police station and requested to confer with him. This request was also refused. Several hours later Escobedo confessed.

At his trial Escobedo's lawyer argued that the confession should be suppressed because it had been obtained after Escobedo had been deprived of his state statutory right to a lawyer as well as his constitutional right to one. The suppression motion was denied and the confession was admitted in evidence. The jury convicted, largely because of the confession, and Escobedo was sentenced to 20 years in prison.

Upon appeal the Illinois Supreme Court affirmed the conviction, relying upon the prior decisions of the Supreme Court of the United States in the *Crooker* and *Cicenia* cases.[76] The Illinois court held that the constitutional right to counsel did not begin in the police station, and that even though the arrestee had a statutory right to counsel the police were entitled to a reasonable period for an interrogation prior to the conference with counsel.

The decision of the Illinois court was reversed by the Supreme Court, five to four, on the basis of a deprivation of the constitutional right to counsel. Although the Court used some very broad language in its opinion regarding a police station right to counsel the

[74] Watts v. Indiana, 338 U.S. 49, 59 (1948).
[75] 378 U.S. 478 (1964).
[76] *Supra* notes 65 and 66.

actual holding seemed to be limited to the particular facts of the *Escobedo* case. The Court said:

"We hold, therefore, that [1] where, as here, the investigation is no longer a general inquiry into an unsolved crime but has begun to focus on a particular suspect, [2] the suspect has been taken into police custody, [3] the police carry out a process of interrogations that lends itself to eliciting incriminating statements, [4] the suspect has requested and been denied an opportunity to consult with his lawyer, and [5] the police have not effectively warned him of his absolute right to remain silent, the accused has been denied 'the Assistance of Counsel' in violation of the Sixth Amendment to the Constitution ... and that no statement elicited by the police during the interrogation may be used against him at a criminal trial. ***

"... We hold only that when the process shifts from investigatory to accusatory—when its focus is on the accused and its purpose is to elicit a confession—our adversary system begins to operate, and, under the circumstances here, the accused must be permitted to consult with his lawyer."

Escobedo was not re-tried; without the confession the prosecution felt that there would be insufficient proof of guilt beyond a reasonable doubt.

The full import of the *Escobedo* decision was unclear, except as regards other cases with a similar fact pattern. Did it mean, for instance, that a suspect was not only entitled to counsel but also to be advised of his right to one? State supreme court decisions differed. Most of them held that no warning was required.

The uncertainty as to what the majority of the Supreme Court had in mind in the Escobedo decision, however, was removed when the Court rendered its decision in *Miranda v. Arizona.*[77] In that case the Court laid down the rule, in unmistakable language, that a suspect in police custody must be warned of his right to counsel prior to any interrogation of him.

[77] 384 U.S. 436 (1966).

The Nature of the Required Warnings Regarding the Self-Incrimination Privilege and the Right to Counsel

The first warning that must be given before any "custodial interrogation" begins is the one regarding the privilege against self-incrimination. The interrogator must tell the suspect: (1) that he has a right to remain silent, and he need not answer any questions; and (2) that if he does answer questions his answers can be used as evidence against him.

The second required warning is with respect to the suspect's right to counsel. He must be told, before he is asked any questions: (1) that he has the right to consult with a lawyer *before* or *during* the questioning of him by the police; and (2) that if he cannot afford to hire an attorney one will be provided for him without cost.

Both warnings must be given in such a way that the suspect clearly understands what he is being told. And he must specifically acknowledge that he is willing to talk without the benefit of counsel.

Even though the two warnings have been given properly and timely to a suspect who thereafter waives his privilege and his right to counsel, they should be repeated whenever a second interrogation has begun, or whenever a written or sound recorded statement is about to be obtained. This seems required by reason of the statements in the *Miranda* opinion that a suspect may, at any time, invoke his self-incrimination privilege and his right to counsel.

The Consequences of an Exercise of the Self-Incrimination Privilege or a Request for Counsel

According to the *Miranda* decision, if a suspect indicates, in any manner whatsoever, that he does not want to answer any questions, or any further questions, the interrogation must cease. The interrogator is not privileged to "talk him out of" his refusal to talk, as was formerly permissible.

If the suspect says, at any time, that he wants a lawyer, the interrogation must cease until he has had an opportunity to confer with a lawyer, and no further questions may be asked of him outside the lawyer's presence or without the lawyer's permission. Nor may the interrogator "talk him out of" his desire for a lawyer.

In instances where the suspect requests a lawyer, but he cannot obtain one, and no lawyer is provided for him, the interrogation must be terminated.

The Waiver of the Self-Incrimination Privilege and the Right to Counsel

The Supreme Court in *Miranda* specifically stated that a criminal suspect could waive his self-incrimination privilege and his right to counsel, but the prosecution would have the "heavy burden" of proving that the waiver was made "knowingly and intelligently." Some insight into what the Court had in mind may be obtained from the following exerpt from its opinion:

> "An express statement that the individual is willing to make a statement and does not want an attorney followed closely by a statement could constitute a waiver. But a valid waiver will not be presumed simply from the silence of the accused after warnings are given or simply from the fact that a confession was in fact eventually obtained."

The Court then went on to point out, however, that a "lengthy interrogation or incommunicado incarceration before a statement is made is strong evidence that the accused did not validly waive his rights." And it further stated that "any evidence that the accused was threatened, tricked, or cajoled into a waiver will, of course, show that the defendant did not voluntarily waive his privilege."

Circumstances Under Which the Warnings Are Not Required

No warnings are required unless the person to be interrogated has been "taken into custody or otherwise deprived of his freedom of action in any significant way." The meaning of "custody" is fairly clear, but what the Supreme Court meant by "freedom of action" is uncertain.

Does it mean that the warnings must be given to a person who is stopped and questioned on the street because of suspicious circumstances, such as the carrying of a suitcase in an alley at 3 a.m. by someone whose clothing or physical appearance gives rise to the impression he is not a resident of the neighborhood? What about the stopping and questioning of a motorist in a traffic violation situation?

It is to be hoped that the Court will hold that in case situations of this type the warnings will not be required, because such police action lacks the aura of "inherent compulsion" that the Court finds in the police station interrogation of an arrestee.

The warnings seem not to be required in instances where the police question bystanders at a crime scene who probably would not be restrained if they attempted to leave.

In view of the Supreme Court's 1966 decision, in *Schwerber v. California*[78] holding that the self-incrimination privilege does not protect a person from the relinquishment, seizure, or observation of physical evidence—e.g., blood for purposes of a chemical test for intoxication—a warning is not required in such situations. Nor is the warning required with respect to the procurement of a specimen of handwriting from a criminal suspect in police custody.[79]

Congressional Attempt to Nullify the *Miranda* Decision

In the earlier discussion of the Congressional abolition of the *McNabb-Mallory* rule,[80] reference was made to the fact that at the same time Congress sought to nullify the *Miranda* case by providing that the test of confession admissibility (in federal cases) was to be the test of voluntariness, and that the absence of the warnings prescribed in *Miranda* were only factors to be considered in determining voluntariness; in other words, the absence of the warnings would no longer categorically outlaw a confession. The precise language used is as follows (81 U. S. C. § 3501):

> "(a) In any criminal prosecution brought by the United States or by the District of Columbia, a confession, . . . shall be admissable in evidence if it is voluntarily given. . .

---

[78] 384 U.S. 757 (1966).
[79] Gilbert v. California, 388 U.S. 263 (1967).
[80] Supra p. 150.

"(b) The trial judge in determining the issue of voluntariness shall take into consideration all the circumstances surrounding the giving of the confession, including (1) the time elapsing between arrest and arraignment of the defendant making the confession, if it was made after arrest and before arraignment, (2) whether such defendant knew the nature of the offense with which he was charged or of which he was suspected at the time of making the confession, (3) whether or not such defendant was advised or knew that he was not required to make any statement and that any such statement could be used against him, (4) whether or not such defendant had been advised prior to questioning of his right to the assistance of counsel; and (5) whether or not such defendant was without the assistance of counsel when questioned and when giving such confession.

"The presence or absence of any of the above-mentioned factors to be taken into consideration by the judge need not be conclusive on the issue of voluntariness of the confession. . . .

"(d) Nothing contained in this section shall bar the admission in evidence of any confession made or given voluntarily by any person to any other person without interrogation by anyone, or at any time at which the person who made or gave such confession was not under arrest or other detention.

"(e) As used in this section, the term 'confession' means any confession of guilt of any criminal offense or any self-incriminating statement made or given orally or in writing." [81]

Since the Supreme Court in *Miranda* said that the rules therein laid down were constitutionally mandated, by all conventional judicial standards the general view prevails among legal scholars that unless the Supreme Court itself "overrules" *Miranda*, it will be difficult to sustain the validity of the Congressional Act. It might, however, look upon a portion of its opinion in that case so as to sanction what Congress has done, without actually overruling *Miranda*. It reads as follows:

"Our decision in no way creates a constitutional straight jacket which will handicap sound efforts at reform nor is it intended to have this effect. We encourage Congress and the States to continue their laudable search for increasingly effective ways of protecting the rights of the individual while promoting efficient enforcement of our criminal laws. However, unless we are shown other procedures which are at least as effective in apprising accused persons of their right of silence and in assuring a continuous opportunity to exercise it, the safeguards [of *Miranda*] must be observed."

---

[81] 18 U. S. C. § 3501.

4

RESTRICTIONS UPON THE LENGTH OF AN INTERROGATION AND THE NUMBER OF INTERROGATORS

In its *Miranda* opinion the Supreme Court stated that regardless of the testimony of law enforcement officers as to the waiver of the self-incrimination privilege and the right to counsel, the fact of a lengthy interrogation would be considered strong evidence that the accused had not validly waived those rights.[82] It is essential, therefore, that the length of an interrogation be a *reasonable* one, taking into consideration all the surrounding circumstances of the particular case. No precise guide is available at the present, and perhaps none is practically feasible.

Even apart from the concern of the courts, criminal interrogators should realize that an effective interrogation can be conducted *without* interrogating an accused person for an uninterrupted period of many hours. Moreover, not more than two interrogators are required; in fact, in most instances one is not only sufficient but also more effective than two or more.[83]

Another good reason for minimizing the number of interrogators is the difficulty that confronts a prosecutor when he has to establish the voluntariness of a confession in a case where several, or many, persons have participated in, or were merely present during an interrogation or confession. Some courts have held that whenever the defense is raised that a confession has been obtained under duress, the prosecution must, if practicable, produce as a witness each and every person who was present during the interrogation or confession.[84] This, obviously, places a great burden on

[82] 384 U.S. at 476 (1966).
[83] See *supra* pp. 5–11.
[84] "An inescapable duty rests upon the prosecution . . . to bring in every police officer and every other person connected with taking the statements in order to ascertain whether they were forced by threats and physical violence." People v. Sloss, 412 Ill. 61, 104 N.E.2d 807 (1952). To the same effect: People v. La Coco, 406 Ill. 303, 94 N.E.2d 178 (1950); People v. Ickes, 370 Ill. 486, 19 N.E.2d 373 (1939); People v. Ardelean, 368 Ill. 274, 13 N.E.2d 976 (1938); People v. Ardenarczyk, 367 Ill. 534, 12 N.E.2d 2 (1937); People v. Jennings, 11 Ill. 2d 610, 144 N.E.2d 612 (1957); People v. Sammons, 17 Ill. 2d 316, 161 N.E.2d 322 (1959); People v. Pale, 20 Ill. 2d 532, 171 N.E.2d 1 (1960); People v. Sims, 21 Ill. 2d 425, 173 N.E.2d 494 (1961) (but note dissenting opinion

the prosecuting attorney, and it may represent a very real danger to the entire prosecution effort where perhaps five, ten, or more witnesses may have to be produced to establish the voluntary character of a confession. In the first place, considerable time and expense will be consumed in producing the testimony of all police officers who were present when the confession was obtained. Secondly, the more witnesses there are to the event, the more likely there is to be a certain amount of inconsistency in their testimonies as to the various details surrounding the confession— even though all of them may be attempting to tell the absolute truth—and his inconsistency is very apt to lend credence to the allegations of duress.

5

THE MENTAL AND PHYSICAL CONDITION OF THE PERSON UNDER INTERROGATION

Under the *Miranda* case rules[85] it is difficult to state with any degree of assurance just what mental or physical conditions will render a waiver or a post-waiver confession invalid. For whatever value they may possess as guide lines, we offer the following analysis of the earlier decisions with respect to the issue of voluntariness:

According to prior decision law, the fact that a confessor is mentally deficient or mentally ill, by itself, will not nullify a confession, although such a condition must be given consideration in ascertaining whether a confession is a voluntary one.[86] The same rule

---

criticism of the rule). *Cf.* People v. Jankowski, 391 Ill. 298, 63 N.E.2d 362 (1945), where the defendant testified that he did not remember making a confession and did not know what he signed, but claimed that a particular officer, whom he named, was the only one who had beaten him, which officer was produced as a witness for the prosecution and denied any abuse. The court held that under the circumstances it was unnecessary to call the other officers as witnesses.

Also see State v. Scarborough, 167 La. 484, 119 So. 523 (1929); State v. Lord, 42 N.M. 638, 84 P.2d 80 (1938); Holmes v. State, 211 Miss. 436, 51 So.2d 755 (1951). *Contra:* Logan v. State, 251 Ala. 441, 37 So.2d 753 (1948).

[85] *Supra* p. 4.

[86] State v. Watson, 114 Vt. 543, 49 A.2d 174 (1946); State v. Ashdown, 5 Utah 2d 59, 296 P.2d 726 (1956); Commonwealth v. Krzesniak, 180 Pa. Super. 560, 119 A.2d 617 (1956); People v. Tipton, 48 Cal. 2d 389, 309 P.2d 813 (1957); State v. Bailey, 233 La. 40, 96 So.2d 34, 69 A.L.R.2d 340 (1957). *Cf* Blackburn v. Alabama, 361 U.S. 199 (1960).

has been applied with respect to a confessor's intoxication,[87] his addiction to drugs, and his being under their influence or in a state of deprivation,[88] or to other physical or mental disabilities.[89]

6

THREATS

Under any test of confession admissibility—whether prior to or subsequent to the *Miranda* decision—a confession was legally invalid if it had been obtained after a suspect had been led to believe that unless he confessed he was in danger of loss of life or bodily harm.[90]

[87] State v. Dorman, 28 Cal. 2d 846, 172 P.2d 686 (1946); Roper v. People, 116 Colo. 493, 179 P.2d 232 (1947); State v. Alexander, 215 La. 245, 40 So.2d 232 (1949); Harper v. State, 206 Tenn. 509, 334 S.W.2d 933 (1960); State v. Isom, 243 N.C. 164, 90 S.E.2d 237 (1955); People v. Pogoda, 9 Ill. 2d 198, 137 N.E.2d 386 (1956); and also annotation in 69 A.L.R.2d 358, 362, in which it is stated: "The case law on the subject . . . may be summarized briefly: proof that the accused was intoxicated at the time he confessed his guilt . . . will not, without more, bar the reception of the confession in evidence. . . . But if it is shown that the accused was intoxicated to the degree of mania, or of being unable to understand the meaning of his statements, then the confession is inadmissible. . . ."

[88] People v. Mendoza, 122 Cal. App. 2d 185, 264 P.2d 223 (1954); Tiner v. State, 271 Ala. 254, 122 So.2d 738 (1960); People v. Townsend, 11 Ill. 2d 30, 141 N.E.2d 729 (1957), but see Justice Schaefer's dissenting opinion that confession was involuntary because the accused, a narcotics addict, had confessed while under the influence of drugs admitted by a police physician to relieve the defendant's withdrawal pains. Also see the decision and opinion of the United States Supreme Court in its reversal of the Townsend case. The Court said: "It is difficult to imagine a situation in which a confession would be less the product of a free intellect, less voluntary, than when brought about by a drug having the effect of a 'truth serum'." 372 U.S. 308 (1962).

[89] State v. Hofer, 238 Iowa 820, 28 N.W.2d 475 (1947) (state of fatigue); Eiffe v. State, 226 Ind. 57, 77 N.E.2d 750 (1948) (intoxication hang-over); Dennison v. State, 259 Ala. 424, 66 So.2d 552 (1953) (accused in weakened condition as result of previous overdose of sleeping pills in suicide attempt); People v. Cobb, 45 Cal. 2d 158, 287 P.2d 752 (1955) (poor physical condition generally); State v. Wise, 19 N.J. 59, 115 A.2d 62 (1955) (severe physical injuries); Commonwealth v. Harrison, 173 N.E.2d 87 (Mass. 1961) (brain injury).

[90] The fear must be that of a "reasonably prudent man." In Simring v. State, 77 So.2d 833 (Fla. 1955), the defendant, at the time of his arrest on an obscene literature charge, urinated in his pants and started "shaking awfully," but the fear thus evidenced was not considered of such a nature as to nullify his confession.

Some states have statutes outlawing confessions made "under the influence of fear produced by threats." See ORE. STAT. §136.540.

In the application of this test a confession is obviously inadmissible if obtained as a result of telling a suspect that unless he confessed he would be hanged, shot, or delivered to a mob outside the jail,[91] or if obtained as a result of physical abuse administered to a fellow suspect in the presence of the person under interrogation.[92]

An extension of the same test also excluded a confession obtained as a result of telling a suspect that unless he confessed he would be sent to the penitentiary for more serious offenses.[93] One court extended the test to include a situation in which the police confronted a suspected arsonist with an accusation of an independent offense, a sex crime, and told him that if that charge were investigated by the police it would create considerable publicity and embarrassment for him.[94]

Another type of threat that has been held to nullify a confession is telling a suspect that unless he confesses the police will apprehend and accuse his wife, his mother, or some other person close to him in affection.[95] A similar effect has been attached to a threat to merely

---

[91] Reason v. State, 94 Miss. 290, 48 So. 820 (1909) (hanging threat). In Edwards v. State, 194 Md. 387, 71 A.2d 487 (1950), the interrogator kept making a "hangman's knot" with a piece of rope as he talked to the defendant. This was considered a threat, especially in view of the defendant's further testimony that the interrogator said that a mob might hang the defendant if he were released. Rollins v. State, 18 Ala. App. 354, 92 So. 35 (1922) (shooting threat); People v. Sweetin, 325 Ill. 245, 156 N.E. 354 (1927) (mob threat); Payne v. Arkansas, 356 U.S. 560 (1958) (mob threat). Compare Thomas v. Arizona, 356 U.S. 390 (1958), in which a member of a posse had roped the defendant as he was apprehended but the sheriff removed the rope immediately, and there was no threat of mob violence or lynching. The confession was held to be admissible. Also compare Kirkendoll v. State, 198 Tenn. 497, 281 S.W.2d 243 (1955), in which the defendants had been removed from one jail to another and were told, truthfully, that it was being done for their own safety. This was held not to nullify the confession, as long as there were no other factors involving threats or promises. In Jones v. State, 188 Md. 263, 52 A.2d 484 (1947), a confession was held admissible even though the defendant contended that his fear of mob violence must have been well-founded since the police took him to a jail a considerable distance away from the scene of the murder for which he was apprehended.

[92] People v. Flores, 15 Cal. App. 2d 385, 59 P.2d 517 (1936).

[93] State v. Miller, 68 Wash. 239, 122 Pac. 1066 (1912); State v. Harvey, 145 Wash. 161, 259 Pac. 21 (1927).

[94] Hooper v. State, 115 So.2d 769 (Fla. 1959).

[95] People v. Mellus, 134 Cal. App. 219, 25 P.2d 237 (1933); People v. Trout,

bring into the police station an invalided wife for questioning.[96] And in a relatively recent Supreme Court case a woman's narcotics conviction was reversed because the interrogators had told her that if she did not "cooperate" she would be deprived of state financial aid and her children would be taken from her.[97]

On the other hand, however, it has been held permissible for an interrogator to ask a question rather roughly,[98] to assume in his various questions that the subject is guilty,[99] to express impatience with the suspect's alleged lying,[100] to tell a suspect that the investigators will secure or have already secured the necessary proof to convict him anyway,[101] or even to tell him that if he desires he can "stick to his story" and run the risk of being convicted and executed.[102] This last statement, however, is one that should be avoided because it is too near the borderline of an actual threat.

The mere fact that the interrogator is armed, or that an officer

---

6 Cal. Rptr, 759, 354 P.2d 231, 80 A.L.R. 1418 (1961). But see Phillips v. State, 29 Wis. 2d 521, 139 N.W.2d 41 (1966), a robbery case in which the interrogator threatened to arrest the suspect's girl friend on a charge of living with him. The Wisconsin Supreme Court said: "We think the statement in reference to the girl friend was motivation rather than coercion because the defendant in his testimony stated that it was a threat more to her than to him." The court concluded that the threat "standing in context with the other facts" was "insufficient to render the confession coerced." Also compare the Mellus case with People v. Mattock, 51 Cal. 2d 682, 336 P.2d 505 (1959) and People v. Kendrick, 14 Cal. Rptr. 13, 363 P.2d 13 (1961).

[96] Rogers v. Richmond, *supra* note 31.

[97] Lynum v. Illinois, *supra* note 36.

[98] Anderson v. State, 133 Wis. 601, 114 N.W. 112 (1907).

[99] People v. Fitzgerald, 322 Ill. 54, 152 N.E. 542 (1926).

[100] Dame v. State, 191 Ark. 1107, 89 S.W.2d 610 (1936). The interrogator's impatience even to the extent of swearing at the subject has been held insufficient to nullify a confession. State v. Dehart, 242 Wis. 562, 8 N.W.2d 360 (1943). Also, upon this point, see Buschy v. People, 73 Colo. 472, 216 Pac. 519 (1923); the second McNabb case, 142 F.2d 904 (6th Cir. 1944); and State v. Henderson, 182 Ore. 147, 184 P.2d 392 (1947).

[101] State v. Johnson, 137 S.C. 7, 133 S.E. 823 (1926); People v. Castello, 194 Cal. 595, 229 Pac. 855 (1924).

[102] State v. Donovan, 40 Del. 257, 8 A.2d 876 (1939). Also see People v. Hubbell, 54 Cal. App. 49, 128 P.2d 579 (1942), in which the court held that telling a subject accused of a sex offense against a child that thirty children would be used as witnesses for the prosecution did not vitiate the confession made thereafter.

had pointed a pistol at the subject when he was arrested, does not affect the validity of a confession.[103]

Advising or imploring a subject to tell the truth is never considered objectionable.[104] Some difficulty arises, however, when the interrogator uses such language as "It would be better for you to confess"; "You had better confess"; "It would be better for you to tell the truth"; or "You had better tell the truth." [105]

A number of courts have held that such statements as "You had better confess," or "It would be better for you to confess," constitute threats or promises which will nullify a confession. Some courts have gone so far as to hold that the same rejection rule applies even when the suspect is merely told "It would be better to tell the truth." [106] There are many cases, however, in which the courts have taken a more liberal attitude, particularly as regards the latter type of expressions.[107] Nevertheless, it is well for interrogators to avoid

[103] State v. Thomas, 161 La. 1010, 109 So. 819 (1926); State v. Kennedy, 232 La. 755, 95 So.2d 301 (1957); State v. Hart, 292 Mo. 74, 237 S.W. 473 (1922); Commonwealth v. Ballem, 386 Pa. 20, 123 A.2d 728 (1956).

[104] People v. Randazzio, 194 N.Y. 147, 87 N.E. 112 (1909); State v. Caldwell, 212 N.C. 484, 193 S.E. 716 (1937); People v. Davis, 10 Ill.2d 430, 140 N.E.2d 675 (1957); State v. Statler, 331 S.W.2d 526 (Mo. 1960).

One state, by statute, provides that "the fact that a confession shall have been made under a spiritual exhortation . . . shall not exclude it." GA. CODE ch. 38, §412 (1933).

[105] For a discussion of the distinctions between a mere adjuration to tell the truth, and telling the subject "It is better to tell the truth," or "It is better to confess," see Edwardson v. State, 255 Ala. 246, 51 So.2d 233 (1950). Also see State v. Robinson, 215 La. 974, 41 So.2d 848 (1949), where the statement "You had better confess," was preceded by, "Boy, I have got you in the palm of my hand."

[106] See in particular the following cases, which have disapproved the use of any form of expressions such as those above mentioned: Biscoe v. State, 67 Md. 6, 8 Atl. 571 (1887); Edwards v. State, 194 Md. 387, 71 A.2d 487 (1950); West v. United States, 20 D.C. App. 347 (1902); State v. Nagel, 25 R.I. 105, 54 Atl. 1063 (1903); People v. Leavitt, 100 Cal. App. 93, 279 Pac. 1056 (1929).

[107] Hintz v. State, 125 Wis. 405, 104 N.W. 110 (1905); State v. Gee Jon, 46 Nev. 418, 211 Pac. 676 (1923); State v. Mayle, 108 W. Va. 681, 152 S.E. 633 (1930); State v. Meyers, 202 N.C. 351, 162 S. E. 764 (1932); Hicks v. State, 178 Ga. 561, 173 S.E. 395 (1934); State v. Tharp, 234 Mo. 46, 64 S.W.2d 249 (1933); State v. Wickman, 39 N.M. 198, 43 P.2d 933 (1935); Commonwealth v. Mabey, 299 Mass. 96, 12 N.E.2d 61 (1937); State v. Thompson, 227 N.C. 19, 40 S.E.2d 620 (1946); Territory of Hawaii v. Sumngat, 38 Haw. 609 (1950); People v. Pugh, 409 Ill. 584, 100 N.E.2d 909 (1951); Barksdale v. State, 200

the use of any expressions such as "You had better...," or "It is better...." [108]

7

PROMISES

There are certain promises that have been held permissible, and there are others that are prohibited.[109] The line of demarcation is usually determined by the following question: "Is the promise one that is likely to cause the subject to make a false confession?"

As a general rule, in order for a promise to invalidate a confession it must have reference to the subject's escape from punishment or the mitigation of his punishment. It is not sufficient if the promise merely offers the subject an opportunity for the gratification of his personal desires and comfort, or for the granting

---

Tenn. 322, 292 S.W.2d 193 (1956), but compare Ann v. State, 30 Tenn. 159 (1850). An interrogator's statement to a Negro subject that, "the best thing that I think you can do is to get down on your knees and tell God about it," was approved in Smits v. State, 248 Ala. 363, 27 So.2d 495 (1946). In State v. Nunn, 212 Ore. 546, 321 P.2d 356 (1958), the court approved the expression, "You ought to get it off your mind."

The most reasonable view, of course, is the one taken by the majority of courts, which examine the expression in the light of all the other conditions and circumstances in the case. For instance, in People v. Ardelean, 368 Ill. 276, 13 N.E.2d 976 (1938), the court even tolerated the expression, "It would be better for you to talk and if you don't it would be too bad," because, said the court, "if sufficient facts are proved showing that a statement of guilt was freely made, a trial court may admit it in evidence, although there may be some evidence of threats or promises." Also see Murphy v. United States, 285 Fed. 801 (7th Cir. 1923), and State v. Wickman, 39 N.M. 198, 43 P.2d 933 (1935).

[108] For a general discussion of the law regarding such expressions see WIGMORE, EVIDENCE §§832, 838 (1940).

[109] An example of a permissible promise is a promise of secrecy. State v. Novak, 109 Iowa 717, 79 N.W. 465 (1899); Markley v. State, 173 Md. 309, 196 Atl. 95 (1938). One state, by statute, authorizes the use of a promise of secrecy. GA. CODE, Ch. 8, §412: "The fact that a confession shall have been made under a spiritual exhortation, or a promise of collateral benefit, shall not exclude it." But compare LA. CODE CRIM. PROC. §451, which requires the prosecution to prove that a confession was not made under the influence of "fear, duress, intimidation, menaces, threats, inducements or promises." Presumably no promises of any kind are permitted. But see State v. Richards, 223 La. 674, 66 So.2d 589 (1953), in which a deputy sheriff, in urging the defendant to con-

of a benefit to some third person.[110] It must also be a promise made by "one in authority"; if made by a private citizen, the promise is generally held not to void the confession.[111]

A promise to the subject that if he confesses he will be released from custody,[112] that he will not be prosecuted,[113] that he will be granted a pardon,[114] or that he will receive a light, or lighter sentence than the law prescribes[115] will invalidate a confession.[116] The same is true even though the interrogator merely states that he will

---

fess, told him that if he was guilty it might be "easier for him." This was held not to nullify a confession, since the officer also told the subject he should not confess unless he was actually guilty.

The types of promises that are prohibited are illustrated in the cases cited in the ensuing footnotes.

[110] See State v. Blair, 118 Vt. 81, 99 A.2d 677 (1953). Also see GA. CODE, *supra* note[106] with respect to "collateral benefits." But see People v. Trout, 6 Cal. Rptr. 759, 354 P.2d 231, 80 A.L.R. 1418 (1961).

[111] WIGMORE, EVIDENCE §828–831 (1940). *Cf.* Simmons v. State, 206 Miss. 535, 40 So.2d 289 (1949), where the defendant's alleged accomplices urged the defendant to confess by promising him assistance in the form of bail. This circumstance, along with certain other factors, was held to nullify a resulting confession.

[112] Such promises have been held improper even when they refer only to a temporary release on bail. Clash v. State, 146 Miss. 811, 112 So. 370 (1927).

[113] People v. Campbell, 359 Ill. 286, 194 N.E. 533 (1935).

[114] WIGMORE, EVIDENCE §834 (1940).

[115] State v. Livingston, 202 N.C. 809, 164 S.E. 337 (1932); State v. Ellis, 207 La. 812, 22 So.2d 181 (1945); State v. Crittenden, 214 La. 81, 36 So.2d 645 (1948); State v. Mullin, 249 Iowa 10, 85 N.W.2d 598 (1957). Also see Leyra v. Denno, 347 U.S. 556 (1954), where a psychiatrist-interrogator, working for the police, promised to help the accused.

[116] But see Lewis v. United States, 74 F.2d 173 (9th Cir. 1934); State v. Ashdown, 5 Utah 2d 59, 296 P.2d 726 (1956), in which an implication of a lesser offense, or possibly immunity, was considered offset by the fact that it came early during the interrogation and that the accused had been warned, and also told that the interrogator did not want a confession from an innocent person; Humphries v. State, 163 Tex. Cr. R. 601, 295 S.W.2d 218 (1956), in which a confession was held admissible even though the interrogator had told the accused that "it was always best to tell the truth, even though it did hurt sometimes, and that if he told the truth it would be better for him in the long run."

A statute of the state of Washington provides as follows: "The confession of a defendant made under inducement, with all the circumstances, may be given as evidence against him, except when made under the influence of fear produced by threats; but a confession made under inducement is not sufficient to warrant a conviction without corroborating testimony." WASH. REV. CODF

do whatever he can to induce the proper authorities to grant such immunity or diminution of sentence.[117]

Promising a subject who is accused of a number of crimes that if he will confess to one he will not be prosecuted for the others will nullify a confession.[118] A promise to a parolee that if he confesses to a murder he will be returned to the neighboring state prison from which he was paroled has been held to constitute a promise of immunity and therefore an improper inducement.[119]

The courts have uniformly held that an interrogator's promise to keep the subject's confession a secret does not affect its validity.[120] In one state such a promise is rendered permissible by statute.[121]

Promises made *after* a confession has been received are held not to affect the validity of the confession, regardless of the nature of the promise.[122] There is a practical danger, however, in making

---

ANN. §10.58.030. Applied and upheld in State v. Meyer, 37 Wash. 2d 759, 226 P.2d 204 (1951), and State v. Winters, 39 Wash. 2d 545, 236 P.2d 1038 (1951). Indiana has a similarly worded statute, vol. 4, pt. 1, 9-1607.

[117] People v. Martorano, 359 Ill. 258, 194 N.E. 505 (1935). In fact, an intimation of such assistance will also nullify a resulting confession. See Edwards v. State, 194 Md. 387, 71 A.2d 487 (1950), where the interrogator showed the accused a letter from a convict which stated: "Next time you get a smart guy . . . show him this letter, from another wise guy, and don't forget to tell him what it cost me for not listening to you."

Also see State v. Woodruff, 259 N.C. 333, 130 S.E. 2d 641 (1963).

[118] See People v. Hurst, 36 Cal. App. 2d 63, 96 P.2d 1003 (1939).

[119] State v. Williamson, 339 Mo. 1038, 99 S.W.2d 76 (1936). Regarding Missouri cases generally, see 20 U. OF KANS. CITY L. REV. 66 (1952).

[120] Supra note 109.

[121] Georgia, supra note 109.

[122] State v. Moore, 124 Ore. 61, 262 Pac. 859 (1928); State v. Williamson, 343 Mo. 732, 123 S.W.2d 42 (1938); State v. Green, 210 La. 157, 26 So.2d 487 (1946). A promise of a lighter penalty, made between the making of an oral confession and the signing of a substantially similar one, does not necessarily render the written confession inadmissible, if upon a consideration of all the circumstances the confession appears trustworthy. State v. La Pean, 247 Wis. 302, 19 N.W.2d 289 (1945).

On a related question, as to the effect of force in securing the signature to the written confession upon the admissibility of the voluntary oral confession, see Gray v. Commonwealth, 293 Ky. 833, 170 S.W.2d 870 (1943) (holding that the written confession was also admissible; but here the defendant admitted that his oral confession, which was the same as the written one, was voluntarily made).

a promise after a confession. Such a promise may be considered by the trial court or jury as corroboration of the defendant's contention that a promise was made to him *before* the confession. It is advisable, therefore, to refrain from making any promises whatsoever, even after the confession.

Expressions such as, "It would be better for you to confess," or "It would be better for you to tell the truth," have been interpreted by a few courts as constituting promises sufficient to invalidate a confession.[123] It is suggested, therefore, that the interrogator avoid the risk incurred by the use of expressions of this nature.

[123] See cases cited *supra* note 106, and also State v. Linn, 179 Ore. 499, 173 P.2d 305 (1946); Kier v. State, 213 Md. 556, 132 A.2d 494 (1957). But compare Penton v. State, 194 Ark. 503, 109 S.W.2d 131 (1937), where the sheriff told the accused that it would go well with him if he told the truth, and the court held that "this was merely an expression of opinion, and the statement was not coupled with innuendo or subtleties calculated to deceive the prisoner. Appellant was only advised to tell the truth"; Merchant v. State, 217 Md. 61, 141 A.2d 487 (1958), in which the subject asked the interrogator if it would be easier on him if he told the truth, and the interrogator said he was making no promises but that "the truth hurts no one." The court held that this statement did not amount to a promise of leniency. Also consider Frazier v. State, 107 So.2d 16 (Fla. 1958), which held that the use of expressions such as "it would be easier on you," without an explanation why it would be easier, did not in and of itself nullify the confession. The court said: "Whether the specific language used amounts to a threat or promise of benefit depends upon the circumstance in which it is used and on warrantable inferences drawn from the language and circumstances."

As regards the confessor's own inferences of leniency from the interrogator's general statements, the Oregon Supreme Court had this to say: "Even if defendant—influenced perhaps by wishful thinking and the hope that springs eternal in the human breast—assumed that he would get more lenient treatment by making a confession, that would not, as a matter of law, make the confession inadmissible. It is not every inducement that vitiates a confession, but only such inducement as involves "any fair risk of a false confession.... If the defendant was motivated by a desire to tell the truth, it does not matter that his desire was buttressed by the hope that telling the truth would also bring leniency." State v. Nunn, 212 Ore. 546, 321 P.2d 356 (1958).

In People v. Klyczek, 307 Ill. 150, 138 N.E. 275 (1923), the Illinois Supreme Court held that the expression, "It would be better to tell the truth," was permissible, but in People v. Heide, 302 Ill. 624, 135 N.E 77 (1922) the court pointed out that the expression may become objectionable if it should be coupled with any other statement suggestive of leniency.

8

"TRICKERY" OR "DECEIT"

Over the years all the reviewing courts that were presented with the problem have held that a confession is admissible in evidence even though it was obtained by the use of trickery or deceit on the part of the interrogator. Only one important qualification has been attached to the rule; the trickery or deceit must not be of such a nature as to induce a false confession.[124]

In accordance with this general rule, it has been held that a valid confession may be obtained by leading the subject to believe that there is more proof of his guilt than actually exists;[125] for instance, he may be told that his fingerprints were found at the scene of the crime, when, in fact, no fingerprints had been discovered.[126] The interrogator might also deceive the subject into believing that his accomplice has confessed and implicated both himself and the subject.[127]

Prior to the new requirement regarding warnings, it was held permissible for an investigator to pose as a fellow prisoner, or even as a friend of the subject, and a confession obtained as a result of such trickery is admissible as evidence,[128] but in all probability that will no longer be allowed because the person seeking the confession is acting in an official "agency" capacity and he is, in effect, conducting a "custodial interrogation."

A confession is inadmissible if obtained by an investigator posing as an attorney for the subject, because of the fact that such a misrepresentation involves a violation of the attorney-client privilege,

[124] Commonwealth v. Cressinger, 193 Pa. 326 (1899); State v. Hofer, 238 Iowa 820, 28 N.W.2d 475 (1947); People v. Everett, 10 N.Y.2d 500, 180 N.E.2d 556 (1962).; WIGMORE, EVIDENCE §841 (3d ed. 1940). This principle is also referred to in the cases subsequently cited.
[125] People v. Thompson, 133 Cal. App. 2d 4, 284 P.2d 39 (1955).
[126] People v. Connelly, 195 Cal. 584, 234 Pac. 374 (1925); Lewis v. United States, 74 F.2d 173 (9th Cir. 1934).
[127] Osborn v. People, 83 Colo. 4, 262 Pac. 892 (1927); State v. Palko, 121 Conn. 669, 186 Atl. 657 (1936); and Commonwealth v. Green, 302 Mass. 547, 20 N.E.2d 417 (1939), in which the accused was shown a fake telegram purporting to come from another police department and revealing that an accomplice had confessed.
[128] People v. White 176 N.Y. 331, 68 N.E. 630 (1903).

which renders confidential any communication between attorney and client.[129]

It has been held permissible for a police officer to pose as a witness to a crime and "identify" the subject as the perpetrator.[130] Also previously sanctioned has been the tactic of an investigator to make fake notes purporting to come from one prisoner to another and thereby eventually procure a statement in the handwriting of one of them admitting his guilt.[131]

A confession's admissibility has been considered unaffected by the fact that during the interrogation a murder suspect is not told that death has resulted from his act but is questioned only about the act itself (e.g., train derailment, assault, etc.)[132]

The foregoing police practices are all illustrative of the general rule that trickery or deceit will not nullify a confession, regardless of the possible objection to such practices from a strictly moral viewpoint. The underlying consideration has been a tacit recognition that practices of this type are required in order to solve crimes where sufficient proof other than a confession is lacking. Moreover, the interests of the innocent are sufficiently protected by the requirement that the artifice involved must not be of a type that is apt to make an innocent person confess.

Although recent Supreme Court opinions have contained derogatory statements about "trickery" and "deceit" as interrogation devices, no case has prohibited their usage. And if they are ever prohibited then the end of effective police interrogations will have arrived, and for a very basic reason: Whenever the police interrogate a person whom they believe to be guilty of a crime they are not doing so for *his* benefit. Deceit, therefore, is inherent in every question asked of the suspect, and in every statement made by the interrogator. So if deceit is impermissible a ban will have to be placed upon all interrogations of criminal suspects. And without some elements of "trickery," such as leading the suspect to believe

[129] People v. Barker, 60 Mich. 277, 27 N.W. 539 (1886).
[130] United States v. Murphy, 227 F.2d 698 (2d Cir. 1955) (dicta).
[131] State v. Dingledine, 135 Ohio St. 251, 30 N.E.2d 660 (1939).
[132] Commonwealth v. Johnson, 372 Pa. 266, 93 A.2d 691 (1953); State v. Hofer, *supra* note 124.

that the police have some tangible or specific evidence of guilt, many interrogations will be totally ineffective.

We again wish to emphasize that the "trickery" and "deceit" involved in many of our recommended tactics and techniques *will not*, and *have not* produced confessions from the innocent. The Supreme Court seems to have tacitly accepted this principle in the 1969 case of *Frazier v. Cupp*[133] when it sustained the validity of a confession obtained from a subject who had been told, *falsely*, that his accomplice had confessed and implicated him.

9

THE LEGAL STATUS OF CONFESSIONS OBTAINED DURING OR AFTER POLYGRAPH ("LIE-DETECTOR") OR "TRUTH-SERUM" TESTS

Polygraph, or so-called "lie-detector" test results—i.e., the opinion of an examiner as to whether a criminal suspect is telling the truth or lying when he denies his guilt—are not generally admissible in evidence, except in instances where the prosecution and the defense have agreed and stipulated upon the admissibility of the test results prior to the administration of the test itself. On the other hand, however, confessions made by the subject before, during, or after the test are admissible, provided, of course, that they meet the other judicial requirements, including the *Miranda* warnings.[134]

"Truth-serum" test results lack the reliability required for judicial acceptance.[135] Accordingly, a denial of guilt during a "truth-serum" test is not admissible as evidence. The same considerations should apply, of course, to a general admission of guilt. A different conclusion might be expected, however, where a "truth-serum" admission of guilt is substantiated by the finding of evidence of guilt at a place disclosed by the subject while under "truth-serum" in-

---

[133] 394 U. S. 731.

[134] For a collection and analysis of the case law on the admissibility of Polygraph test results as well as of admissions obtained by the examiner, consult REID & INBAU, TRUTH AND DECEPTION: THE POLYGRAPH ("LIE-DETECTOR") TECHNIQUE (1966).

[135] See excellent discussion of truth-serum tests and the various legal problems involved in 52 NORTHWESTERN U. L. REV. 666 (1957).

fluence. In such a situation, that part of the admission referring to the discovered proof of guilt is established as trustworthy and perhaps should be accepted as evidence. All of this presupposes, of course, that the subject willingly submitted to the "truth-serum" test, after having received the *Miranda* warnings.[136]

10

THE STATUS OF EVIDENCE OF GUILT DISCOVERED AS A RESULT OF DISCLOSURES IN AN IMPROPERLY OBTAINED CONFESSION

Up until a few years ago the courts held, and a few statutes specifically provided, that evidence of guilt could be used against an accused even though it was obtained as a result of disclosures he made in an improperly obtained confession. For instance, if during the course of a coerced confession a burglary suspect told where he had concealed the stolen property, that property could be used as evidence, along with that part of the confession pertaining to its location.[137] The theory back of such holdings or statutory revisions was that the confession rule was intended only as a safeguard against untruthful and untrustworthy admissions, so it was considered proper to use that which proved to be reliable regardless of the method by which it was obtained.

Under recent court decisions, and particularly those of the of the Supreme Court, the prosecution may no longer be privileged

---

[136] For the case law prior to Miranda, see *supra* note 135.

[137] State v. Garrison, 59 Ore. 440, 117 Pac. 657 (1911); Baughman v. Commonwealth, 206 Ky. 441, 267 S.W. 231 (1924); Patton v. State, 201 Miss. 410, 29 So.2d 96 (1947) (reversed by United States Supreme Court for other reasons, 332 U.S. 463); Harris v. Commonwealth, 301 Ky. 818, 193 S.W.2d. 466 (1946); State v. Cocklin, 109 Vt. 207, 194 Atl. 378 (1937); McCoy v. State, 170 N.E.2d 43 (Ind. 1960).

A Georgia statute, §38-413, provides: "Any material facts discovered by a confession by an accused may be proved, and the fact of its discovery by reason of such information, though the confession shall be rejected."

In Texas there is a statutory provision to the effect that whenever any material part of a confession is substantiated by circumstantial evidence (finding the loot or body, etc.) the entire confession becomes admissible. Tex. Code Crim. Proc. §727. But the effect of this provision has been nullified because of a conflict with another Texas statute (§727a, C.C.P.) rendering illegally seized evidence inadmissible. Colley v. State, 158 S.W.2d 1014 (Tex. Cr. 1942).

to make use of evidence of guilt derived from a coerced confession, or even, it now seems, from one otherwise improperly obtained.

The first step in this direction, insofar as the states were concerned, was in the 1952 case of *Rochin v. California*.[138] In this case the Supreme Court held that it was a violation of due process for a state to use evidence of a narcotics violation that had been obtained as the result of a stomach pumping operation on the suspect. Having taken this position in the *Rochin* case it seemed reasonable to assume that the Court would not tolerate the use of evidence obtained from a coerced confession. For a while, however, it appeared that the Court might not annul evidence derivatively obtained from other improperly obtained confessions not involving coercive procedures. One basis for this impression was the fact that the Court had not imposed the *McNabb-Mallory* rule upon the states as a constitutional requirement.

However, the net effect of the Court's rulings in *Mapp v. Ohio*,[138] *Fahy v. Connecticut*,[140] *Wong Sun v. United States*,[141] *Escobedo v. Illinois*,[142] and *Miranda v. Arizona*[143] seems to be that no state may use evidence derivatively obtained from disclosures made during a confession which itself would not be usable on due process grounds.[144] In federal cases, of course, the law is unmistakably clear that no derivative use may be made of confessions obtained either by due process violations or by interrogation practices violative of the *McNabb-Mallory* rule or any other rule of similar nature. The Circuit Court of Appeals for the District of Columbia even applied the *McNabb-Mallory* exclusion to nullify the significance of the finding of a dead body found where the defendant said he buried it.[145]

---

[138] 342 U.S. 165 (1952).
[139] 367 U.S. 643 (1961).
[140] 375 U.S. 85 (1963).
[141] 371 U.S. 471 (1963).
[142] 378 U.S. 478 (1964).
[143] 384 U.S. 436 (1966).
[144] The California Supreme Court, on its own initiative, adopted this rule. People v. Ditson, 20 Cal. Rptr. 165, 369 P.2d 714 (1962).
[145] Killough v. U.S., 319 F.2d 241 (1962).

11

ONCE IMPROPER INTERROGATION METHODS HAVE BEEN USED, IS IT POSSIBLE, LATER ON, TO OBTAIN A LEGALLY VALID CONFESSION?

Assume that coercion has been employed in the interrogation of a suspected or accused person, or suppose that he has been threatened or offered a promise of leniency, following any of which he may or may not have confessed. Is it possible, at some subsequent time, to obtain a legally valid confession from him? Or suppose a non-coerced confession has been obtained from a suspect without having first warned him of his constitutional rights, is it possible to interrogate him at a later time and obtain a legally valid confession?

Over the years, the courts, both state and federal, have held that even though improper interrogation methods have been used, there is still a possibility of obtaining a legally valid confession later on by properly interrogating the subject under different conditions and circumstances than those which prevailed originally.[146] The United States Supreme Court itself, a number of years ago, held this to be so in both state and federal prosecutions, despite its "civilized standards" (McNabb-Mallory) concept of confession admissibility in the federal courts,[147] and despite the fact that the first confession in the state case was a coerced one. However, this general rule was subject to some important qualifications, and there are now grave

---

[146] The usual position of the courts in such cases finds expression in the majority opinion in Lyons v. Oklahoma, 322 U.S. 596 (1944), where the United States Supreme Court said: "If the relation between the earlier and later confession is not so close that one must say the facts of one control the character of the other, the inference is one for the triers of fact, and their conclusion, in such an uncertain situation, that the confession should be admitted as voluntary cannot be a denial of due process."

The following cases are illustrative of the application of this general rule: State v. Foster, 136 Iowa 527, 114 N.W. 36 (1907); State v. Williamson, 343 Mo. 732, 123 S.W.2d 42 (1938); State v. Lorain, 141 Conn. 694, 109 A.2d 504 (1954); Fields v. State, 284 P.2d 442 (Okla. Cr. 1955); Boyd v. State, 230 Ark. 991, 328 S.W.2d 122 (1959); United States ex. rel. Weber v. Ragen, 176 F.2d 579 (7th Cir. 1949); Watts v. United States, 278 F.2d 247 (D. C. Cir. 1960); State v. Scarberry, 180 N.E.2d 631 (Ohio App. 1961). Also see *supra* note 132.

[147] United States v. Bayer, 331 U.S. 532 (1947); also Lyons v. Oklahoma, *supra* note 146.

doubts that the present Court would tolerate the use of any subsequent confession if the earlier one had been coerced.

In all of the earlier cases involving this problem the courts said that a presumption exists that the influence of the first improper interrogation was a continuing one.[148] The prosecution, therefore, had the burden of proving that when the subject confessed later on he was no longer dominated or affected by the influence of the earlier improper interrogation practices. Moreover, the courts have demanded a very high degree of proof to offset the presumption that prevails in favor of the accused.[149]

Whenever an interrogator is called upon to interrogate a person who has been mistreated or threatened in any way, he should be informed (and the conditions and circumstances surrounding the interview should so indicate) that no further mistreatment or threats

[148] State v. Henry, 196 La. 217, 198 So. 910 (1940); State v. Jugger, 217 La. 687, 47 So.2d 46 (1950); Huntley v. State, 250 Ala. 303, 34 So.2d 216 (1948); Holt v. State, 151 Tex. Cr. R. 399, 208 S.W.2d 643 (1948); People v. LaCoco, 406 Ill. 303, 94 N.E.2d 178 (1950); State v. Whitman, 67 N.W.2d 599 (N.D. 1954); Ladner v. State, 231 Miss. 445, 95 So.2d 468 (1957); People v. Brommel, 15 Cal. Rep. 909, 364 P.2d 845 (1961); United States v. Shanks, 12 USCMA 586 (1961).

In his dissenting opinion in Malinski v. New York, 324 U.S. 401 (1945) at p. 438, Justice Rutledge said: ". . . the conclusion would seem doubtful in any case that a later confession could be entirely voluntary or uncoerced, where an earlier one had been compelled. A man once broken in will does not readily, if ever, recover from the breaking. . . . No change in circumstances can wholly wipe out its effects upon himself or upon others." In the same case (p. 433) Justice Murphy expressed the view, as a dissenting judge, that "Once an atmosphere of coercion or fear is created, subsequent confessions should automatically be invalidated unless there is proof beyond all reasonable doubt that such an atmosphere has been dispelled and that the accused has completely regained his free individual will."

Consider the six to three decision in Leyra v. Denno, 347 U. S. 556 (1954), which held that a psychiatrist's promises to the accused nullified the resulting confession and that the influence thereby created carried over to a subsequent confession.

Even where earlier mistreatment has been administered by private persons, the resulting influence may nullify a confession obtained by law enforcement authorities later on. People v. Berve, 51 Cal. 2d 286, 332 P.2d 97 (1958).

[149] People v. Sweetin, 325 Ill. 245, 156 N.E. 354 (1927); People v. Jones, 24 Cal. 2d 601, 150 P.2d 801 (1944); People v. Thomlison, 400 Ill. 555, 81 N.E.2d 434 (1948); Edwards v. State, 194 Md. 387, 71 A.2d 487 (1950); People v. Rogers, 413 Ill. 554, 110 N.E.2d 201 (1953); Lee v. State, 236 Miss. 717, 112 So.2d 254 (1959).

will occur, and if a previous objectionable promise has been made it should be revoked in unmistakable terms. Moreover, none of the persons who were in any way involved in the previous interrogation should be present at the subsequent one.[150] Then the subject should be given all the warnings now required by the *Miranda* case, and there should be one or more impartial witnesses present, or at least in a position to observe and hear the entire interrogation.

Although, as previously stated, the courts have held that improper interrogation methods do not necessarily nullify a later confession obtained under different and proper conditions and circumstances, it is very likely that future decisions may make a distinction based upon the nature of the impropriety. In all likelihood the Supreme Court will hold that if physical violence has been used, or perhaps even the threat of such violence, any later confession becomes a legal nullity, regardless of the conditions and circumstances under which it was obtained. On the other hand, the Court may hold that non-violent interrogation practices such as a promise of leniency will not necessarily bar the use of a confession obtained later on under proper conditions and circumstances. And the Court has already committed itself, in the *Miranda* opinion, to the rectification of a failure to issue the required warnings at the time of the first interrogation. In *Miranda* the Court said: "We do not suggest that law enforcement authorities are precluded from questioning any individual who has been held for a period of time by other authorities and interrogated by them without appropriate warnings. A different case would be presented if an accused were taken into custody by the second authority, removed both in time and place from his original surroundings, and then adequately advised of his rights and given an opportunity to exercise them." [151]

12

IS AN ORAL CONFESSION COMPETENT LEGAL EVIDENCE?

An oral confession is competent legal evidence, and it may be proved by anyone who heard it.[152]

---

[150] As an example of the necessity of having previous abusers absent, see Jones v. State, 184 Wis. 50, 198 N.W. 598 (1924).

[151] P. 496.

[152] State v. Lu Sing, 34 Mont. 31, 85 Pac. 521 (1906); State v. Coy, 140 Kans.

For all practical purposes, of course, a written and signed confession has a decided advantage over one that is unwritten or unsigned. An offender who is confronted with a written and signed confession will have considerable difficulty convincing a judge or jury that he did not make the confession, but where the only proof of a confession is the word of another person or persons, the offender is in a far better position to effectively disclaim the alleged confession. Nevertheless, they are both equally admissible as evidence, the only difference being the feature of the greater weight or credibility usually given to the written and signed confession.

13

LEGAL REQUIREMENTS REGARDING THE FORM OF A WRITTEN CONFESSION

A written confession need not be in any particular form. It may be typewritten or handwritten, and it may be in either a narrative or question and answer form.[153] Moreover, it need not be a verbatim record of what the confessor said orally, as long as he acknowledges the written confession after he has read it or after it has been read to him.[154]

The person under interrogation, or whose confession is about to be reduced to writing, should not be placed under oath; otherwise the confession may be rejected on the theory that the oath consti-

---

284, 36 P.2d 971 (1934); Douberly v. State, 184 Ga. 577, 192 S.E. 226 (1937); People v. Leving, 371 Ill. 448, 21 N.E.2d 391 (1939); People v. Thompson, 133 Cal. App. 4, 284 P.2d 39 (1955). Also see Evans v. United States, 122 F.2d 461 (10th Cir. 1941), where it was held that oral statements made by the accused, which he did not want incorporated into the written statement, were nevertheless admissible in evidence.

In Texas, however, by statutory provision, a confession must be in writing and signed by the defendant before it is admissible in evidence. TEX. CODE CRIM. PROC., Art. 38.22 (1965).

[153] Roesel v. State, 62 N. J. 216, 41 Atl. 408 (1898); State v. Brasseaux, 163 La. 686, 112 So. 650 (1927); Sherman v. State, 38 Ala. App. 106, 77 So.2d 495 (1954).

[154] State v. Boudreaux, 67 Nev. 36, 214 P.2d 135 (1950); Cooper v. State, 205 Md. 162, 106 A.2d 129 (1954); Blackburn v. State, 38 Ala. App. 143, 88 So.2d 199 (1955); Garcia v. State, 163 Tex. Cr. R. 146, 288 S.W.2d 513 (1956); State v. Howard, 238 La. 595, 116 So.2d 43 (1959).

tuted compulsion, or because of a concern that the jury may regard the oath as a virtual guarantee of the confession's trustworthiness.[155]

[155] Bianchi v. State, 169 Wis. 75, 171 N.W. 639 (1919), and Flamme v. State, 171 Wis. 501, 177 N.W. 596 (1920), in both of which the prosecuting attorney placed the accused under oath before the interrogation. The Wisconsin court said: "The witness is under a species of extra-moral duress to tell the truth ... the testimony was not voluntary." In states such as Florida which, by statute (ch. 34 . . 4), empowers a prosecuting attorney to summon witnesses to appear before him and to be questioned, the same considerations may prevail to render a confession invalid.

People v. Foley, 8 N.Y. 2d 153, 168 N.E.2d 514 (1960), in which the oath was administered by a justice of the peace before the subject made his confession. In holding that the confession was inadmissible at the murder trial, the New York Court of Appeals said: "The jury may well have regarded the fact that the confession was sworn to before the magistrate in the courtroom as a virtual guarantee of its trustworthiness, as overwhelming proof that the statement contained a true account of what had happened and, indeed, the fact that it had been sworn to before a judicial officer was heavily relied upon at the trial to overcome the defendant's repudiation of it and his claim that he had 'blacked out' and was not aware of what he was doing when he committed the homicide." Compare People v. Randall, 9 N.Y. 2d 413, 174 N.E.2d 507 (1961), where the accused first made an oral confession, then a written one after a notary public had administered an oath to him, following which the accused swore before a magistrate to the truth of the confession. In upholding the validity of the confession the New York Court of Appeals said: "On the trial, the People at no time exploited the fact that the confession had been sworn to before the Magistrate. Rather, the defendant and his witness brought it out, and emphasized it. Under these circumstances, we do not think that the Foley case (supra), and the cases decided thereunder, necessitate a reversal. An oral confession voluntarily was made and subsequently a written confession voluntarily was executed and sworn to before a notary. Only thereafter did the Magistrate become involved in the confession, and the People did not attempt to take advantage of his participation. The defendant, by his own acts, and by the acts of his counsel, made the incident known to the jury. Here there was no prejudice to defendant by any act of the People.... We do not mean to condone the act of the troopers and the Magistrate, but on this record, we fail to see how defendant was harmed except by his own acts."

In People v. Jackson, 23 Ill. 2d 258, 178 N.E.2d 299 (1961), the accused, who was unrepresented by counsel, was called upon by the prosecutor to testify under oath at the preliminary hearing of a murder charge. He admitted his guilt, and the admissions were used as evidence against him at his trial. Upon appeal the Illinois Supreme Court reversed the conviction on the ground that the preliminary hearing admissions were obtained in violation of the defendant's constitutional rights. The Court said, "By reason of their very nature, such proceedings are cloaked with the solemnity and authority inherent in counts, and there exists the highest duty to see an accused is fairly

As recommended earlier, the warnings given at the outset of the interrogation should be repeated as the written (or recorded) confession is about to be taken.[156]

Whenever possible, the person taking the written confession should be someone other than the attorney who will prosecute the case, but if he is the only one available, the person who makes the shorthand record or who writes out or types up the confession should be the one to testify at the trial. In this way the prosecutor will avoid the dual role of attorney and witness, a practice which the courts look upon with disfavor.[157]

After an oral confession has been reduced to writing, the confessor should be permitted to read it or else it should be read to him, or, perhaps better yet, he should be given the original copy to examine as a carbon copy is read to him. Any changes or corrections should be made by the confessor, where possible, in his

---

and properly treated and his rights observed." The rights involved are referred to in the following excerpt from the court's opinion: "where an accused is unattended by counsel and does not become a witness of his own volition, a judicial confession made at a preliminary hearing may not be properly introduced into evidence at the subsequent trial, unless the proof affirmatively shows (1) that the accused had independent knowledge or was advised by the court of his right to refuse to testify; (2) that he was advised or knew that any statements made could be used against him, and (3) that he knowingly and intelligently waived his constitutional privilege against self-incrimination. In such a manner, preliminary hearings at which judicial confessions are made, as well as the confessions themselves, will not be suspect of unfairness or judicial pressure, and both the letter and the spirit of the constitutional guaranty will be observed."

Contra: State v. Sanders, 227 S.C. 287, 87 S.E.2d 826 (1955), where the court held that the oath administered by a notary public not only did not vitiate the confession but that "it would seem that the solemnity of the oath would add to the trustworthiness of a written confession." *Accord:* State v. White, 27 N.J. 158, 142 A.2d 65 (1958). Also see Hawaii statute (vol. 2, ch., 222–226), providing that a confession shall not be rejected merely because it was made under oath.

Perhaps a distinction is warranted between cases where the oath is administered by a non-judicial officer, outside of a courtroom (e.g., by a notary public), and cases where the oath is administered by a judicial officer (a justice of the peace or magistrate). The reasons for excluding a sworn confession are far more compelling in the latter situation.

[156] *Supra* p. 125.
[157] See *infra* p. 210.

own handwriting, and in that event he should be asked to place his initials in the margin alongside the change or correction. As previously stated,[158] some errors should be made intentionally on the written confession for the very purpose of having the confessor insert corrections and thereby evidence the fact that he actually read the confession before signing it.[159]

If the confessor should refuse to sign the written confession, may the unsigned copy be used as evidence?

Some courts will admit an unsigned copy of a confession in evidence, provided a witness or witnesses testify that it is an accurate account of what the witness heard the defendant say.[160] Other courts will admit the unsigned confession if the prosecution offers proof that the confession was read by or to the defendant and he acknowledged it to be true.[161] Some courts, however, hold that if the written confession is both unsigned and unacknowledged, it can only be used to refresh the recollection of the witness who testifies as to what the defendant had confessed to orally.[162]

As will be subsequently discussed,[163] the confession should re-

[158] *Supra* p. 126, wherein we also suggest that a female stenographer is to be preferred over a male stenographer, to more effectively counteract an unwarranted defense contention of coercion.

[159] *Supra* p. 132 Also see People v. Shelton, 388 Ill. 56, 57 N.E.2d 473 (1944) as an illustration of the persuasive effect of this practice.

One state, South Carolina, requires that whenever a written statement is taken from anyone during the course of an investigation, that person must be furnished by the investigators with a copy thereof. S.C. CODE §1-64 (1960 Supp.).

[160] Bosko v. People, 68 Colo. 256, 188 Pac. 743 (1920); State v. Dierlamm, 189 La. 544, 180 So. 135 (1938); Prather v. State, 137 P.2d 249 (Okla. Cr. 1943); Mobley v. State, 85 N.E.2d 489 (Ind. 1949). Also see People v. Fitzgerald, 17 Cal. Rptr. 129, 366 P.2d 481 (1961); People v. Hanson, 31 Ill. 2d 31, 198 N.E. 2d 815 (1964).

[161] State v. Folkes, 174 Ore. 568, 150 P.2d 17 (1944); State v. Rios, 17 N.J. 572, 112 A.2d 247 (1955); State v. Saltzman, 241 Iowa 1373, 44 N.W.2d 24 (1950); State v. Landrum, 96 Ohio App. 333, 113 N.E.2d 705 (1953); State v. Smith, 27 N.J. 433, 142 A.2d 890 (1958); Tiner v. State, 271 Ala. 254, 122 So.2d 738 (1960) (but here the court held that reversible error was committed by the trial court in deleting from the end of the statement a notation by the transcriber that the defendant had refused to sign it).

[162] State v. Haworth, 24 Utah 398, 68 Pac. 155 (1902). State v. Cleveland, 6 N.J. 316, 78 A.2d 560 (1951).

As regards the unsigned confession matter generally, see 23 A.L.R.2d 919.

[163] *Infra* p. 209. Also see *supra* p. 136.

late to one crime only, unless it is so closely related to some other offense that the confession must necessarily deal with the other offense as well. Another precaution to follow is to avoid the incorporation into the confession of prejudicial statements such as one whereby the confessor is told that his accomplice has placed all the blame on him and he is asked if that is true. In the face of the confessor's denial that he is solely to blame, the reference to the accomplice's statement constitutes hearsay evidence that may jeopardize the confession's admissibility or result in the reversal of a conviction based upon its usage at the trial. On the other hand, if one subject is shown the written confession of his alleged accomplice and he acknowledges the accomplice's confession to be true, that confession may be considered the equivalent of his own.[164] The better practice, of course, is to take another and separate confession rather than rely upon the first confession alone, primarily because of the difficulty to be encountered if the two confessors are granted separate trials.

14

VOICE-RECORDED AND SOUND MOVIE CONFESSIONS

The point is well-established, by many court decisions, that voice-recorded and sound movie confessions are admissible as evidence.[165] All that is basically required is the testimony of someone

[164] People v. Siemsen, 153 Cal. 387, 95 Pac. 863 (1908); State v. Dunlap, 61 N.J. Super. 582, 161 A.2d 760 (1960).

[165] Commonwealth v. Roller, 100 Pa. Super. 125 (1930); Fikes v. State, 263 Ala. 89, 81 So.2d 303 (1955) (reversed by the United States Supreme Court on other grounds); People v. Hayes, 21 Cal. App. 2d 320, 71 P.2d 321 (1937); State v. Lorain, 141 Conn. 694, 109 A.2d 504 (1954); State v. Spencer, 74 Idaho 173, 258 P.2d 1147 (1953); Sutton v. State, 237 Ind. 305, 145 N.E.2d 425 (1957); State v. Triplett, 248 Iowa 339, 79 N.W.2d 391 (1956); State v. Alleman, 218 La. 821, 51 So.2d 83 (1950); State v. Gensmer, 235 Minn. 72, 51 N.W.2d 680 (1951); Sanders v. State, 237 Miss. 772, 115 So.2d 145 (1959); State v. Perkins, 355 Mo. 851, 198 S.W.2d 704 (1946); Williams v. State, 93 Okla. Cr. 260, 226 P.2d 989 (1951); State v. Reyes, 209 Ore. 607, 308 P.2d 182 (1957); Kirkendoll v. State, 198 Tenn. 497, 281 S.W.2d 243 (1955); State v. Salle, 34 Wash. 2d 183, 208 P.2d 872 (1949); Monroe v. United States, 234 F.2d 49 (D.C. Cir. 1956); Thomas v. Davis, 249 F.2d 232 (10th Cir. 1957). In People v. Dabb, 32 Cal. 2d 491, 197 P.2d 1 (1948), the court upheld the admissi-

who can testify that the contents of the recording or of the film and sound track are an accurate reproduction of what actually occurred. Some courts, however, have prescribed certain detailed procedures that the prosecutor should follow in the authentication of the recording or the sound film, and particularly as regards the latter. These procedures require testimony that the instrument used accurately records and reveals what was said or done, that it was properly operated, that the speakers and participants are identified, and that the recording is otherwise authentic and correct.[166]

A sound recording's admissibility is unaffected by the fact that it can be tampered with by means of deletions and changes or that it may be turned on or off at will during the recording of the confession and thereby omit some of what the confessor said. As several courts have pointed out, the opportunities for such practices are equally applicable to stenographic recordings of confessions.[167]

Partial inaudibility of the recording is no reason, in itself, for rejection of the entire recording as evidence.[168]

The fact that the confessor did not know that his confession was being recorded has been held not to affect the confession's admissibility.[169] A different result has been reached, of course, in states which have statutes prohibiting the electronic recording of a person's conversation without his consent.[170]

Once a recording has been admitted in evidence, some courts have held that it is proper for the trial court to permit the jury to

---

bility of a sound movie of the defendant re-enacting the crime to which he had confessed.

Pertinent to the general subject consult: 9 U. OF PITTSBURGH L. Rev. 28 (1947) and 58 A.L.R.2d 1024.

[166] State v. Williams, 49 Wash. 2d 354, 301 P.2d 769 (1956); Wright v. State, 38 Ala. App. 64, 79 So.2d 66 (1954); Ray v. State, 213 Miss. 650, 57 So.2d 469 (1952). Also see Solomon v. Edgar, 92 Ga. App. 207, 88 S.E.2d 167 (1955), involving the procedures employed in a civil case.

[167] Williams v. State and State v. Gensmer, supra note 165.

[168] State v. Salle, supra note 165; Cape v. United States, 283 F.2d 430 (9th Cir. 1960). Also see Wright v. State, supra note 166.

[169] State v. Alleman and State v. Lorain, supra note 165.

[170] See ORE. STAT. §165.540; ILL. REV. STAT., ch. 38, §14.

take it, along with a playback instrument, into the jury room so that they may hear the recording again.[171]

15

IN CASES WHERE A PERSON CONFESSES SEVERAL CRIMES, IS IT PROPER TO INCORPORATE ALL OF THEM INTO ONE CONFESSION?

It is a general rule of law that in the course of a criminal trial for one offense, evidence may not be heard which establishes or tends to show that the accused committed another crime wholly independent of the one for which he is being tried.[172]

Although there are several exceptions to the general rule,[173] the only exception of direct concern to the interrogator is the one which permits a statement of the details of some other crime or crimes when the latter cannot be separated from the former. In other words, if the confession is to a rape within a burglarized home, a reference to the burglary is unavoidable, but if the subject committed a burglary of one home and later committed a rape within another home, the offenses may be separately described, and in such instances a separate confession should be taken of each one. To combine them into one confession will render the confession inadmissible as evidence, unless the reference to the unrelated crime can be deleted from the confession without destroying its evidential value or producing some prejudicial effect upon the defense.[174]

---

[171] People v. Walker, 150 Cal. App. 2d 594, 310 P.2d 110 (1957); and State v. Tripplett and State v. Reyes, *supra* note 165. Such a practice may be subject to attack in certain jurisdictions, however, on the theory that since the recording is heard out of the presence of the defendant, he is deprived of his right to be confronted by the witnesses against him. See, for example, People v. White, 365 Ill. 499, 6 N.E.2d 1015 (1937), involving jury experimentations in the jury room.

[172] Hergenrother v. State, 215 Ind. 89, 18 N.E. 784 (1939).

[173] For example, where the evidence of another crime tends to establish (a) the absence of mistake or accident on the part of the accused when he did the act for which he is being tried; (b) the intent or motive with which the act was committed; (c) the identity of the accused; and (d) the scheme, plan, or system used in the commission of the offense.

[174] People v. Oden, 20 Ill. 2d 470, 170 N.E.2d 582 (1960).

Not only should the confession ordinarily be confined to one crime, but it should also avoid any reference to or contain any question about another offense for which the subject was arrested or convicted. This, too, would be violative of the principle that a person's guilt or innocence should be determined without consideration being given to his otherwise bad character.[175]

16

MAY A PROSECUTING ATTORNEY WHO OBTAINS A CONFESSION TESTIFY AS A WITNESS AND ALSO SERVE AS PROSECUTOR?

Although there is no specific law or rule of court that forbids a prosecuting attorney to testify as a witness in his own case, the courts have expressed their disapproval of the practice.[176] Moreover, under certain conditions and circumstances such a practice may constitute reversible error or even amount to a denial of due process.[177] For these and for other considerations as well, no prosecutor should accept the dual role of prosecutor-witness if he can possibly avoid it.

[175] State v. Dietz, 5 N.J. Super. 222, 68 A.2d 777 (1949).

[176] Zeidler v. State, 189 Wis. 44, 206 N.W. 872 (1926); Adams v. State, 202 Miss. 68, 30 So.2d 593 (1947); Frank v. State, 150 Neb. 745, 35 N.W.2d 816 (1949); Maund v. State, 254 Ala. 452, 48 So.2d 553 (1950); Butler v. State, 229 Ind. 241, 97 N.E.2d 492 (1951). Cf. People v. Burwell, 44 Cal. 2d 16, 279 P.2d 744 (1955), where both prosecutors trying the case testified to incriminating statements made by the accused and the court held: "This in itself was not improper. A district attorney is not precluded from testifying as to material facts within his knowledge." Also, as regards the general issue of a prosecutor testifying as a witness, see Adams v. State, 202 Miss. 68, 30 So.2d 593 (1947), and 149 A.L.R. 1305. Also consider Canon 19 of the Canon of Professional Ethics, condemning the practice of a lawyer testifying for his client in a civil case.

[177] See Irvin v. Doud, 271 F.2d 552 (1959), in which one of the two prosecutors who tried the state murder case against the defendant testified about incriminating statements made by the defendant during the investigative stage of the case. The defendant contended that the prosecutor's conduct in testifying was unethical and a violation of due process. The majority of the court held that "the most that can be said is that this conduct was error which did not have such a substantial effect upon the outcome as to strip the trial of due process." One of the three federal circuit court judges, however, pointed out in his dissent that in the prosecution's closing argument the prosecutor-witness commented upon the evidence, including his own, and that "such conduct was offensive to the rights of the defendant to a fair and impartial trial." (Case reversed by Supreme Court, but for other reasons, 366 U.S. 717 (1961).

In the larger communities with prosecution staffs consisting of several assistant prosecutors, the prosecutor-witness problem is a relatively easy one. If one prosecutor obtains the confession and has to testify as a witness, the case can be assigned to one of his colleagues for trial. In the smaller communities, however, there may be only one prosecutor and no assistants. Moreover, the other local law enforcement or investigating officers may be inexperienced or unskilled as interrogators, and the responsibility will thereby go by default to the prosecuting attorney himself. What, then, is the way out of the prosecutor-witness dilemma, when the prosecutor obtains a confession and its use as evidence is essential?

If legal provisions exist for the appointment of a special prosecutor, some courts have suggested that this be done,[178] but this is rarely possible, and there are some obvious practical considerations that militate against the adoption of this alternative, even when it is otherwise quite feasible.

It is our suggestion that whenever an oral confession is obtained by the prosecutor who must also try the case, arrangements should be made to have a stenographer, preferably a woman, take shorthand or stenotype notes of the confession and then, after it is typed, be present when it is read by or to the confessor and signed by him. The stenographer may then be used as a witness to the confession and to its voluntariness, and thereby render it unnecessary for the prosecutor to testify at all, except possibly as a rebuttal witness in the event that the defendant alleges that the prosecutor himself employed improper methods in obtaining the confession.

The above described witness procedure is probably a good one to follow even in jurisdictions whose courts have established the rule that when the defendant claims his confession was obtained by force or other improper means, all persons present at the interrogation or confession must be offered as witnesses. As between the two requirements—the production of all witnesses, and the avoidance of the prosecutor-witness practice—a court would probably carve out an exception to the former requirement. Even if the

[178] State v. Magnuson, 46 S.D. 156, 191 N.W. 460 (1922).

prosecutor should be required to testify, either upon demand of the trial court or by reason of other compelling circumstances, he will then be taking the stand with reluctance and out of necessity. His witness appearance under such circumstances is unlikely to draw appellate court criticism.

CRIMINAL INTERROGATION—
A PRACTICAL NECESSITY

One completely false assumption accounts for most of the legal restrictions on police interrogations. It is this, and the fallacy is certainly perpetuated to a very considerable extent by mystery writers, the movies, and TV: whenever a crime is committed, if the police will only look carefully at the crime scene they will almost always find some clue that will lead them to the offender and at the same time establish his guilt; and once the offender is located, he will readily confess or disclose his guilt by trying to shoot his way out of the trap. But this is pure fiction; in actuality the situation is quite different. As a matter of fact, the art of criminal investigation has not developed to a point where the search for and the examination of physical evidence will always, or even in most cases, reveal a clue to the identity of the perpetrator or provide the necessary proof of his guilt. In criminal investigations, even of the most efficient type, there are many, many instances where physical clues are entirely absent, and the only approach to a possible solution of the crime is the interrogation of the criminal suspect himself, as well as others who may possess significant information. Moreover, in most instances these interrogations, particularly of the suspect himself, must be conducted under conditions of privacy and for a reasonable period of time; and they frequently require the use of psychological tactics and techniques that could well be classified as "unethical," if we are to evaluate them in terms of ordinary, everyday social behavior.

To protect ourselves from being misunderstood, we want to make it unmistakably clear that we are not advocates of the so-called "third degree." We are unalterably opposed to the use of any interrogation tactic or technique that is apt to make an innocent person confess. We are opposed, therefore, to the use of force, threats, or promises of leniency—all of which might well induce

213

an innocent person to confess; but we do approve of such psychological tactics and techniques as trickery and deceit that are not only helpful but frequently necessary in order to secure incriminating information from the guilty, or investigative leads from otherwise uncooperative witnesses or informants.

Our position, then, is this, and it may be presented in the form of three separate points, each accompanied by case illustrations:

1. Many Criminal Cases, Even When Investigated by the Best Qualified Police Departments, Are Capable of Solution Only by Means of an Admission or Confession from the Guilty Individual or upon the Basis of Information Obtained from the Questioning of Other Criminal Suspects.

As to the validity of this statement, we suggest that consideration be given to the situation presented by cases such as these. A man is hit on the head while walking home late at night. He does not see his assailant, nor does anyone else. A careful and thorough search of the crime scene reveals no physical clues. Then take the case of a woman who is grabbed on the street at night and dragged into an alley and raped. Here, too, the assailant was unaccommodating enough to avoid leaving his hat or other means of identification at the crime scene, and there are no other physical clues. All the police have to work on is the description of the assailant given by the victim herself. She describes him as about six feet tall, white, and wearing a dark suit. Or consider this case, an actual one in Illinois. Three women are vacationing in a wooded resort area. Their bodies are found dead, the result of physical violence, alongside a foot trail, and no physical clues are present.

In cases of this kind—and they all typify the difficult investigation problem that the police frequently encounter—how else can they be solved, if at all, except by means of the interrogation of suspects or of others who may possess significant information?[1]

There are times, too, when a police interrogation may result not

---

[1] For other case illustrations of the practical necessity for the interrogation process in criminal investigations, and for a discussion of the broader social and legal aspects of this issue, see the chapter by one of the present authors entitled *Law Enforcement, the Courts, and Individual Civil Liberties* in KAMISAR, INBAU & ARNOLD, CRIMINAL JUSTICE IN OUR TIME 96–136 (1965).

only in the apprehension and conviction of the guilty, but also in the release of the innocent from well-warranted suspicion. Here is one such actual case within our own professional experience.

The dead body of a woman was found in her home. Her skull had been crushed, apparently with some blunt instrument. A careful police investigation of the premises did not reveal any clues to the identity of the killer. No fingerprints or other significant evidence was located; not even the lethal instrument itself could be found. None of the neighbors could give any helpful information. Although there was some evidence of a slight struggle in the room where the body lay, there were no indications of a forcible entry into the home. The deceased's young daughter was the only other resident of the home, and she had been away in school at the time of the crime. The daughter could not give the police any idea of what, if any, money or property had disappeared from the home.

For several reasons the police considered the victim's husband a likely suspect. He was being sued for divorce; he knew his wife had planned on leaving the state and taking their daughter with her; and the neighbors reported that the couple had been having heated arguments, and that the husband was of a violent temper. He also lived conveniently near—in a garage adjoining the home. The police interrogated him and although his alibi was not conclusive his general behavior and the manner in which he answered the interrogator's questions satisfied the police of his innocence. Further investigation then revealed that the deceased's brother-in-law had been financially indebted to the deceased; that he was a frequent gambler; that at a number of social gatherings which he had attended money disappeared from some of the women's purses; that at his place of employment there had been a series of purse thefts; and that on the day of the killing he was absent from work. The police apprehended and questioned him. As the result of a few hours of competent interrogation—unattended by any abusive methods, but yet conducted during a period of delay in presenting the suspect before a committing magistrate as required by state statute—the suspect confessed to the murder. He told of going to the victim's home for the purpose of selling her a radio, which she accused him of stealing. An argument ensued and he hit her over the head with a mechanic's wrench he was carrying in his coat pocket. He thereupon located and took some money he found in the home and also a diamond ring. After fleeing from the scene he threw the wrench into a river, changed his clothes, and disposed of the ones he had worn at the time of the killing by throwing them away in various parts of the city. He had hidden the ring ir the attic of his mother's home, where it was found by the police after his confession had disclosed its presence there. Much of the stolen money was also recovered or else accounted for by the payment of an overdue loan.

Without an opportunity for interrogation the police could not have solved this case. The perpetrator of the offense would have remained at liberty, perhaps to repeat his criminal conduct.

2. *Criminal Offenders, Except, of Course, Those Caught in the Commission of Their Crimes, Ordinarily Will Not Admit Their Guilt unless Questioned under Conditions of Privacy, and for a Period of Perhaps Several Hours.*

This point is one which should be readily apparent not only to any person with the least amount of criminal investigative experience, but also to anyone who will reflect momentarily upon the behavior of ordinary law-abiding persons when suspected or accused of nothing more than simple social indiscretions. Self-condemnation and self-destruction not being normal behavior characteristics, human beings ordinarily do not utter unsolicited, spontaneous confessions. They must first be questioned regarding the offense. In some instances, a little bit of information inadvertently given to a competent interrogator by the suspect may suffice to start a line of investigation which might ultimately establish guilt. On other occasions, a full confession, with a revelation of details regarding a body, the loot, or the instruments used in the crime, may be required to prove the case; but whatever the possible consequences may be, it is impractical to expect any but a very few confessions to result from a guilty conscience unprovoked by an interrogation. It is also impractical to expect admissions or confessions to be obtained under circumstances other than privacy. Here again recourse to our everyday experience will support the basic validity of this requirement. For instance, in asking a personal friend to divulge a secret, or embarrassing information, we carefully avoid making the request in the presence of other persons, and seek a time and place when the matter can be discussed in private. The very same psychological factors are involved in a criminal interrogation, and even to a greater extent. For related psychological considerations, if an interrogation is to be had at all, it must be one based upon an unhurried interview, the necessary length of which will in many instances extend to several hours, depending upon various factors, such as the nature of the case situation and the personality of the suspect.

3. In Dealing with Criminal Offenders, and Consequently Also with Criminal Suspects Who May Actually Be Innocent, the Interrogator Must of Necessity Employ Less Refined Methods Than Are Considered Appropriate for the Transaction of Ordinary, Everyday Affairs by and between Law-Abiding Citizens.

To illustrate this point, let us revert to the previously discussed case of the woman who was murdered by her brother-in-law. His confession was obtained largely by the interrogator's adoption of a friendly attitude in questioning the suspect, when concededly no such genuine feeling existed; by his pretense of sympathizing with the suspect because of his difficult financial situation; by his suggestion that perhaps the victim had done or said something which aroused the suspect's anger and which would have aroused the anger of anyone else similarly situated to such an extent as to provoke a violent reaction; and by his resort to other similar expressions, or even overtures of friendliness and sympathy such as a pat on the suspect's shoulder. In all of this, of course, the interrogation was "unethical" according to the standards usually set for professional, business, and social conduct, but the pertinent issue in this case was no ordinary, lawful, professional, business, or social matter. It involved the taking of a human life by one who abided by no code of fair play toward his fellow human beings. The killer would not have been moved one bit toward a confession by subjecting him to a reading or lecture regarding the morality of his conduct. It would have been futile merely to give him a pencil and paper and trust that his conscience would impel him to confess. Something more was required—something which was in its essence an "unethical" practice on the part of the interrogator; but, under the circumstances involved in this case, how else would the murderer's guilt have been established? Moreover, let us bear this thought in mind. From the criminal's point of view, *any* interrogation of him is objectionable. To *him* it may be a "dirty trick" to be talked into a confession, for surely it was not done for his benefit. Consequently, any interrogation of him might be labeled as deceitful or unethical.

Of necessity, criminal interrogators must deal with criminal offenders on a somewhat lower moral plane than that upon which ethical, law-abiding citizens are expected to conduct their everyday affairs. That plane, in the interest of innocent suspects, need only be subject to the following restriction: Although both "fair" and "unfair" interrogation practices are permissible, nothing shall be done or said to the subject that will be apt to make an innocent person confess.

If we view this whole problem realistically, we must come to the conclusion that an interrogation opportunity is necessary and that legislative provision ought to be made for a privately conducted police interrogation, covering a reasonable period of time, of suspects who are not unwilling to be interviewed; and that the only tactics or techniques that are to be forbidden are those which are apt to make an innocent person confess.

There are other ways to guard against abuses in police interrogation short of taking the privilege away from them. Moreover, we could no more afford to do that than we could stand the effect of a law requiring automobile manufacturers to place governors on all cars so that, in order to make the highways safe, no one could go faster than twenty miles an hour.

The only real, practically attainable protection we can set up for ourselves against police interrogation abuses (just as with respect to arrest and detention abuses) is to see to it that our police are selected and promoted on a merit basis, that they are properly trained and adequately compensated, and that they are permitted to remain substantially free from politically inspired interference.

In the hands of men of this competence there will be a minimum degree of abusive practices. Once again we suggest that the real interest that should be exhibited by the legislatures and the courts is with reference to the protection of the innocent from the hazards of tactics and techniques that are apt to produce confessions of guilt or other false information. Individual civil liberties can survive in such an atmosphere, alongside the protective security of the public.

INDEX